From War to the Rule of Law

AF872877

The series 'Verkenningen' comprises studies commissioned by the WRR that are deemed to be of such quality and importance that their publication is desirable. Responsibility for the contents and views expressed therein remains that of the authors.

Scientific Council for Government Policy (WRR)
Lange Vijverberg 4-5
P.O. Box 20004
2500 EA The Haque
Tel. + 31 70 356 46 00
Fax + 31 70 356 46 85
E-mail: info@wrr.nl
Internet: http://www.wrr.nl

SCIENTIFIC COUNCIL FOR GOVERNMENT POLICY

From War to the Rule of Law

PEACEBUILDING AFTER VIOLENT CONFLICTS

Joris Voorhoeve

Amsterdam University Press, Amsterdam 2007

Front cover illustration: US Army Soldier helps an Iraqi policeman to adjust his armband in Falluja, June 2003. © Reuters / Radu Sigheti

Cover design: Studio Daniëls, Den Haag
Layout: Het Steen Typografie, Maarssen

ISBN 978 90 5356 867 5
NUR 754

© WRR/Amsterdam University Press, Den Haag / Amsterdam 2007

All rights reserved. Without limiting the rights under copyright reserved above, no part of this book may be reproduced, stored in or introduced into a retrieval system, or transmitted, in any form or by any means (electronic, mechanical, photocopying, recording or otherwise) without the written permission of both the copyright owner and the author of the book.

"The long-term goal of relatively well-ordered societies should be to bring burdened societies and outlaw states into the Society of well-ordered Peoples."

John Rawls, *The Law of Peoples*, Harvard University Press (2001, p. 116)

CONTENTS

PREFACE

The vocation of the Dutch Scientific Council for Government Policy is to make sure that the results of important scholarly work find their way into the realm of political decision-making. Democracy is as much about power as it is about learning. In order to pursue future-oriented policy-learning, the council favours research-informed dialogues between those who have the time to do research and those that have accepted the responsibility to design policies and to make decisions. In this book, the subject matter of these policies and decisions is as important as it is complex and challenging: the domain of international peace-building operations. These operations, many of which are systematically explored and evaluated in this study, most of the time follow many years of violent conflicts and civil wars, atrocious assaults on human dignity and international military intervention. Many countries and policymakers have experienced the dilemmas and uncertainties that accompanied these operations, that have often not been much of a success.

The author of this book, professor Joris Voorhoeve, serving as a member of the Dutch Council of State, is especially qualified and motivated to contribute to this important field of study. Having served not only in politics (notably as minister of Defence during the tragic failure of UN peace-keeping efforts in Bosnia), but also as a professor of international relations at Leyden University, he wholeheartedly accepted the invitation to contribute to the body of knowledge that might help us to improve our efforts to make future peacekeeping and –building missions more successful. Such an effort demands an interdisciplinary and future-oriented approach, one that dares to transcend and challenge the usual divisions of policymaking routines and responsibilities.

The Scientific Council is proud to be able to publish the results of the research that Voorhoeve was carrying out as a special guest of the Council. Indeed, the most vexing questions of political and other social sciences are how political violence can be avoided, how conflicts can be settled peacefully and how the safety of human beings and their basic rights can be ensured. Voorhoeve explores these urgent and difficult questions which need to be solved after a country has been ravaged by war. Most war-torn societies return to political violence within a few years. Wars, civil wars and other forms of contemporary political violence tend to repeat and multiply themselves. To make the 21st century more peaceful than the 20th, it will be essential to better diagnose the pathology of different types of wars, and develop more effective therapies for building sustainable peace.

The most rewarding approach is, of course, prevention of armed conflict. Where prevention failed, a curative approach is needed to prevent a relapse of war. This study focuses on the curative approach: how to rebuild a war-torn country in such a way that the causes of the violence are reduced or removed.

As many decision makers and scholars already found out, this is a vast and complex area. The present study explores the many questions with the aim to suggest policy improvements. Peacebuilding can be most effective as a joint effort of the population concerned with the aid of many members of the international community. Also today, the Netherlands participates in several peace operations in the world and is also engaged in civilian peacebuilding. The author has suggested, on the basis of his research, a series of recommendations that will help to improve decision making. As a center of international law, the Netherlands can especially focus on assisting war-torn countries to (re-) build the rule of law which is essential for sustainable conditions for human dignity, good governance and peaceful conflict settlement. The council hopes that this study will be of great use for all those involved in this important responsibility.

Prof. dr. W.B.H.J. van de Donk
Chairman of the council

1 WHY THIS STUDY?

"Currently, half the countries emerging from violent conflict revert to conflict within five years".

Kofi Annan, *In Larger Freedom*, UN Doc. 59/2005

War, civil war and other political violence often revisit countries after brief periods of 'peace' or armistice. Some countries are ravaged by multifarious violent conflict during two to four decades. Many cease-fires and peace agreements do not cure the underlying social pathology which led to the bloodshed in the first place. I started this study to explore how a country which has gone through civil war might be helped to avoid the next war.

The journey which this explorative study maps out begins at the cease-fire line. It proceeds through the rough and risky terrain of post-war looting, military rule, interim government, and 'transitional' justice. We will pass refugee camps and come across heinous war criminals. Our destination is the promise of a peaceful state in the distance, where stable and possibly good governance gives comfort to the traveller. Grave threats to basic human rights dominate the entire region. The grey zone between war and peace is a source of life-threatening problems, not only to its inhabitants, but also to people in distant countries, far away from the violence.

Around the turn of the twentieth to the twenty-first century, it became clearer than ever before that war, civil war and massive, violent political crimes in a state anywhere in the world can also pose risks to the well-being of other states, even on different continents. In the era of global communications, the news about political violence travels fast. Streams of refugees knock on the doors of other states. The effects of different forms of terrorism, violent and oppressive governments, failing or collapsing states, widespread, abject poverty and virulent, endemic diseases, as well as other sources of instability, can hardly ever be contained to the areas of origin.

National stability and legal order, including human rights, suffer from lawlessness and instability of states elsewhere, as well as from the volatility of the world's political system. The serious deficiencies which exist in the maintenance of human rights in many regions have a troublesome impact on stable states which are trying to uphold those rights. Anarchy, violence and the absence of the rule of law in several states undermine the maintenance of the global legal order.

The imperative of human solidarity prompts us to help avoid violence. It is not only in the enlightened interest, but also in the narrower self-interest of well-developed societies that try to respect all human rights, to foster the rule of law in other societies. There can be no solid international peace without legal order.

There is no effective legal world order when its foundations, the legal order of stable states, are holes or crumbling stones. Encouraging effective states, based on the rule of law, is a major task of foreign policy and civil society.

Fostering the rule of law in foreign societies is a daunting task, however. The efforts of the international community to help build up the rule of law in other states are not always successful. The assistance by the United Nations, the European Union, NATO and many other international bodies, as well as many donor countries and humanitarian or legal assistance organisations are often late, weak, short, divided or ill-designed. Three examples from the mid-1990s illustrate this point.

In 1994 the UN Security Council decided not to provide additional peacekeepers for Rwanda, after a multilateral peace operation in Somalia had become a fiasco. While the UN turned a blind eye to Rwanda, about 800,000 people were killed in a genocidal wave of politically mobilised group hatred.[1]

In 1995, when the UN's peacekeeping effort in Bosnia collapsed, two enclaves, Srebrenica and Zepa, full of Bosnian refugees, were overrun. UN blue helmets from the Netherlands were unable to prevent this. The Serb attackers deported the women, elderly and children to Central Bosnia, but massacred about 7500 men. At the time of writing, the man who ordered the executions, Gen. Mladic, was still to be tried for war crimes.

In 1994-5, the UN decided to intervene in a small and extremely poor Caribbean peninsula, Haiti, to end an illegitimate, suppressive regime and install a democratically elected president, Aristide. While the UN's peacekeeping operation in Haiti was carried out successfully from a military point of view, the further development of the country and its political, legal and economic system was a failure.

Twelve years later (at the time of writing), Haiti was in as bad a state as before. Bosnia appeared to be a relatively successful post-conflict peacebuilding operation, but if foreign peacekeeping forces would leave, local war might break out again. In Rwanda, the future was still heavily mortgaged by inadequate provision of justice vis-à-vis the genocidaires and, understandably, no real reconciliation among Tutsi's and Hutu protagonists.

These three examples show how mixed the experience is of countries which have suffered massive violent political crimes. One can easily add other mixed examples: the UN operations in Sierra Leone, Liberia and Ivory Coast are seen (at the time of writing) as successful. In recent years, Iraq, Afghanistan and Sudan dominate the news. The US, Great Britain and a small group of supporting states took it upon themselves, without approval of the UN Security Council, to remove a very oppressive regime in Iraq and encourage this country to become a democracy. The huge human and economic costs appear to make this intervention very unwise, and the outcome seems very unsettling to large segments of the population and the Persian Gulf region, to say the least.[2]

A coalition of NATO members has been attempting since 2001 to build up Afghanistan after decades of war and civil war, in the hope of a better future for the population. In Sudan the UN and the African Union seem powerless to stop genocidal campaigns encouraged by the government. In many other African states, the African Union and the UN have tried to end murderous political violence, in some cases with success.

As the words of UN Secretary-General Kofi Annan, quoted at the start, indicate, about half of the countries which have gone through civil war fall back into violence in only a few years. In 2006, a World Bank study concluded that 1/3 of countries returns to civil war within 5 years and 1/3 within 10 years, meaning only one in three can avoid a new war for 10 years or longer.[3] This shows that national and international efforts to maintain, re-establish, and develop peaceful structures are often not yet successful. How can it be done better?

Purpose, Method and Limitations

In the light of past failures and limited successes, it is necessary to get an overview of the most relevant issues encountered by assistance programmes for post-conflict peacebuilding, in particular in establishing the rule of law, and to suggest ways to improve international action. The purpose of this brief explorative study is to gain such an overview.

The literature on various peacebuilding operations has grown rapidly over the last fifteen years, and this exploration is not a complete summary of all issues. Its purpose is more modest: to make a practical, provisional attempt to point out the main questions which often arise across very different cases. It is based on various case studies and a number of general works published between 2000 and the middle of 2007. It was inspired by many visits to countries in South Eastern Europe, the Middle East, the Caribbean, Asia and Africa between 1984 and 2005. Involvement of the author in decisions about peace operations in Haiti, Bosnia, Cyprus, West Sahara, Eastern Congo, Albania and other cases motivated this study, particularly the disastrous fall of Srebrenica (Bosnia) and subsequent massacre of Bosnian men and boys.

A chronological overview of main peacebuilding operations is presented in Table 1.1. Cases which received special attention for the purpose of the present study are marked. Operations mentioned in this table were selected by three criteria:

- The post-conflict solution was sought in a unitary or federal political entity.
- The peacebuilding process was strongly influenced by external actors.
- Part of the peacebuilding process was focussed on reform of the rule of law.

Table 1.1 Peace Operations since 1960

Geographical location	Period of operations	Executing agency
Congo *	1960-1964	United Nations (MONUC)
Dominican Republic	1965-1966	United Nations (DOMREP)
Lebanon *	1978-present	United Nations (UNIFIL)
Angola *	1988-1999	United Nations (several missions)
Namibia	1989-1990	United Nations (UNTAG)
Cambodia *	1991-1993	United Nations (various missions)
El Salvador *	1991-1995	United Nations (ONUSAL)
Mozambique *	1992-1994	United Nations (ONUMOZ)
Somalia *	1992-1995	United Nations (UNOSOM) initially under American lead
Bosnia Herzegovina *	1992-present	United Nations (UNPROFOR), later NATO (IFOR/SFOR) and EU in concordance with OSCE and the Council of Europe
Rwanda *	1993-1996	United Nations (UNOMUR/UNAMIR)
Haiti *	1993-present	United Nations (various missions) and OAS, USA and France
Liberia*	1993-1997	United Nations (UNOMIL) and ECOWAS (ECOMOG)
Liberia*	2003-present	Initially ECOWAS (ECOMIL), followed by United Nations (UNMIL)
Tajikistan (ceasefire monitoring)	1994-2000	United Nations (UNMOT), OSCE, CIS
Croatia	1994-1998	United Nations (various missions), EU, NATO
Sri Lanka	1987-1990	India unilateral
FRY Macedonia *	1995-present	UN (UNPREDEP), NATO (Amber Fox and Essential Harvest)
		EU (Proxima) with OSCE and the Council of Europe
Croatia (Eastern Slavonia)	1996-1998	UN (UNTAES)
Guatemala	1997	United Nations (MINUGUA)
Sierra Leone*	1998-present	UN (UNOMSIL/UNAMSIL), ECOWAS & British forces
Central African Republic	1998-2000	United Nations (MINURCA and BONUCA) regional states joint in MISAB
East Timor *	1999-2005	UN (various missions), initially under Australian lead
Kosovo *	1999-present	UN (UNMIK), NATO (KFOR) and EU, supported by OSCE and COE
Dem. Rep. of the Congo	1999-present	UN (MONUC)
Albania *	1997-2002	Italian-led multinational force with EU and OSCE
Lesotho	1998-1999	South African (lead nation) and Botswana forces
Afghanistan *	2001-present	NATO and UN
Iraq	2003-present	Mainly American, British and other coalition forces
Solomon Islands	2003-present	Regional Assistance Mission, under Australian lead
Burundi *	2003-present	Initially African Union (AMIB), as of June 2004 UN (ONUB)
Ivory Coast*	2004-present	ECOWAS (ECOMICI), UN (UNOCI), AU
Sudan (North-South)	2005-present	UN (UNMIS), AU
Sudan (Darfur)	2004-present	AU (AMIS), expansion of role UN under discussion

Many of these cases have been analyzed in studies mentioned in the annex. For *illustrative* purposes, several cases are summarized in textboxes throughout this book. These boxes of just one page do not claim to be complete, of course. They only serve to remind the reader of various crises which received worldwide attention since the Congo crisis of 1960, which can be seen as the first major peacebuilding operation of the UN in an (immediately) failing state. For analysis of these country cases, we refer to Further Reading at the end of this book. The line of thought in this explorative study is guided by practical considerations concerning priorities and their interrelationships. Chapter 2 starts with a general overview. In chapter 3 a tentative, simple theory of peacebuilding is formulated. It also presents lists of states whose people are most in danger of political violence.

Chapters 4 and 5 provide an overview of the vexing questions encountered in the first phase after a violent conflict has ended. They focus on how to improve personal security for the population and lay the foundations for a future legal order. Chapter 6 discusses what criteria might be used when deciding which countries to support with peacebuilding programs. It also gives preliminary cost estimates of such programs. Chapter 7 takes a look at the possibilities for a larger role of the EU in support of peacebuilding. Chapter 8 makes recommendations for improvement of international assistance and further studies.

The subject of this exploration is constantly changing due to new cases, new research, and unfolding events. I acknowledge the valuable contributions which many authors have made and are still being added to the field. It is my intention to add to this book in the coming years, as time allows, to close some gaps in this exploration and add other subjects, such as experiences with conflict *prevention* programmes in a number of countries. An important limitation of this exploration is that the recent, sobering experiences with post-conflict peacebuilding in Iraq and Afghanistan have not been fully included. These subjects require extensive additional study. For all these reasons, this exploration has to remain unfinished and is of a provisional nature. It should be seen as a 'growth document' that may, notwithstanding its shortcomings, still be of some help to others who also are working in the unpredictable 'post-war zone'. I welcome criticism and suggestions at j.voorhoeve@raadvanstate.nl

July 16, 2007

NOTES

1 The UN Security Council had refused to expand the peacekeeping force and strengthen its mandate, as had been urged by the head of mission, Gen. Dallaire, to deal with the escalating violence. See further: Roméo Dallaire, *Shake Hands with the Devil; the Failure of Humanity in Ruanda*, Toronto, Random House of Canada, 2003.

2 Preliminary cost estimates are: at least 70.000 Iraqis killed by internecine, terrorist and economic violence, combat operations and other causes related to the war; 4 million Iraqi refugees and internally displaced persons; 25,000 wounded US and UK soldiers; about 3500 US soldiers killed, and a total US expenditure since the beginning of combat operations till mid 2007 of $ 500 billion, including economic reconstruction costs. Sources: CNN, July 1, 2007; UNHCR; Iraq Body Count; and the government of Iraq. Note that a cross-sectional cluster sample survey of the medical journal *The Lancet* puts the total number of deaths at about 650,000 in 2007. This is disputed by the governments of Iraq, the US and UK.

3 K. Samuels, *Rule of Law Reform, Conflict Prevention Paper 37*, World Bank 2006. www.worldbank.org/conflict.

Congo – The first large peacebuilding mission of the UN

This large Central African country was a colony of Belgium until June 30, 1960. Without any preparation, it was suddenly granted independence, which resulted in political and social instability because of mutiny and the secession of the mineral-rich province of Katanga. A UN-led mission, ONUC, was quickly authorized on July 14, 1960 to restore order and help establish a government.

Within days after the independence, Congolese members of the Force Republique mutinied, and attacked white civilians. As a result, Belgium sent forces to protect its nationals. In the midst of chaos, Tshombe, the leader of Katanga, declared Katanga independent and hired Belgian military and Western mercenaries to prevent government troops from retaking the province. Prime Minister Lumumba of the Congolese government requested that the UN dispatch troops to restore order and oust the Belgian 'aggressors'. In total, 20,000 personnel were contributed to ONUC by approximately 30 countries.

Over the next three years, UN troops forced the removal of foreign mercenaries and suppressed the Katanga secession, while civil elements of the mission provided a wide range of humanitarian, economic, and civil assistance to the new Congolese regime. Given the unprecedented nature of ONUC and the lack of prior experience, doctrine, expert staff or administrative structure for this operation, the United Nations performed remarkably well. Democratic objectives were subordinated by the Security Council to establishing stability and territorial integrity. Large-scale civil conflict was averted for more then a decade following the UN departure.

These achievements came at considerable cost in lives, money and controversy. The costs associated with the UN operation to end the Katanga secession were huge. The Secretary-General of the UN was killed in what seemed to be a plane crash. The corrupt and bloody nature of the following Mobutu dictatorship cast a pall over UN achievements in the Congo.

For the next 25 years the UN restricted its military interventions to interpositional blue-helmet peacekeeping, where all the parties to a conflict agreed with UN intervention and where the use of armed force by UN troops was limited to self-defence. The UN learned that peace enforcement is costly and controversial, even when done well. It was a massive operation, improvised by a very conscientious UN Secretary General, Dag Hammarskjöld.

See also text box on Congo since Mobutu

2 AN OVERVIEW OF PEACEBUILDING

"If civilization is to survive, we must cultivate the science of human relationships – the ability of all peoples, of all kinds, to live together and work together in the same world, at peace."

Franklin D. Roosevelt, in a draft speech before he died in 1945

2.1 WHAT IS PEACEBUILDING?

Everything necessary for normal human life starts with the absence of violence. The core tasks of any government are to provide physical peace, public security and basic freedoms to its citizens. The common purpose of various forms of democratic government is to create conditions which enable its population to satisfy their needs and desires and enjoy human rights, to the extent that this does not harm others.

Of course, no country is Utopia. Thomas More's Utopia was a fantasy island without international relations. There were no external security concerns. In the real world, the core tasks of maintaining peace, security and freedom require international action. In the intertwined world of the 21st century, it is in the national interest of democratic states to help end war, civil war, terrorism and gross and persistent human rights violations outside their own states, to the extent possible. (The degree to which this is feasible is discussed in the following chapters.) Rapid global communications quickly spread unrest beyond state borders. Territories which are plagued by political violence, large scale crime, pandemic diseases and absolute poverty upset and 'infect' distant nations.

In this study, post-conflict peacebuilding means building or reconstructing a country after its government, institutions, population and economy have been ravaged by large-scale armed conflict. Experience shows that after an internal or international war, and after a successful foreign military intervention, a peace enforcement action or peacekeeping operation, there are serious reconstruction problems which take a long time to resolve. Military intervention is usually difficult and controversial in itself, but it is also the beginning of new, tough challenges. At the end of a conflict there is often no consolidated central power, no functioning legal order, no good governance, no democracy, and no protection of human rights. In many cases most of the population lives in poverty – already endemic or worsened by the war. Hatred between groups exacerbated by wartime violence and abuses often increases the risk of a return to war. Most wars sow the seeds of new violence.

Post-conflict reconstruction faces the same challenges and requires the same efforts as state-building in places where the state collapsed for reasons other than war. In both instances, the lack of a functioning government and a collapse of the rule of law are the central problems. The problem of failing and ineffective states is most pressing in large parts of Africa, some states in the Middle East, the Caucasus region, South-Eastern Europe, and around the Caspian Sea. Some are also found in South East Asia, the Pacific, Latin America and the Caribbean region.

It is not only states destroyed by war and failing or collapsed states that leave holes in the international legal order. There are also areas within geographic states which do not effectively fall under that state's legal order, such as remote valleys, mountains, jungles far removed from the state's institutional reach, or territories where existing governments are only loose structures with little claim to actual control beyond the government's quarters in the capital. Many such territories have become havens for drug barons, heavily armed tribal potentates, pirates, training camps for terrorist organizations, child armies and rebel groups operating across borders into neighbouring states. Conversely, there are also states in anarchy, with very weak central governments, but in some regions or provinces, local order is maintained by traditional or alternative authorities in better ways than the central government is able to do for the country as a whole.

Peacebuilding should be pursued in ways which lower the risks that a country falls back into violence. This requires many years of intensive efforts by all communities in the country itself, and long-lasting, well-guided assistance from other countries and international organisations – the so-called international community which, in fact, consists only of a relatively small number of interested states, international organisations, and many NGOs, often rather small.

2.2 A HISTORY OF FAILURE?

Although the UN peace operation in the newly independent Congo in 1960-64 helped to prevent secession of Katanga and stopped much bloodshed, it could not create a stable country. Congo, later Zaire and then the Democratic republic of Congo again, was ill-prepared by its colonizers for independence. It is still too large and diverse to grow rapidly into a stable, sustainable and effective state. Congo experienced more than four decades of violence, exploitation, bad government and civil war.

The entire Great Lakes region in Africa has become a political disaster area which is much worse in the late 20th and early 21st century than ever before. The genocide in Rwanda in 1994 made the headlines. The following years, many more in this region have been killed or maimed for life: perhaps more than 5 million people died in the Great Lakes region as the result of the war since 1994. Some died directly in fighting, but the vast majority died from poverty and disease exacerbated by the war.

Thirteen years after the humanitarian intervention to end bloodshed and hunger in Somalia, that country is still a shambles, lacking an effective central government. The Transitional Federal Government, appointed in 2004, was unable to

Somalia

During the colonial period, Somalia was divided into British, Italian and French Somaliland. In 1960, Britain and Italy withdrew, which lead to unification of the northern and southern part and the establishment of Somalia as a state.

Between 1969 and 1990, a socialist military dictatorship ruled the country. At the end of the 1980's the authority of this government declined when the end of the Cold War was coming close and the population became disillusioned about life under military rule.

In 1991, resistance movements overthrew the regime. Since then, Somalia has suffered from instability and anarchy. In 1991-1992, a severe civil war destroyed large parts of agriculture and food distribution, causing widespread famine. Talks between the parties led to a ceasefire; a small UN peacekeeping force (UNOSOM) was sent in April 1992 to monitor this ceasefire and protect humanitarian aid.

The violence continued and in December 1992 the United States led an operation (UNITAF) to establish a secure environment (authorized by the UN to use 'all necessary means'). The tasks of UNITAF were taken over by UNOSOM II in March 1993; the mandate also included disarmament, mine-clearing, repatriation of refugees, and the reestablishment of national institutions in the country. The UN troops suffered significant casualties (for example in the 'Battle of Mogadishu') and withdrew from Somalia in March 1995, although the rule of the government was not restored.

Somalia became the example of a 'failed state'. Northern groups declared an independent Republic of Somaliland. Competing warlords ruled over smaller territories.
The Transitional National Government (TNG) came to existence in Somalia in 2000 but lacked authority because of opposition from warlords. Between 2003 and 2006, a transitional constitution was created, followed by the election of a president, a prime minister and the establishment of an interim government. The UN supported this process.
In June 2006, 'Islamic court' militias defeated Mogadishu warlords and took control of the capital. The militias tried to expand over the rest of the country, but the interim government of Somalia responded with the help of Ethiopian forces. Heavy fighting between these parties, combined with severe droughts and floods, led to a grave humanitarian situation. The UN Security Council authorized an African Union peacekeeping mission; the first troops flew into Somalia in March 2007.

UN operations in Somalia taught that a profound analysis of the tribal political situation is needed before a humanitarian operation. Objectives should be limited to what is feasible in a limited number of years. A failure in one case can make the UN too risk-averse or even negligent in the next one (Rwanda).

overcome the complete anarchy that reigned before. It was incapable of establishing itself in Mogadishu and had no effective control over Somalia or its territorial waters. In 2006, it lost almost all control in the uprising of the Islamic Courts movement. Neighbouring Ethiopia intervened militarily. At the time of writing, it was unclear which direction the country would take.

Fortunately, there are also examples of relatively successful peacebuilding efforts. Since the Dayton Peace Agreement of 1995, Bosnia is at peace, although twelve years on, tensions in the country are still too strong to allow for a withdrawal of international troops. Mozambique is an African example of a very poor country that has experienced peaceful growth, some freedom, and has held several elections, after a long war of decolonisation followed by civil war. Its success story is partly explained by relatively large assistance over a long period of time, in particular from some member states of the European Union, which adopted Mozambique as a 'donor darling' for development assistance.

In general, development cooperation with poor countries, as it grew since the 1960s, was first focussed on fighting poverty and improving socio-economic conditions after a country became independent. Originally, development cooperation steered clear of political questions such as mismanagement of the country by its own leadership.

Similarly, peace operations were originally limited to establishing military peace and trying to maintain it. The two, development cooperation and peace operations, were separate activities, far removed from each other, carried out by different organisations, under the responsibility of Ministries which did not communicate much with each other. A merger of peace enforcement, peacekeeping, and peace support operations, with such civilian tasks as emergency assistance, peacebuilding activities and development cooperation has become the norm only recently. In a small number of countries, the international donors have pioneered an integrated approach, for example in Kosovo and East Timor.

However, such joint operations often lack clear leadership and a common purpose of the various donors. In Bosnia, 450 international organisations, large and small, have been working since 1996, with different mandates, sometimes in fragmented ways. A common complaint heard from staff engaged with the various facets of peacebuilding in the field is: we are doing too little and our work is too fragmented; the causes of the violence are not really tackled.

2.3 ELEMENTS OF PEACEBUILDING

There is often no clear division between war and peace. There is rarely one exact date marking the transition from one to the other. Violence tends to linger on after a cease-fire. Reconstruction has to start in an environment of insecurity. As a result, the new (interim) government has to begin many of the tasks of peacebuilding and reconstruction at the same time, in a high risk environment.

The main elements of peacebuilding are: establishing security, renewal of government institutions, (re)starting the rule of law, possibly sowing the seeds of democracy, and socio-economic rehabilitation and development. In the beginning, emergency powers are needed for stabilisation. Ruined infrastructure needs to be repaired. Mines have to be cleared. Refugees need protection and assistance to return safely to their homes.

The sense of security and faith in the future will increase if an international peace force disarms and demobilises former warring parties, disbands paramilitary forces, reintegrates combatants and builds law-abiding security forces, including professional police, embedded in a new legal order. Progress towards democracy needs to be entrenched through national, regional and local elections. Prosecution, arrest and trial of war criminals is needed, while a new professional justice system has to be built up, for which officials have to be (re)trained and laws have to be enacted. These tasks are formidable, as they encounter much opposition from old vestiges of power.

Good government, based on an internally recognised and legitimate legal order with clearly defined powers, accepted by the population, is the basis for lasting internal peace. In countries outside the OECD-area (comprised of Europe, North America, Australia, New Zealand, Japan, South Korea and Mexico) donors are tempted to transplant European multi-party democracy. They might instead help to create conditions for power sharing, pluralism and inclusive participation in political decision making. Security for individuals and respect for basic human rights are crucial. An independent, well-functioning, professional justice system and independence of the media are the best checks on corruption and abuse of power.

Peacebuilding requires patience. Instant solutions and quick fixes, often advocated by donors who think that their electorates are averse to long-term involvement, do not bring lasting stability. Peacebuilding takes more nerve and stamina than fighting wars. Ten weeks of military intervention often need to be followed by ten years of peacebuilding, to avoid a return to bloodshed. In many capitals, one can admire statues of generals who have won a war. Statesman and diplomats who avoided wars by caution and compromise are less frequently immortalized.

Countries that provide troops for peacekeeping or enforcement actions are generally inclined to withdraw them as soon as possible to reduce casualties among their own troops and limit domestic criticism and high expenses, but international forces often remain crucial to stabilising the country. Their presence is usually required for several years to allow peacebuilding to proceed. These stabilising forces should be strong enough to deter resumption of hostilities. Experience in Afghanistan and Iraq shows that frequent terrorist acts can seriously undermine peacebuilding. Organising, training and supporting a new police structure helps shifting domestic security tasks from military to civilian control. It is important to encourage visible, domestic ownership of the security sphere and weaken the criticism that foreign troops are an occupying force.

One can categorise these manifold activities in eight elements:

Table 2.1 Overview of peacebuilding activities

Task	Activities	Main Organisations
1. Ending violence	Political and diplomatic actions to arrange a cease-fire and facilitate a peace agreement. Deterrence of war, civil war and terrorism by military security.	UN, NATO, regional organisations or ad hoc coalitions
2. Emergency assistance	Food, medicine, water, shelter.	Red Cross, NGOs, UN-agencies, regional organisations
3. Disarmament, demobilisation, reintegration and de-mining	Reduction of weapons and troops; collection and destruction of munitions; charting mine fields; demining of roads.	UN, NATO, regional security organisations
4. Economic reconstruction	Restarting the economy; encouraging employment; reducing poverty; Reconstruction of infrastructure Return of investors.	World Bank, IMF, Specialised UN organisations, EU, bilateral donors
5. Transitional justice; reconciliation	Trials of local war criminals; reconciliation programmes and 'truth commissions'; trauma assistance, especially for women, children, wounded soldiers.	Legal assistance organisations; social and religious organisations; educational institutions; local govt. and media
6. Legal Order	Monitoring, advising and training of police and prosecutors; training of judges; renewal of laws; renewal of prison system; renewal of courts; trials of war crimes suspects.	UN, regional organisations, NGOs, bilateral donors, war crimes tribunals, International Criminal Court
7. New (democratic) government	New constitutional order; elections for new leadership at local, regional and national level; political party formation.	UN, regional organisations, OSCE, IDEA, various NGOs and bilateral aid
8. Refugee return	Return and resettlement of refugees and displaced persons.	UNHCR, World Bank, OCHA, bilateral donors, NGOS

It goes without saying that reality is more complex than this overview. The pattern of required steps differs from country to country. The eight tasks of table 2 are not equally urgent, and overlap each other. In order to succeed, each task is often dependent on the effective execution of the others.

In the chaos after political violence, many essential steps need to be taken by local, national and international leaders at the same time. Many forms of international assistance are urgent. It is hard to prioritise: more troops to ensure security, more medical aid, repair of drinking water systems, rebuilding bridges and houses, electricity, and the list goes on. Everything needs to be there at once, which is of course not possible. Priorities have to be set and proper sequencing has to be managed. How all activities could be sequenced will be indicated in chapter 8. Needless to say, this 'optimal sequencing' is only a general indication, as the best time to start, the duration of the activities and their relative priorities differ from case to case.

2.4 INTERNATIONAL ORGANIZATIONS

Since the early 1990's, several international organizations have entered the fields of peacebuilding *inside* their member states. At the global level, the United Nations and many of its special agencies and programmes have developed policies and programmes to help secure peace after a conflict. Related efforts have been made for conflict prevention. Many of their activities will be mentioned in the following chapters, but this exploration does not contain a complete summary of what each is doing.

At the turn of the century, the UN took new initiatives to bring more coherence to the still fragmented and ineffective system of international organisations working in the field of peacebuilding. The UN decided in 2005 to establish a permanent Peacebuilding Commission. It began work in 2006 as a subsidiary body of the UN Security Council. Hopes that this would become a strong new institution have not as yet been fulfilled. At the UN summit of September 2005, the Peacebuilding Commission was defined as an *advisory* body. The UN General Assembly also proposed in September 2005 to establish a 'Peacebuilding Fund' from voluntary contributions. In 2006, a Central Emergency Response Fund was indeed set up with contributions totalling $250 million.

The Peacebuilding Commission should provide recommendations and information to improve the coordination of all relevant actors within and outside the United Nations, develop best practices, help to ensure predictable financing for early recovery and extend the period of attention paid by the international community to post-conflict recovery. The Commission is to give its advice in *consensus*. This advisory character and the required consensus will reduce its power, effectiveness and ability to reach agreement swiftly, as countries with contrary views can delay or prevent decisions. The recommended participation and size of its meetings is very large, if not unwieldy. It might have been better to establish a smaller commission of Security Council members and major countries and organisations involved in large assistance programmes.

The Peacebuilding Commission intends to form subcommittees for individual countries in need of assistance. In the fall of 2006, two country cases were started: Burundi and Sierra Leone. At the time of writing, no evaluation was possible of the effectiveness of the Commission. The first task was to design with like-minded countries effective subcommittees that will enhance coordination of donor countries, international organisations and NGOs in specific cases and avoid vagueness and slowness that could threaten the Peacebuilding Commission.

The UN General Assembly of September 2005 also supported the establishment of a Democracy Fund at the United Nations. In 2006, it made its first round of funding decisions. Its projects support reform of constitutions, advice to political parties, electoral laws, election preparation, election oversight and other activities for democratisation.

Of increasing importance for peacebuilding are the policies and programmes of the European Union. That is why a separate chapter 7 is devoted to an analysis of EU policies in this field.

After this indicative overview, we will attempt, in the next chapter, to distinguish types of countries in trouble, and try to formulate a general approach to effective peacebuilding.

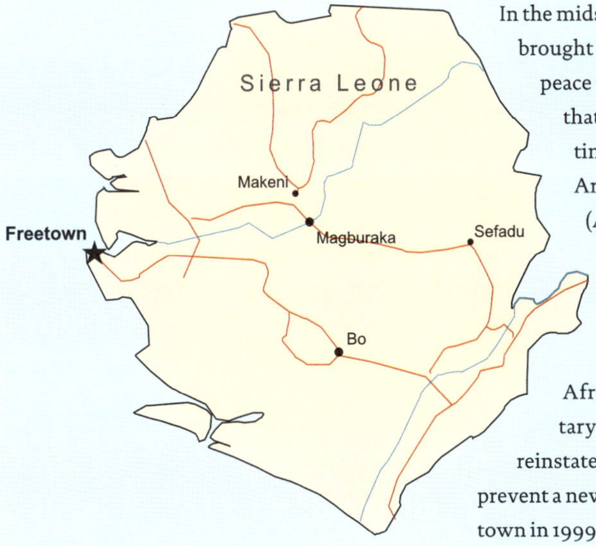

Sierra Leone is a relatively small West African country of about 6 million inhabitants who have an average life expectancy of barely 40 years. The country became internationally known for its 'blood' diamonds that helped finance the gruesome civil war lasting from 1991 to 2002. Independence from Britain in 1961 was followed by political instability and economic trouble. Corrupt leaders and military coups succeeded each other.
Stevens became prime minister after the 1968 elections and the first president after having declared the Republic in 1971. He was succeeded by Momoh 1986 who paved the way for a more democratic constitution in 1991.

That same year, civil war broke out. The combination of a weak state, poverty and corruption enabled Sankoh's Revolutionary United Front (RUF) to recruit unemployed youth. In 1992, the government was overthrown by Strasser's Republic of Sierra Leone Military Forces (RSLMF). During the following years the RUF waged war against the RSLMF and seized significant areas by using terror tactics. In 1995 the RUF captured Freetown. Anarchy broke out and thousands were killed, mutilated, or raped. Strasser used a private army to destroy important RUF headquarters and recapture Freetown. In the midst of war, presidential elections brought Kabbah to power. Subsequent peace talks resulted in the Abidjan Accord that officially ended the war for the first time. The following year, Koromha's Armed Forces Revolutionary Council (AFRC) took power and continued the war. Nigeria's initial intervention failed, though it returned under the flag of the Economic Community of West African States (ECOWAS) with its military wing ECOMOG. The intervention reinstated Kabbah in 1998, but could not prevent a new RUF and AFRC invasion of Freetown in 1999. In 1998 the UN sent an observer mission to Sierra Leone, which was replaced by UNAMSIL that received a broader mandate to protect citizens.

The 1999 Lomé peace agreement called for an immediate cease fire and set up a power-sharing government of national unity. The year 2000 witnessed the outbreak of large scale fights between rebels, the government and UN peace forces. British troops intervened to protect the UN-peace forces and bring some stability. The second Abuja Agreement, signed in May 2001, started disarmament, demobilization and reintegration of former rebels. The president declared peace in 2002. UNAMSIL left the country in 2005.

Since then, Sierra Leone's authorities have carried full responsibility for interior security with the help of the UN Integrated Office (UNIOSIL) and an International Military Advisory and Training Team (IMATT). Sierra Leone has struggled to combat the causes of the war: extreme poverty, unemployment, corruption, and a weak state. The Special Court for Sierra Leone put on trial suspects of war crimes. The country's future now appears brighter; democratic institutions are being built under guidance of the international community.

3 TOWARDS TYPOLOGY AND THEORY

It would be a mistake to generalise quickly about peacebuilding operations. All countries and wars are different. There are at present 192 member states of the United Nations and a number of autonomous but not fully sovereign nations and territories. These countries all have their distinct characteristics. The same applies to wars, civil wars, and other forms of contemporary armed conflict and political violence. No manifestation can be said to be the same as another. Comparative analysis of various cases offers insight, but the number of variables that differ between countries is so large that modesty is necessary when searching for general theory. The large number of variables and the immeasurability of many of them make generalisations about international politics, comparative politics and violent conflicts very complex. In some areas of research, useful generalisations are nearly impossible, or remain so abstract that they are almost meaningless. As is the case with human beings, generalisations about states, too, need to be supplemented by a precise analysis of the separate features of each individual case and its unique combinations.

3.1 A DEDUCTIVE TYPOLOGY

Nonetheless, for the sake of overview, some classification is needed of states in various kinds of trouble. Let us start with deduction, without reference to possible statistical measurement, which will be discussed later. To begin with, the majority of states are in a *state of peace* only in the minimal sense of an absence of war (negative peace). Usually, in a state which is not experiencing internal war, most of the means of violence are in the hands of the governments' military and police forces. In between these 'states in peace' and 'states in or at war' are states which seem at peace, but their peace is brittle, threatened by looming external or civil war, terrorism, widespread crime, drugs lords and armed gangs.

Next to this, one can distinguish among states according to quality of government system. It is clear that some countries in peace are governed well and others very badly. Good government is effective and legitimate. (For a definition of good governance, see section 3.2). As legitimacy and effectiveness are related but separate dimensions, let us first look at legitimacy.

Legitimacy in a broad, sociological sense means that the majority of the population accepts the authority of the government on the basis of laws, traditional rules and norms, and cultural values, instead of 'acceptance' of the rulers due to a fear of the government's oppressive and coercive power.

Authoritarian regimes which uphold their laws generally rule *by* law, but this is not the same as the rule *of* law. The rule of law requires legitimacy in a stricter, legal sense, meaning that all authority is wielded only under laws which have been approved voluntarily by freely elected representatives of the population.

Acceptance by the population reflects various types of approval. Is the government widely accepted because it rests on democratic structures of representation and the rule of law, or because of traditional authority patterns seen by most of the population as 'normal', even if there is no rule of law? Or would the government and state institutions be rejected if people were given a chance to express themselves? Degrees of internal acceptance and legitimacy in a broad sense could be used as the second 'dimension' of a categorisation of states.

A third aspect, *effectiveness*, means that a government and its apparatus are able to carry out government decisions and make citizens and institutions behave accordingly. A precondition for effectiveness is that the government's authority is at least passively accepted by the population, and that the state has a monopoly over the means of physical coercion (often abbreviated by the loose and wider notion of 'power'). This coercive monopoly can ensure domestic peace between opposing interests inclined to use force against each other or the state itself. This monopoly can also safeguard national security from external threats. Coercive monopoly maintains the domestic legal order against the use and threat of violence by others than the state. This monopoly also indirectly enforces the main laws and institutions for the economic system.

An effective government provides all necessary public services and collective goods such as safety for the population, an effective justice system, education, basic health care, physical infrastructure and protection of the natural environment. Government effectiveness means that the state's main aims are met and that the government's main policies and institutions are accepted and carried out by the population. The effectiveness of government is, for instance, low in many African states, as the government does not provide many useful services, while different tribes feel little solidarity with a 'post-colonial' state structure imposed on them, often dividing the tribe among different governments.

The two aspects just mentioned, effectiveness and acceptance, would by themselves lead to a fourfold classification. Examples of ineffective and illegitimate governments abound; they form a motley collection of states run by groups which grabbed the means of suppression to advance their political agenda and ideology or personal interests. Portugal is a good example of a country which moved with international assistance in two decades from traditional, well integrated but rather ineffective and not very legitimate, to being effective and very legitimate. An opposite example, moving from relatively effective/legitimate (at least in African terms) to ineffective/illegitimate is Zimbabwe in the last ten years of Mugabe's rule. A number of communist countries in the post-WW2 era had relatively effective but illegitimate governments. And an example of a legitimate but ineffective government was India in the first decades after independence. It has become increasingly effective since. This simple typology can of course be developed into greater precision by specifying more variables.

In addition to the three aspects dealt with up to this point – security, effectiveness and acceptance – we should consider the reach of the *government domain*.

Domain refers to the functional areas and sectors of society over which the government exerts control. The US government (federal and states), for instance, has a limited domain relative to society. It leaves many sectors relatively free. The US tax revenue or government expenses divided by national income are very low compared to other OECD member states. The domain of the Northwest European governments, which try to maintain a social welfare state, is much bigger. Government domain is, however, not to be seen as the opposite of freedom: some human rights, particularly socio-economic and cultural rights, are guaranteed better in states with a large domain than in those with a limited scope of regulation.

This typology based on security, acceptance, effectiveness and domain, yields in theory at least 36 different pigeon holes, if domain is divided in large or small; effectiveness in effective or ineffective, acceptance in illegitimate, traditional, or democratic, and if security is divided in high, medium or low.

One should add a fifth, economic factor for consideration, like income per capita, or a composite indicator for the prevalence of prosperity or its opposite, poverty. How to combine absolute poverty figures with income inequality and other indicators of economic ill health of a country is left aside for the moment. Let us assume such an indicator can be made carefully, and just call this dimension *poverty*. This fifth dimension has a complex relationship with peace. Poverty in the sense of a very low income per capita could exist in history along with political stability and low frequency of war and civil war, in traditional societies which underwent little or very slow change.

The frequency of political violence tends to rise when economic modernization and social change pick up speed. Civil strife correlates with change and with rising expectations. During the transition from a stable, traditional society to a highly developed, modern society, political violence occurs much more frequently. This rising unrest tends to decline after the transition is more or less completed and prosperity is enjoyed by a high proportion of the population. This phenomenon contradicts the hope that economic development, by satisfying consumer needs and providing more employment, directly reduces wars and civil wars. As most less-developed nations are in transition, a relatively low level of income per capita correlates since the Second World War with a high frequency of violence. This depends also heavily on related, other economic factors, like a very unequal distribution of income which is seen as highly unjust by the population. The complex relation between poverty and violence also works the other way round: oppression, civil wars and international wars strongly reduce the capacity of a country to create more wealth and reach a state of steady economic progress. Frequent violence undermines confidence in the near future and reduces the propensity of the population, the business elite and foreign companies to save and invest in that country.

The five aspects of the nature of the state mentioned above – *security, acceptance, effectiveness, domain and poverty* – are not independent from each other. It is clear that national security influences acceptance, domain and effectiveness, while acceptance, effectiveness and domain also influence each other. Insecurity and ineffectiveness correlate highly with poverty. For brief, descriptive purposes or comparisons, however, this typology may be a handy scheme to indicate the different contexts in which peacebuilding and rule-of-law assistance programmes operate. Low effectiveness, low legitimacy, high insecurity, small domain and widespread poverty signal 'red alert'. High effectiveness, high legitimacy, high security, large domain and little poverty indicate a solid state. For example, we can see that the government of Afghanistan is ineffective, people are insecure and poor, and the government has a small domain, but has increased in legitimacy due to recent internationally organised elections. Yet its acceptance by regional leaders and various ethnic groupings is not secure. China on the other hand is effective, secure, has a large domain, and its acceptance is relatively high (not democratic but not considered illegitimate). Though the People's Republic of China has been very successful since the early 1980s in eliminating much poverty in Eastern coastal regions, a major source of inner tension is rising economic inequality, regionally and socially, due to remaining poverty in the areas which are far away from its bustling cities.

A weakness of the typology just outlined is that most states are not internally homogeneous. Some governments may represent a small part of the population rather well but suppress and exploit the rest. Examples are states whose governments are dominated by one out of many tribes, or by a closed political elite bent on increasing their benefits from state positions. Such governments are often supported by systems of patronage and *clientelism*, which may appear to be ' democratic', as those who benefit from ruling others and have much influence over the media can be able to channel voting behaviour in favour of electoral victories. But the system breeds corruption. Resentment, and a lack of trust among those who do not profit or are suppressed, will weaken the state in the long run.

Here, a policy remark comes to mind. In situations as those just mentioned, it is risky to give assistance to an unrepresentative government without strict conditions. Preaching reform to oppressive elite is likely to remain without results. No diplomat or aid minister should entertain the illusion that a *cleptocratic* power circle is eager to cut its revenue. Those in power try to increase it and will say 'yes' to the donors' conditions, but fail to act upon them in a *bonafide* fashion once foreign funds have been secured.

Fortunately, many corrupt governments are not monolithic. It is not impossible to find institutions which are run by people of good intent who can use foreign training and expert advice while their government is of a rather evil nature.

Foreign donors may have to walk a tight-rope assisting these persons, without drawing too much attention from distrustful government leaders. Such investments run the risk of failure once the top officials clamp down, but they also can sow some seeds of change. This needs to be determined case-by-case, weighing the risks and opportunities.

In such instances, it may still be possible to help improve the professional civil service officers at the middle and lower level, especially of offices that appear able to shield themselves to some extent from corruptive influences from the top, like parts of the court system, which may benefit from professional training.

A donor may also choose to strengthen non-governmental institutions. Helping civil society to organize itself better and increase awareness of human rights may encourage social change from below in due course. This, too, is not without risk, as authoritarian leaders may take harsh counter measures.

3.2 GOOD GOVERNANCE AND HUMAN RIGHTS

Good governance can be defined as the fair and efficient management of a country's public resources in a sustainable fashion, as well as the upholding of laws and institutions that encourage optimal private management of people's lives and private resources, without trespassing basic human rights and freedoms. The general purpose is to optimise conditions for sustainable enjoyment of human rights.

Perhaps good governance could be codified in a set of internationally accepted norms, if possible in treaty form, by organs of the United Nations.[1] Many elements of such a code are already available from international human rights treaties, UN documents, the EU Handbook on Good Government, and from individual country statements and academic sources.[2]

Officially, there is an *international consensus on human rights* as defined in treaties which have been signed by almost all governments and representatives of major philosophies and religions. Differences in emphasis and interpretation will always exist but do not reduce the general validity of the aspiration of human rights. It is sometimes argued that human rights as formulated in the relevant international treaties are too individualistic and not taking into account 'Islamic culture', 'collectivist Asian values', or 'African culture'. The universal human rights treaties fit a cosmopolitan view and equal rights philosophy, which assumes that all human beings deserve fair chances to a happy life. This differs from ways of thinking which emphasise not the ethical rights of all human beings, but supposed privileges of nations, peoples, (small) communities, certain people with a particular set of characteristics (such as religious, cultural, linguistic, racial or ethnic features) and their membership of privileged groupings.

As many of the human rights of the international treaties are not equally respected and upheld in most states, one might distinguish, of course, among human rights of a first order, particularly the rights needed to enjoy physical security, and a second or third group of rights which are essential for freedom of expression and freedom from want. The obvious distinction between political rights, on the one hand, and socio-economic and cultural rights on the other, has been made in the UN conventions. Communal or *group* rights and other particular identities are notions that are not easy to square ethically with equal *human* rights. Moreover, rights of particular groups are difficult to define.

Why may certain people *not* belong to the group, and on what ethical ground can they be excluded from equal rights? Group rights which do not relate to objective criteria such as the rights of children or the rights of women run into tricky questions. It is beyond the area of this study on reconstruction assistance to further discuss these differences in the notions of human rights and their impact, however important they are. We simply proceed on the basis of the two most important UN treaties which are also the foundations for several other protocols and conventions that are binding for all nations and people.[3]

In general, improving respect for human rights has become a widely agreed aim for national and international assistance, which has been reconfirmed many times by the international community over the past few decades. One can remain sceptical about the gap between words and deeds, but should not be relativist as to the general ideal, which is supported by the world's main religions and philosophies. We return to this in section 5.13.

3.3 WARNING SIGNALS

Which practical indicators exist to get a quick overview of the war risks different peoples are exposed to? The Fund for Peace[4] has designed a system to assess if a state risks state failure and civil war. This conflict assessment methodology CAST (Conflict Assessment Tool) uses twelve indicators of a social, economic or political nature:

A Social Indicators
1. mounting demographic pressures
2. massive movement of refugees or internally displaced persons creating complex humanitarian emergencies
3. legacy of vengeance-seeking group grievance or group paranoia
4. chronic and sustained human flight (educated, middle class)

B Economic Indicators
5. uneven economic development along group lines
6. sharp and/or severe economic decline

C Political Indicators
7. criminalisation and/or de-legitimization of the state
8. progressive deterioration of public services

9. suspension or arbitrary application of the rule of law and widespread violation of human rights
10. the state's security apparatus operates as a 'state within a state'
11. rise of factionalised elites
12. intervention of other states or other external political actors

The CAST methodology enumerates five qualities which reflect the capacity of a state to cope with the risks of state failure:
1. a competent police force and corrections system
2. an efficient, professional civil service
3. an independent judicial system that works under the rule of law
4. a professional and disciplined military accountable to a legitimate civilian government
5. a strong executive/legislative leadership capable of national governance.

The CAST analysis supports the view that the rule of law has a strong impact on the risk that a state falls (again) into civil war. The CAST analysis is used to make an index of states which are most at risk of falling into civil war, as shown in the text box and on the map.

3.4 AN ATTEMPT AT THEORY

Pondering the practical challenges posed by peacebuilding begs the question if theoretical generalisation is possible as a way to gain an overview, notwithstanding the observation at the outset that all countries and wars are different. The purposes of a peacebuilding theory might be: 1. to help diagnose the political pathology of countries; 2. to help determine feasible goals, optimal treatment, and suitable sequencing of actions; 3. to select countries in need for assistance programs; 4. to better allocate limited resources; 5. to find the best 'agents of change' (improvement) in countries in need; and also 6. to develop crisis prevention strategies. Such theory may exist, but we have not yet identified it. This new field of study might not yet be ready for such achievements, but the need is great and new studies may help to make progress in the next few years.
In the present explorative study, the purpose is more modest: to find elements of a possible theory that might help to improve assistance to building the rule of law in post-conflict societies.

There are different approaches and frameworks used in the peacebuilding literature, such as a liberal/universalistic strand which focuses on human rights, and more constructivist strands that focus on local culture. The subject area of assistance for building the rule of law in foreign countries is relatively new as an academic and policy field. On the other hand, history offers endless cases of building and reforming states and their various legal systems, sometimes with outside assistance, or under strong external pressures.

Failed States index

Foreign Policy Magazine has published with the assistance of the Fund for Peace an index that gives an indication of the weakest states in the world.[5] State structures can fail 'by explosion, implosion, erosion or invasion.' A state that is failing loses control over territory and its monopoly over the means of force. Next comes the inability to provide basic services.

The indicators cover a wide range, such as corruption, criminal behaviour, large-scale displacement of the population, rapid economic decline, sharp inequality, persecution or discrimination, and environmental decay.

The index depicts the world's weakest states. Its 12 social, economic, political and military indicators are used to rank 177 states in order of vulnerability to violent internal conflict and deterioration of the society.

The ranking in the right column shows the 60 most vulnerable states as published in 2007. The left column shows a recent, more comprehensive index (which is not necessarily better) which measures both the internal and external peacefulness of countries. This Global Peace Index is discussed in the GPI textbox hereafter.

For brevity, we have omitted the indices attributed to separate countries and show the rank of countries according to both indices *in reverse*. The table starts with the worst cases: numbers 1 and 2 are the most inclined to state failure, etc. The lower the number, the higher the risks.

Global Peace Index and Failed States Index

Worst Rank	Ranking Global Peace Index	Ranking Failed States Index
1	Iraq	Sudan
2	Sudan	Iraq
3	Israel	Somalia
4	Russia	Zimbabwe
5	Nigeria	Chad
6	Colombia	Ivory Coast
7	Pakistan	Congo
8	Lebanon	Afghanistan
9	Ivory Coast	Guinea
10	Angola	Central African Republic
11	Sri Lanka	Haiti
12	Uzbekistan	Pakistan
13	India	North Korea
14	Myanmar	Burma/Myanmar
15	Algeria	Uganda
16	Zimbabwe	Bangladesh
17	Thailand	Nigeria
18	Uganda	Ethiopia
19	Ethiopia	Burundi
20	Venezuela	East Timor
21	Azerbaijan	Nepal

Worst Rank	Ranking Global Peace Index	Ranking Failed States Index
22	Philippines	Uzbekistan
23	South Africa	Sierra Leone
24	Honduras	Yemen
25	Iran	Sri Lanka
26	United States	Rep Congo
27	Yemen	Liberia
28	Trinidad Tobago	Lebanon
29	Guatemala	Malawi
30	Turkey	Solomon Islands
31	Kenya	Kenya
32	Saudi Arabia	Niger
33	El Salvador	Colombia
34	Papua New Guinea	Burkina Faso
35	Bangladesh	Cameroon
36	Ecuador	Egypt
37	Cambodia	Rwanda
38	Serbia	Guinea Bissau
39	Brazil	Tajikistan
40	Macedonia	Syria
41	Jamaica	Equatorial Guinea
42	Ukraine	Kyrgyzstan
43	Mexico	Turkmenistan
44	Indonesia	Laos
45	Syria	Mauritania
46	Cameroon	Togo
47	Bosnia Herzegovina	Bhutan
48	Dominican Republic	Cambodia
49	Egypt	Moldova
50	Equatorial Guinea	Eritrea
51	Moldova	Belarus
52	Peru	Papua New Guinea
53	Bolivia	Angola
54	Malawi	Bosnia
55	Croatia	Indonesia
56	Nicaragua	Philippines
57	Senegal	Iran
58	Namibia	Georgia
59	Jordan	Bolivia
60	Kazakhstan	Guatemala

The Striking differences between both indexes are discussed in the following textbox on the Global Peace Index, after the Failing State Map.

The Failing State Map

The ranking on the failing state index is based on the score on the 12 indicators of the CAST system mentioned in section 3.3. Each rating is from 0 to 10, with 0 being the lowest intensity (most stable) and 10 being the highest intensity (least stable). The total score is the sum of the 12 indicators, and is on a scale of 0-120.

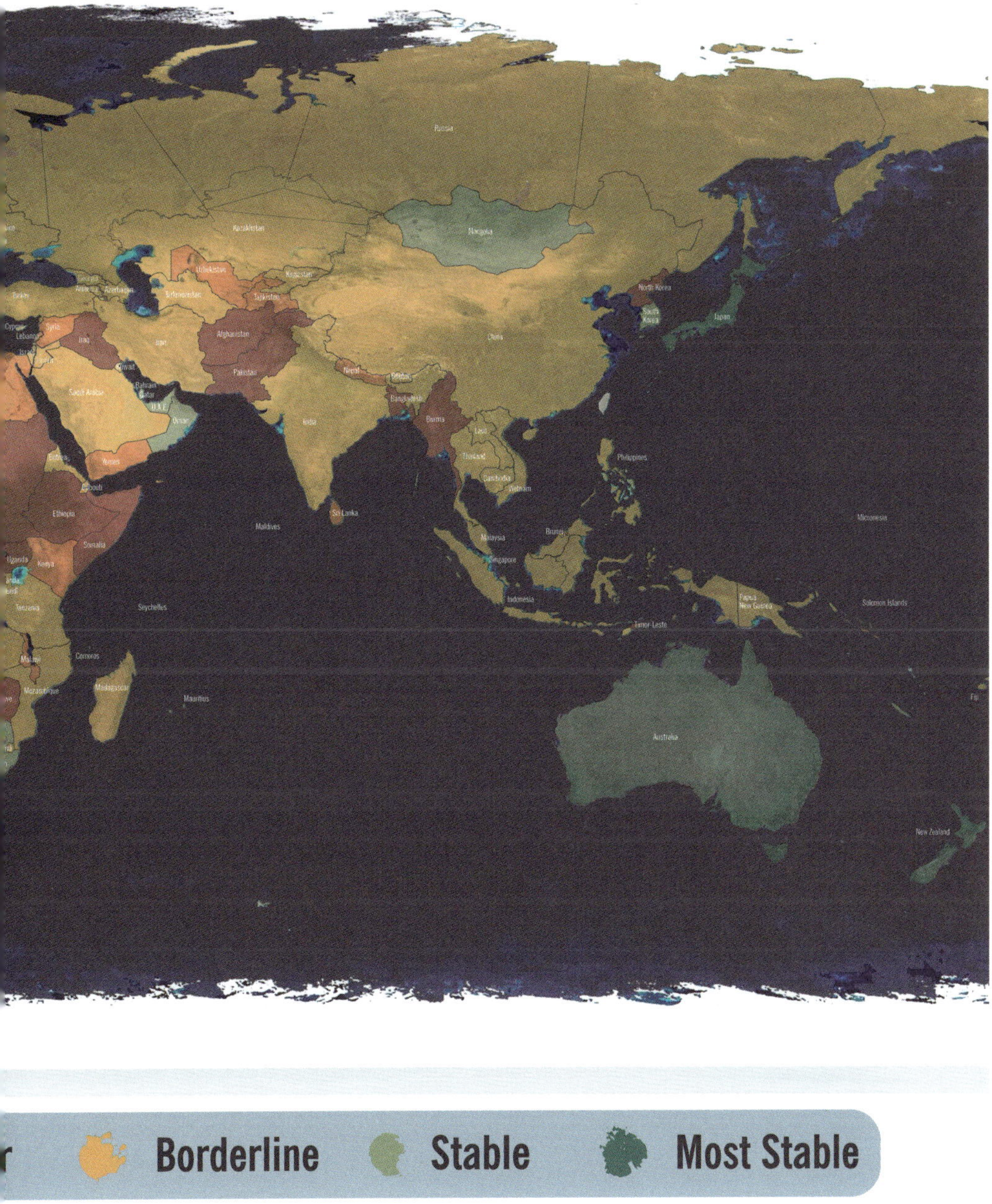

The 60 most vulnerable countries are *critical* (red), *in danger* (orange), and *borderline* (yellow). *Stable* states are light green and *most stable* is dark green. These ratings and colours are no predictions but indicate *vulnerability* to collapse or violent conflict.

The Global Peace Index

In 2007, a Global Peace Index was designed. This GPI ranks 121 nations on their 'state of peace'.[6] The index consists of 24 indicators, ranging from domestic peace, violent crimes, military expenditure, and relations with neighbouring states, to respect for human rights. It was made by a team of scholars, brought together by S. Killelea, and calculated by the Economist Intelligence Unit. We have reversed the numbering and left out the country index scores, to make an easy comparison with the Failed States Index in the previous textbox, showing worst cases first.

The GPI reflects the state of peace in nations based on three sets of indicators: aspects of violent conflicts, aspects of societal security and measures of militarization.

A. *Violent conflict*
- Number of external and internal violent conflicts in 2000-05
- Number of deaths from organised external conflict
- Number of deaths from organised internal conflict
- Indicators of organised internal conflict
- Relations with neighbouring countries

B. *Societal security*
- Level of distrust in other citizens
- Displaced persons as percentage of the population
- Political instability
- Disrespect for human rights (Political Terror Scale)
- Potential for terrorist acts
- Homicides per 100,000 people
- Other violent crime statistics
- Violent demonstrations
- Prisoners per 100,000 people
- Internal security officers and police per 100,000 people

C. *Militarization*
- Military expenditures as a percentage of GDP
- Armed services per 100,000 inhabitants
- Imports of major conventional weapons per 100,000 inhabitants
- Exports of major conventional weapons per 100,000
- UN deployments 2006-07 (percentage of armed forces)
- Heavy weapons per 100,000 inhabitants
- Access to small arms
- Other indicators of military capabilities

Two weighted indices were calculated: a measure of how a country is at peace domestically, and a measure of to what extent it is at peace with other countries. The overall index consists for 60 percent of the measure of internal peace and 40 percent for external peace. Different weights, e.g. 50-50 or 25-75, would attribute more peacefulness to states which are not so much at peace within themselves but are not engaged in international conflicts. The assumption of 60-40 is arbitrary but defensible; it is not a weakness of the index, but its effect on the ranking should be noted.

The index encompasses 95 percent of the world's population. Lack of data resulted in the exclusion of a number of less-developed countries. It is likely that most of these countries would be in the group of worst cases. According to this index, small, stable and democratic countries are relatively most peaceful. Most of those are European democracies and members of the European Union. Island nations also tend to be more at peace, probably due to fewer external sources of tension.

Most regions other than Western Europe show a wide variation in rankings. Asia is the next most peaceful region but with wide variation. Most sub-Saharan African states are in the serious trouble zone. Three of the world's major states score badly. The United States has high levels of military expenditure and involvement outside its borders as a (self-appointed) 'global policeman'. The United States does not show up well due to a very high percent of jailed population and high levels of homicides, as well as high defence expenditure and involvement in the wars in Iraq and Afghanistan. Large states which score much better on GPI are Japan (5), Germany (12) and France (33).

Of special interest are the worst cases on the list: countries which are most under the stress of violence, according to GPI: Iraq and Sudan. Russia's lack of peacefulness seems surprising, but is the result of much domestic violence, the war in Chechnya and relatively high military expenditure. Israel is a special case. Its democratic nature would give a better showing, if it were not for high defence expenditure, internal counter-insurgency measures and frequent violent tensions with its neighbours.

The GPI arrives at a ranking of 121 countries. The 60 worst cases are shown in the previous text box comparing the GPI and the Failing States Index. Of course, this GPI ranking reflects the statistical basis, and is neither a value judgment on actual peacefulness at present, nor on peaceful intent. The indicators reflect statistical data between 2000 and 2006. Of interest is that most developing countries are in the worst ranks.

Next to the 24 main statistical indicators, the authors of the GPI used 33 other indicators of the competence and quality of governments, strength of institutions, political process, international openness, demography, integration in the region, religion, culture, education and well-being.

Comment:
The resulting scores may appear somewhat arbitrary if one looks at differences between similar countries or unexpected high or low rankings. Many features of being at peace internally and externally cannot be measured statistically. Many statistics are not entirely reliable. Important qualities of a social system can often not be measured. The *bon mot* attributed to Albert Einstein, "What can be counted does not count, and what counts cannot be counted" applies here to some extent too. But of equal value is the opposite remark, attributed to Maynard Keynes, when questioned about the figures underlying his general theory of employment: "Do you have better ones?"

The value of this new index is still to be proven. One way is to check how it correlates with various factors. These were calculated by the authors and show some interesting results. The more corruption in a country, the less it is at peace. There is a significant correlation between democracy and internal peace, but the external peace measure is not significantly correlated with democracy. Democracies tend not to make war against each other, but they are involved in military operations against non-democratic states.

GPI may be a step forward in measurement, categorisation and analysis of the state of peace of various countries. It is a first go, and clearly not as refined as e.g. the democracy index of Freedom House, which is the result of a long process of sophistication. As long as there are no longitudinal GPI figures and as long as it consists of some arbitrary measures and not always reliable data, the index is to be used as an indication only, not as a scientific fact.

Comparison of Global Peace Index and Failed States Index

Both systems of measurement agree that Sudan and Iraq were the worst cases in 2005-6. Both measurements also agree that sub-Sahara Africa is the world's region with the largest number of troubled states. Differences between both systems are first of all due to different purposes. The Failing States Index measures vulnerability to collapse and violence. The Global Peace Index measures the internal and external state of peace of a country and combines these in one measure. Other differences are due to other methods and data. Some countries are not included in one index because of lack of data, but are included in the other. This leads already to incomparability of rank orders. Fourth, the GPI includes measures of being involved in external tensions, wars and peace operations, while the failed states index focuses on internal aspects.

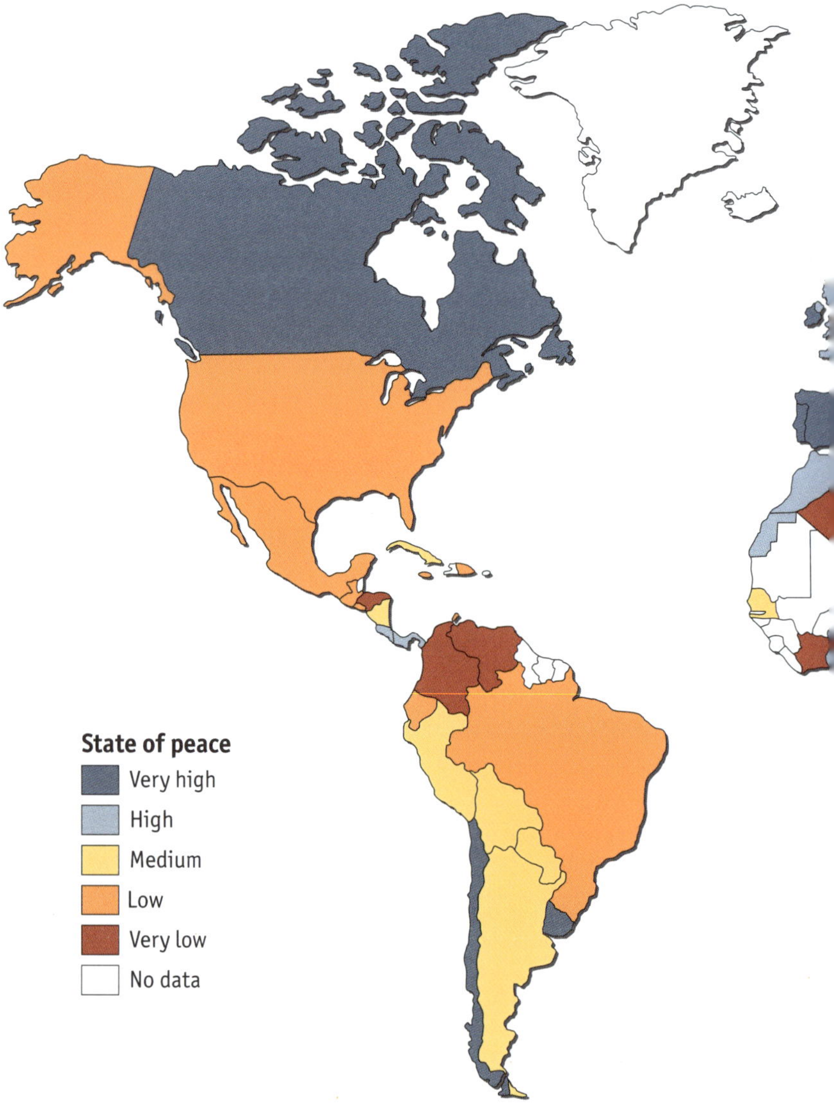

Source: Economist Intelligence Unit.

The GPI gives countries with a high defence spending and high involvement in external military activities a lower score on 'peacefulness', but this may distort the picture of the position and policies of various countries in two directions. A superpower like the US has high defence spending, which is related, to some degree, to much lower defence spending by many of its allies, in so far as they feel covered by the US defence umbrella. Those which feel protected score as 'more peaceful' than the protector itself, which is odd, if not unjust. For instance, the defence expenditures of European NATO allies and Japan and South Korea should not be considered in isolation from their relations with the US.

Further analysis is needed of the underlying data to come to more meaningful comparisons and conclusions and contribute to refinement.

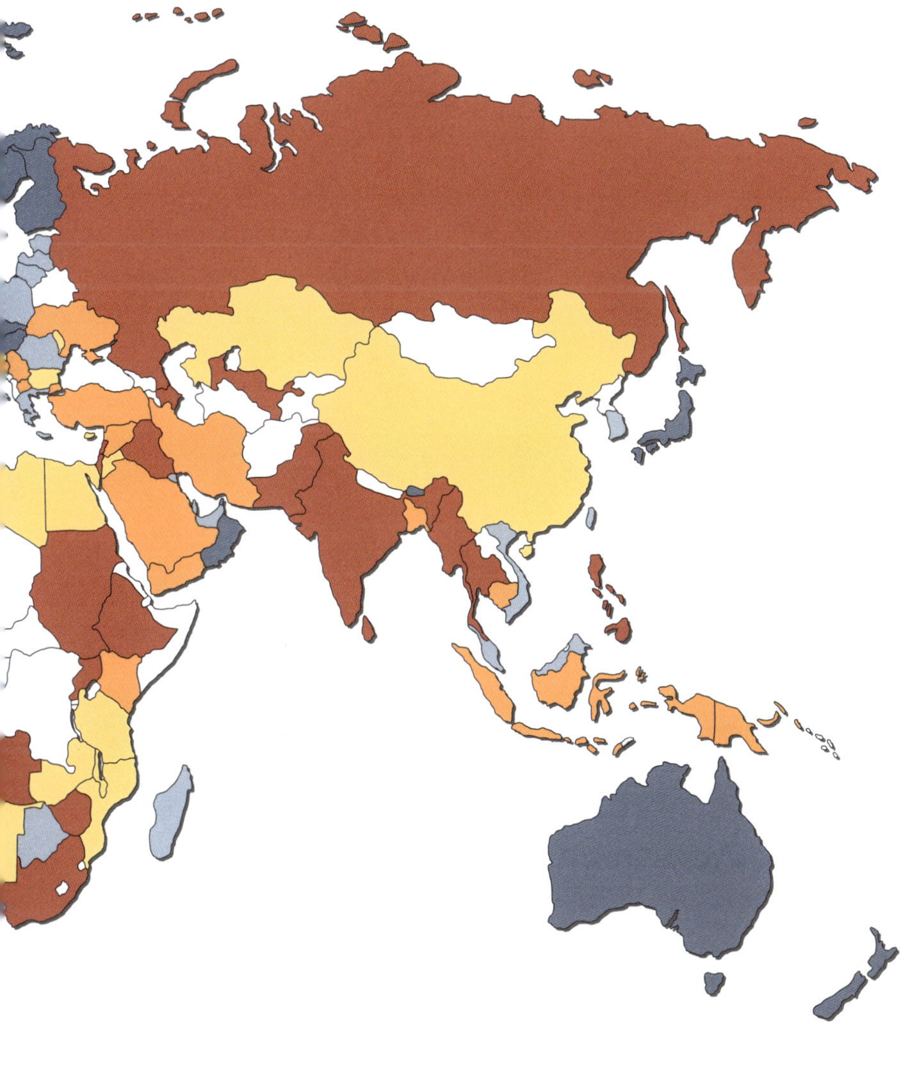

To formulate a 'proto-theory' that might be applicable to many contemporary cases of external rule-of-law assistance, one should ideally find a theory which can be verified, improved or falsified by testing its underlying hypotheses in case studies. This requires a very complex scholarly study, and can be expected to arise in the course of the years out of a growing body of academic research and policy debates.

Many general works and case studies seem, however, to be based on more or less *implicit* theoretical thoughts. For the purpose of the present exploration, it may be useful to attempt a formulation of a more explicit 'proto-theory', however simple at first sight. The following thinking, in brief notions, might be of some use:

The chances of (in the sense of opportunities for) the establishment of the rule of law, as measured by actually implemented respect for human rights, depend mainly on:

- The stability of the state's main institutions, in particular the maintenance of the state's *monopoly on armed forces and police*. This 'monopoly factor' is a prerequisite for the absence of civil war and frequent large-scale political inter-group violence. This monopoly does not at all by itself guarantee the rule of law, as it may also serve a totalitarian ruler or an oligarchic state which does not uphold human rights.
- At least as important is the degree to which the rule of law is engrained in the *population's demand for legal order*. This endogenous demand flows from the values, norms and expectations of the population as shaped by their belief systems, morality, broader culture and other roots of the notion of justice.
- This demand for legal order has led to a *supply of legal and judicial institutions and professionals*. The institutions, which are domestic sources of legal order, comprise the courts, the offices of public prosecutors, the police, human rights institutions and advocacy groups, and academic or professional training institutes, as well as the Ministries of Justice and Interior, and the legislative system. This 'supply' is a broad category which should, of course, be subdivided further. The quality (values, experience, and other personal characteristics) of leadership is of crucial importance within this 'supply' factor. (A case in point is the leadership of Nelson Mandela in South Africa during a period which had a high propensity to social violence. A negative example is the lack of effectiveness of the first elected leaders of Haiti after the UN peace operation. Ineffectiveness contributed to a return of domestic violence after the first peace operation.)
- As noted above, there is a complex correlation between the rule of law and various aspects of economic development. For the sake of peacebuilding theory, we might abbreviate these various economic phenomena (income per capita, income inequality, unemployment, percentage of the work force employed in the service sector, etc.) as 'prevalence of prosperity'. We refer to the discussion about the poverty factor in section 3.1.We presume that, within

this factor 'prevalence of prosperity', one of the most potent determinants of success in building post-conflict rule of law is employment opportunities for males in the age groups that are most inclined to violent behaviour, either for political or economic reasons, or other forms of social violence.

- Even though we can observe that the *domestic* demand and supply of the legal order are crucial variables, it should also be noted that *international* pressure and *incentives* for human rights and legal order are an important factor, as nations respond to international influences and pressures in favour of human rights and legal order, in particular to the strength of international human rights regimes which apply to them, notably regional human rights treaties and courts, like the European Convention on Human Rights, concluded among members of the Council of Europe.

The policies of the Allied Powers after 1945 towards Germany, Japan and Italy encouraged these states to reform rapidly and become rule-of-law societies. The policies of the European Community and the Council of Europe towards Greece, Portugal and Spain influenced these countries to make reforms and adapt to their regional environment. Similarly, several countries of Central and Eastern Europe have adopted rapid reform programs in the 1990's to gain access to the Council of Europe, the European Union and the North Atlantic Treaty Organisations. It is true that not all these reform programs have been completed. Romania and Bulgaria, for instance, still have some distance to go, but the reformist influence from the outside is clearly discernible. A similar effect is exerted in the countries that arose out of the civil war in the Former Yugoslavia, notably Slovenia, Croatia, Bosnia-Herzegovina and Macedonia. Such effects are expected in Kosovo, Montenegro and Serbia in the future. These can also be observed in Albania. There is little doubt that the reformist mood in Turkey in the 1990's and beginning of the 21-st century has to some extent been encouraged by its wish to gain access to the European Union and meet the Copenhagen criteria of democracy, human rights, modern effective administration and a social market economy.

This factor could be summarized as the *external context*, consisting of (1) the *exogenous demand* for reform as experienced by the country in need of reform; (2) the *benefits expected* by the country from adjustment to such external demands, and (3) the *international assistance* which is offered for the (re)construction of legal order and respect for human rights. The volume and quality of external assistance for the rule of law can be an important contribution helping to build up rule of law in recipient countries.

- Finally and as a matter of course, *time* is of the essence, as matters improve or decay over a period of time. Disruption and destruction can happen overnight, but building and reconstruction takes many years, if not decades.

Summarizing these remarks, one might say that:

The degree to which the basic human rights, related to personal security, are respected in a country is a function of:

(a) the state's monopoly over the legal use of armed force and police,
(b) the domestic supply of rule-of-law institutions and legal professionals, and leaders of its main institutions in the police, legal and judicial sector.
(c) the political and religious leadership of the country, security sector leaders and media leaders,
(d) the endogenous demand for the rule of law as felt by the population and opinion leaders,
(e) the absence of poverty, in particular no high unemployment for males in the age groups for soldiers, militia and young violent criminals,
(f) the strength of international human rights treaties and institutions,
(g) international economic and political benefits (including desired membership of international organisations) which are expected to be gained from adapting to rule-of-law standards,
(h) international assistance for peacebuilding, in particular for the rule of law, and
(i) time.

These summarized 9 main variables form complex sets of interrelationships which are, of course, not described by this cursive section, but are still hidden inside this 'box'. These variables need to be specified further. For instance, the state's monopoly on legitimate coercive power rests on physical means (police and security sector personnel in numbers, leadership, quality and equipment), as well as on persuasive, 'soft' influence of the national political and normative leadership. Leadership may be the strongest factor, as discussed above, but at the same time, this factor is very qualitative, psychological and value-driven. It is the least predictable and probably not measurable by any indicators as used in international statistics.

International peacekeeping presence and police assistance can strengthen or even temporarily supplant the monopoly on legitimate coercive power. Whether their temporary presence is adequate, depends, of course, on the nature and size of domestic and foreign threats to peace and public order.

International assistance is offered by bilateral and multilateral donors. Donor assistance varies greatly in quality and quantity. The World Bank Group, UNDP, the EU and many bilateral donors can form a strong external factor for building up legal order, if they have adequate resources, well-designed policies and if they coordinate well. But in most peacebuilding operations their actions are relatively small and not well-coordinated.

It is often assumed that more external assistance is better than less. But this depends on many other factors. The wrong type of assistance can do more harm than good. There can also be counter-productive results. Good intentions can have bad effects, particularly if no thorough social, political and anthropological analysis is made before action is undertaken. External assistance can also have seemingly counter-productive results in the short run, as it can weaken the acceptance by the population of their plight under a traditional, authoritarian regime. Rising expectations and rapidly changing power shares tend to make a country less stable during its transition to modernity.

This observation means one should be careful not to encourage civil war by the wrong kind of international assistance at the wrong time, but design this assistance with the specific urgent problems of the country concerned in mind, particularly the requests from civil society insofar as it represents the needs of the population. Donors should, for instance, avoid giving only little assistance during the first phase of transition, and then give up. This may weaken traditional justice mechanisms, or increase harsh counter measures by the government. Once a demand for change has been encouraged, it is necessary to help the population and the state's organs through the difficult transition before a stable state is achieved. Short, little and wrong aid might be worse than no assistance at all.

3.5 THREATS TO THE PEACE

The manifold threats to a peaceful legal order can be analyzed in five classes or levels: (1) *persons* inclined to political violence (we do not discuss here non-political criminal violence); (2) *groups* inclined to political violence, be they ethnic, religious, economic or other; (3) the *leadership* of such groups, which mobilize and apply this violent inclination; (4) the *temptation or propensity* of state institutions and their leaders *not* to subdue, manage or channel away such violence, but to mobilise the group hatred in an effort to ride the tiger to further their personal goals of control over the state and its resources; (5) the actors in the *external international system*, comprising particularly other states, international companies and international opinion leaders. These five levels (the personal, the social, the political, the state and the international system) each have their own propensity to violence as well as inhibitions against violent conflict behaviour.

Peacebuilding aims at reducing the propensities to violence and increasing the inhibitions at these five levels. Success at one level may be destroyed by failure at another. Excellent national institutions for peaceful conflict settlement may be undercut or destroyed by the weaknesses at the international level, as many peaceful states have experienced in history. And reversely, a peaceful national or regional international system can be upset by aggressive non-state entities at a personal and small group level, like terrorist cells.

Peacebuilding needs to be balanced and comprehensive at all five levels to reach an enduring peace. A daunting task indeed, with high risks at all levels.

3.6 PRACTICAL QUESTIONS

The assistance countries need and the chances for (re)establishment of rule of law depend mainly on the answers to three questions: What kind of peace has been established; what kind of conflict raged; and what kind of government system was in place before the violence?

To start with the last question, if before the war there was an effective, accepted rule of law government, peacebuilding is more likely to be smooth and speedy than if the government was ineffective and illegitimate.

The kind of conflict which raged before a peace agreement makes an enormous difference to post-conflict peacebuilding activities. Was it an international war in which the country was defeated but the regime did not change afterwards? Or was the regime changed or removed while much of the administrative capacity of the state was continued after a purge at the top? In the latter case, there may be better chances for a successful renewal of the state and the government, like Germany, Italy and Japan in 1945. Was the war a civil war leading to division and secession (like the split between India and Pakistan in 1947), or was the attempted secession suppressed (like Katanga from Congo in 1960, or Biafra from Nigeria in 1967-1970)? Was there multi-party fragmentation and religious or ethnic separatism (like in Yugoslavia in 1991-95), or massive political killings (*politicide*) (as in Cambodia in 1977), or inter-group genocide (like in Rwanda in 1994)? Was the conflict an expansion of a country or a (re)unification of a divided state (like Vietnam)? Was it a war of liberation from a foreign ruler, like decolonisation, as in so many countries in the period 1945-1990? Was the conflict a combination of territorial, religious, cultural, ideological, ethnic and economic factors (like Israel-Palestine)? Was the violence the result of long-lasting state failure and collapse (like Haiti in 1994 and 2005)?

The third group of questions concerns the nature of the peace. Is there a victorious group creating a new power order? Did the old regime re-establish its own order? Was there (temporary) domination by a foreign power, and is this power motivated to establish the rule of law? Was a civil war 'settled' by foreign intervention, while no domestic power group established control over the country, and was the internal conflict only suppressed and frozen by international peacekeeping, with a high risk that the conflict will erupt again? The answers to all these questions determine most of the obstacles and opportunities for peacebuilding and the establishment of the rule of law, as we will see in chapters 4 and 5.

3.7 FURTHER STUDY

This chapter did not arrive at a comprehensive theory of peacebuilding, or a sectoral theory of building the rule of law in post-conflict societies. But we could identify many important factors influencing the chances of success of international assistance.

One deductive typology and two different, inductive statistical approaches were discussed. These approaches might lead to a more general theory in the future. Some of the underlying hypotheses should be tested in further studies. This chapter did not offer a complete overview of the literature, but may have served the present, limited purpose of an exploration.

NOTES

1 E. Hirsch Ballin, 'Ontwikkelingsbeleid en Goed Bestuur', The Hague, 2001, WRR report 58, pp. 232-4.
2 See, e.g., *Handbook Good Government,* Ministry of Foreign Affairs, The Hague, 2004.
3 International Covenant on Civil and Political Rights, 1966, and the International Covenant on Economic, Social and Cultural Rights, 1966.
4 Fund for Peace www.fundforpeace.org.
5 www.fundforpeace.org/programs/.
6 www.visionofhumanity.com.

The success of UNTAES was a positive precedent for peace throughout the former Yugoslavia. UNTAES provided the necessary stability to enable Croatia and the Federal Republic of Yugoslavia to normalize their relations and enter into bilateral agreements, including a 'soft border regime' and the re-establishment of normal commercial and traffic links, essential to the economic development of the Danube border area. UNTAES has also ensured that developments in its area did not have a negative effect on the situation in Bosnia and Herzegovina. Within UNTAES area, there has been no large outflow of new refugees and reintegration has been peaceful. Demilitarization was completed in 1996 and that year a Transitional Police Force was established. Local and regional elections were conducted in 1997. The same year, 6,000 Croats and 9,000 Serbs returned to their homes.

Many other international organizations have supported Croatia by monitoring commitments and providing reassurance to the population. The OSCE mission in Croatia continued to monitor the return of refugees and civil rights violations till 2007. Croatian Serbs continue to have problems with restitution of property and acceptance into the assistance programmes.

Croatia In 1918, Croats, Serbs, and Slovenes formed a kingdom known as Yugoslavia since 1929. Following World War II, Yugoslavia became a federal Communist state under Marshal Tito. Although Croatia declared its independence from Yugoslavia in 1991, it took four years of bitter fighting before Serb military withdrew. On 23 August 1996 Croatia and the Former Republic of Yugoslavia signed the Agreement on Normalisation. Under UN supervision, the last Serb-held enclave in eastern Slavonia was returned to Croatia in 1998. The number of refugees and internally displaced persons reached 4,200-7,000 Croats and Serbs.

The 1996 UN Mission (UN Transitional Administration for Eastern Slavonia, Baranja and Western Sirmium UNTAES), which lasted until 1998, was successful. The UN supervised demilitarization and safe return of refugees and displaced persons in cooperation with UNHCR. The UN established a temporary police force; undertook civil administration, and organized elections.

4 (RE) ESTABLISHING ORDER

"No amount of good intentions can substitute for the fundamental ability to project credible force."

Panel on UN Peace Operations, UN A/55/305-S/2000/809

As everything begins with physical safety and negative peace, i.e. the absence of war or the threat of massive political violence, restoring and maintaining basic public security is always the number one priority. People who have personally only experienced peace and watch gross injustices in other countries via the media often find this priority for safety difficult to appreciate. To many, justice seems the most urgent concern. But those who have lost beloved ones in war and are threatened by daily violence will put water, food, medical aid and a secure public order on the top of their agenda.

The crucial question, how to end civil war, is not the focus of this study, but is the subject of war and conflict management studies, diplomatic and mediation analysis and parts of international public law. Our analysis starts with the assumption that there is a cease-fire, that the war has ended, and that the country needs to be rebuilt.

After a cease fire, peace and order have to be maintained with military and police forces of national or international origin. Usually, violent criminals, looters and parts of the former warring parties abuse the lack of government power to commit heinous crimes in the lull after the war. A power vacuum invites a crime wave. The population, tired of the war, expects peace but often gets serious personal insecurity after major combat ends.

The measures for restoring stability and maintaining the peace are usually outlined as part of the cease fire agreement, or in the mandate of a peacekeeping mission, imposed by foreign powers with or without a UN Security Council mandate. Troops are then contributed by UN members on the basis of the UN Stand-by Agreement, or peacekeeping is mandated to another international organisation (NATO, AU, EU), or an ad hoc coalition of countries, usually with a UN mandate but sometimes without. Generally, it takes several weeks if not months before peacekeepers arrive. In the meantime, violent economic, political and other crimes rise rapidly.

Post-conflict peacebuilding may be compared to emergency medical care after a life-threatening trauma. There is often a 'golden hour', when medical intervention, or its absence, determines the chance of healthy survival. This may be the case with countries too, after a war[1]. This crucial time may last only a few weeks or months. Re-establishing basic public order and security in a collapsed social organism is somewhat comparable to getting the heart of a patient pumping again.

4.1 TRANSITIONAL SECURITY

The first task of creating (imposing) peace, order and physical security is often carried out without a complete legal basis and without a complete government. This *transitional security* involves restoring public order after a war, and putting a stop to political violence, widespread crime and looting. Transitional security also tries to prevent citizens from resorting to mob justice and malfeasance. Revenge actions by defeated parties have to be stopped.

The main purpose of transitional security is to provide physical security to allow the rebuilding of the country's institutions and the resumption of regular daily life. The legal basis for transitional security is usually (assumed) emergency powers. Transitional security imposed by foreign peacekeeping troops, with or without strong participation of troops of the country concerned, is generally based on mandates by the UN Security Council. Transitional security enforced by the military and police resembles military rule. It is desirable to bring this under the legal authority of a legitimate government as soon as possible.

Solid transitional security fills the power vacuum after state or government collapse. It is the key to a successful transition from war to lasting peace and the development of a stable state.
Often, transitional security can be legally based on a combination of national emergency law, a UN Security Council Resolution, the right of self defence and international treaties.
It may be unavoidable to integrate former warring parties into the new state's armed and police forces to maintain transitional security, as foreign forces are scarce. Forming entirely new and 'clean' national forces takes too much time and may be impossible anyway. For example, it is possible that the US and Britain have made their purpose of reconstructing Iraq in 2003-2006 more difficult than necessary by dissolving large sections of the Iraqi forces immediately after their defeat.[2]

As soon as there is an armistice, establishing transitional security is the key to effective delivery of humanitarian and emergency relief. Humanitarian relief usually begins already during the war, relying on negotiated rights of passage with armed factions, such as Operation Lifeline Sudan, or any of the ICRC operations in war zones around the world.
As soon as there is a cease-fire, former warring parties have to be controlled, limited to certain areas, and partially or entirely disarmed. Light and heavy weapons need to be collected. Borders have to be secured and suspected war criminals must be arrested. Such and other measures of transitional security, when successful, start the road to the future rule of law.

In most international peace operations, the contribution of *military* forces is less of a problem than *policing* capacity. The scarcity of international police capacity is a pressing problem. Regular army units are not trained for maintaining public order, countering looters and terrorists, or arresting suspects of war crimes. *It is, therefore, necessary to have three systems of rapidly deployable police officers that can monitor, give advice and train local police forces. These should be available at the national donor level, the level of regional organisations like the EU, ASEAN and the AU, and the global (UN) level.*

Once the situation is stabilised, former combatants need to be demobilised and reintegrated; either as part of a new national military force, or retrained and reintegrated into civilian society. This *security sector reform* comprises not only the armed forces but also the old police, security and intelligence services. A number of bilateral and NGO donors and international organisations have set up expertise centres for security sector reform with experts who can be rapidly deployed abroad to advise countries which have an expressed need. For example, some capacity for this exists in the UK Foreign Office Global Conflict Prevention Pool, which has a Security Sector Reform Centre. UNDP has also set up an SSR section.

Private military and security companies are employed by many governments and donor governments in various war and peace operations, for protection of national or international authorities, training of military, police or intelligence services, management or operation of detention facilities, clearing of mine fields, and various other security activities. Not only governments in danger use private military and security services. Oil, gas or other mining companies hire such security services. Sometimes governments or armed opposition groups employ individual private military as advisors, or mercenary soldiers for protection or even civil war fighting.

The use of private security firms for reconstruction efforts, protection, training and other, non-war fighting tasks by a number of legitimate governments is a fact of life which cannot be outlawed internationally. Often, however, the legal basis of their activities, legal responsibility and liability remains unclear. It is advisable for governments employing such firms to define their legal basis, rules of engagement, responsibility and liability under national and international law.

4.2 FOREIGN PEACEKEEPERS AND PUBLIC ORDER

A vexing question is the imposition of transitional security by mostly foreign troops. In peace operations in the 1990's, the contributing states and international organisations limited the mandate of their troops to light military tasks and the protection of humanitarian convoys. The Security Council and the governments of the intervening soldiers and their military commanders were afraid of 'mission creep', i.e. the expansion of strict peacekeeping tasks to more and more tasks approaching military rule. But many field commanders, confronted with the insecurity of the population, were inclined to interpret their tasks more broadly, and often moved to expand duties out of sheer necessity. The notion of 'mission creep' can also be used in the different meaning of extension of the mission in time without a clearly defined end state that would allow exiting from the country in trouble.

Types of UN Peacekeeping

Traditional or 'first generation' UN peacekeeping operations require the consent of the conflicting parties. The mandate is based on Chapter 6 of the UN Charter. Acting under this part of the Charter, the UN is not allowed to impose the will of the UN Security Council on the parties. UN troops with blue helmets and white vehicles are present to monitor a cease-fire and facilitate emergency aid, but not to fight the parties and enforce a political solution. The UN troops are impartial and are therefore clearly visible to all. The troops are sent by nations voluntarily. They are only lightly armed and are allowed to use violence for self-defence only. There are also unarmed (military) observers. These troops are in the conflict area under the leadership of the Secretary General of the UN and under the political responsibility of the Security Council. These 'first generation' peacekeepers control buffer zones, monitor cease-fire lines and observe violations of agreements between the parties. A good example is the small UN Peacekeeping Force in Cyprus since 1964, which helped keep Greek and Turkish Cypriots from returning to civil war.

This type of peacekeeping offers no solution if the parties continue to fight, if humanitarian aid to the population is obstructed by warring parties, and if they continue to suppress, kill, and violate the population.

A 'second generation' peacekeeping mission has a broader mandate to include securing delivery of humanitarian assistance, supervising the return of refugees, disarming militias, removing mines, monitoring police treatment of citizens, providing security for international interim administration and helping to organise elections. A good example is the UN Transitional Authority in Cambodia between 1991 and 1993. This kind of broader mandate is sometimes referred to as 'Chapter 6 1/2', i.e. in-between the chapters 6 and 7 of the UN Charter. Chapter 7 holds the possibility of enforcement action. But '6 1/2' type of peacekeeping can be made ineffective by warring parties, as the mandate does not allow enforcement against their will.

In 'second generation' peacekeeping the UN troops may, in principle, have the right to secure the implementation of their mandate and actively remove obstacles which the warring parties put in the UN's way. But in practice, the UN Security Council and the UN Secretary General do not have the heavy military means and firepower, or the necessary tactical speed and surprise to prevail in war fighting. *Examples of partially or totally failed peace operations are the ones in the former Yugoslavia (UNPROFOR), Somalia (UNOSOM) and Rwanda (UNAMIR).* The Security Council and the UN members failed to provide the relatively small UN forces with adequate mandates, means, instructions and command lines.

These three very serious failures led to a UN study named after its chairman Brahimi in 2000 which made many recommendations for improvement.[3] The report interpreted the rule of 'impartiality' as neutrality between the parties, but also allowing all necessary means to ensure respect for the UN Charter and the objectives of the UN's mandate. The use of arms against warring parties is justified when necessary for these purposes, Brahimi concluded.

Some of Brahimi's recommendations have been carried out, such as reorganisation of the UN Secretariat. But the core problem remains that the UN depends on military contributions from its member states, which are often inadequate and arrive in the troubled area after long delays.

In 2000, the UN Security Council decided, for the first time, in successive resolutions that UN peacekeeping troops (blue helmets) should have the right not only to defend themselves as in previous mandates but also to use force to implement their mandates, protect citizens attacked by warring parties and break blockades of humanitarian convoys, as these could be defined as threats to international peace and security.[4]

Since that year, the UN can deploy not only classic (blue helmet) UN peacekeepers, but also robust peacekeepers (with heavy deterrence capacity). The heaviest peacekeeping, or rather peace enforcement with all-out war fighting capacity, is likely to be left, however, to multinational coalitions of the willing, under the leadership of a large power, but based on a UN mandate.

The UN has called on an alliance (NATO) to carry out military heavy peace operations, ranging from implementation of a peace treaty like the Dayton Peace Agreement which ended most of the civil war in the former Yugoslavia in 1995, to more dangerous peace operations, including enforcement action in Afghanistan (2005). It has also called upon coalitions of willing states to carry out military missions to end a war, like in East Timor (1999).

The UN continues to run a varied array of peace operations in different countries, ranging from unarmed observation to robust peacekeeping. The UN has also mandated other organisations to carry out light and heavy peace missions, or ad hoc coalitions of states willing to do so. In addition, peace operations occur at the initiative of a group of member states without explicit approval by the Security Council, but under the leadership of states which seem willing to run the heavy political and other costs of acting without the consent of the UN.

In a study of peace operations in Cambodia, Somalia, Bosnia and Kosovo, Dr. Brocades Zaalberg shows the rapid growth of military peacekeeping into primary state building tasks in post-conflict countries.[5] This widening of tasks was driven by the needs of the local population on the ground, which saw international soldiers and expected them to provide security and to block serious political and civilian crimes.

In Cambodia, the goal of the UN blue helmet force shifted from demilitarisation of warring factions to facilitating national elections. While the military mission failed to disarm the Khmer Rouge, the political task of helping to prepare elections was completed with success.
In Somalia the goal shifted from protecting humanitarian aid convoys to improvised, temporary security for population groups in certain areas. In the end, both tasks failed.

After the failure of UNPROFOR in Bosnia in 1995, in 1996 the goal shifted first to keeping former warring parties apart, and later on to assisting civilian administration, improving police, supporting elections, and helping to reintegrate the various enemies into one state. These tasks were carried out with some success, at least more than in many previous operations. In Kosovo, the task of protecting the Kosovar Albanians changed in part to protecting members of the Serb minority and helping international interim administration to take control. These tasks were carried out with partial success. The future will reveal whether Kosovo and Bosnia, both entities being products of international intervention, will grow into stable and independently functioning political states that can live in peace within themselves and with their neighbours. They will, however, most likely continue to need various forms of external support, particularly from the European Union, for a long time.

Although national authorities of troop contributing countries always try to avoid 'mission creep' (ever more responsibilities for their soldiers), in reality the missions 'creep' very fast. A wide, practical interpretation of mandates has often helped to attain a relatively successful outcome, or at least better than what would have been achieved if the local commanders had not taken the liberty to respond to circumstances.

The gap between restricted military mandates and actual security needs for the population is caused, of course, by the differentiated thinking in capitals of Western countries and secretariats of international organisations. In the mindsets of politicians and civil servants, a separation of military and civilian powers is imperative. They are used to ensure civilian control over military actions. But their peacekeepers find themselves in the opposite situation, where serious violence rules, and were governments and reliable police forces are nearly absent in the beginning of the operation. The latter are brought in only once the security situation allows for more civilian personnel.

Many assumptions underlying military plans soon prove incorrect during the battle or peace operation. When plans fall to pieces, the commander has to improvise. "Intervening forces (tend) to fall victim to the law of unintended consequences which, during times of chaos, operates at exponential levels."[6]

In headquarters and ministries of countries sending troops, it was thought in the 1990's that the peacekeepers should confine themselves to pure military tasks, like securing military peace, separating armed factions and disarming them. Gradually, civil-military cooperation (CIMIC) entered, first in a technical sphere, like heavy engineering tasks to rebuild infra-structure. This was first seen as a big expansion of military tasks. But in the local circumstances, this expansion soon proved inadequate. What use are new bridges if civilians are still killed on both sides? CIMIC requires public security, that is: law and order, to function effectively. And that is what local peacekeeping commanders, with inadequate police efforts and absent local government, tried to do: protect the population from criminals and warlords.

In addition, peacekeeping forces started humanitarian and emergency work: providing drinking water, food, repairing schools and local power stations, hospitals, etc. This was at first watched with a certain reservation by international relief agencies. Wasn't this their work, and should the military not stay in their tanks or compounds? The soldiers found this kind of work necessary for its own sake, and also to fraternise with the population, reducing misconceptions and providing useful intelligence about who were the local troublemakers, arms dealers and gang leaders. Simple, quick impact assistance which helps to improve daily life is a reward for cooperating with peacekeeping forces and may undercut spoilers of the peace.

Where the re-establishment of public safety, basic law and order are the most urgent concerns, the cooperation of the military peacekeepers with national and international police officers, civilian or military, is of the utmost importance. In most peace operations, there is a relative lack of professional police capacity, to help fill the public security gap. Often, peacekeeping troops have to run an improvised police and judiciary system, as well as a detention system, to curb rampant crime, in the absence of an official system.

In the 1990's, the troop contributing nations regarded such martial-law-like powers as undesirable as they are contrary to the doctrine at home of a separation of powers. But this misconception failed to recognise a simple truth: there can be no legal order, security and justice in a power vacuum, which gives criminals and warmongers a free hand. Separation of powers is an excellent principle for a well-ordered society in which the population is secure.

The adaptability of foreign forces to functioning in this vacuum differs from country to country. Military forces of nations which emphasise heavy and fast military action are inclined to limit the role of their military to fighting. They prefer to act in a heavy handed fashion and rather leave law and order to others. Military forces of nations that have considerable experience in blue-helmet peacekeeping tend to adjust faster to the needs of the local population and try to improvise to help fill the gap of absent government. These differences can be useful. They may lead to a practical division of labour: a big power with much deterrence capacity having the lead in enforcing peace, and the other, smaller powers having the lead in the civil military interface of transitional security and public order. This division, however, can also lead to confusion and resistance among the population, if the heavy and the light operations are not clearly distinguishable, not coordinated, and if the heavy operations cause many civilian victims, which make the population turn also against the lighter, less aggressive military forces from other nations.

Once enemy forces are defeated, the primary purpose of peace operations is stabilisation, public security and order. The daily needs of the population are crucial. Now, emergency assistance can reach the people in need. This martial law phase follows the war phase, and is in turn followed by a transitional or provisional civilian administration, which prepares the way for a new civil government.

Cambodia's 14 million inhabitants are predominantly Khmer Theravada Buddhist with Muslim Cham and other minorities. Cambodia is the remnant of the Angkor Empire. In 1887 it became part of French Indochina and was occupied by Japan during the Second World War. Cambodia became a constitutional monarchy after gaining independence from France in 1953.

In 1960, Prince Sihanouk became head of state. He publicly announced Cambodia's neutrality in the Vietnam War, but permitted North Vietnamese troops and Vietcong to maintain military bases in Cambodia and to use the harbors for weapon shipments. Prime Minister Lon Nol used Sihanouk's temporary absence to depose him. Supported by the US, Lon Nol struggled to remove the Vietnamese army bases and stop shipments of arms through Cambodian harbors. Sihanouk had meanwhile become the primary spokesman for the united communist parties, the Khmer Rouge.

The Khmer Rouge captured Phnom Pen in 1975 and changed the country's name to Democratic Kampuchea. Pol Pot ordered deportations and executions which took over 1.5 million lives. Many more died of starvation due to an oppressive agrarian communist ideology.

The Vietnamese invasion in 1978 initiated a war that would last 13 years. The Khmer Rouge fled into the hills of Western Cambodia while Vietnam occupied the country until the early nineties.

In 1989, UN-administered peace negotiations in Paris commenced. The 1992 Paris Peace Accords called for democratic elections and provided the UN with the authority to guard the ceasefire. The 1993 elections were sabotaged by the Khmer Rouge, which controlled up to 15 percent of the country. The new government voted for a constitution that established a multiparty democracy within the constitutional monarchy. Sihanouk became king.

In 1997, differences between faction members of governing parties FUNCINPEC and CPP turned violent. Hun Sen (CPP) staged a coup and killed dozens FUNCIPEC party members. FUNCIPEC members initially fled, but returned after the 1998 elections to form a new government with the CPP. Elections four years later led to a stalemate between the FUNIPEC and CPP. It took a year of negotiations to form a coalition government.

Since then, coalition governments have been formed and a new constitution has been adopted. Corruption and suppression of the opposition through defamation laws frustrate the process of democratization. Extreme poverty and income inequality may be a source of future conflicts.

4.3 EMERGENCY RELIEF

Peacebuilding can only be successful if the most pressing needs for people's survival are met. Those who stayed in country during the conflict will usually have suffered severely as food is often difficult to come by and most health facilities will not have functioned. Refugees who return may have been susceptible to disease and death from the rigours of the flight or the living conditions in camps. It will take time and effort for government facilities to become fully operational.

Most of those dying in emergency situations from disease and hunger are children and women, as they are most vulnerable. Many diseases can be prevented by hygiene and use of clean water; or easily treated like malaria or respiratory infections. Fast relief can save many lives.

Mental health needs are to be addressed, too, due to post traumatic stress or prior mental illness. Specific programs need to deal with brainwashed child soldiers. Mines have often maimed countless adults and children, which requires extensive orthopaedic programs. Social welfare is urgent for female headed households or care for orphans.

In most conflict and post-conflict situations, there is an increased risk for HIV/AIDS. Women and children are more exposed to exploitation or having to exchange sex for resources. Armed forces, including peace keepers, often also play a role in increasing the transmission of HIV. Health facilities frequently lack supplies for safe sex. Prevention of HIV/AIDS in emergency situations is therefore critical.[7]

Food is often lacking in post conflict situations as harvests may have failed or people are afraid to go into the fields because of land mines. Food rations may need to be distributed while de-mining is to occur and the provision of seeds and tools is necessary in order to rework the land. Usually children and pregnant women are malnourished and require specialised care and supplementary feeding. Safe water and adequate sanitation require that power plants are restarted. Wells have to be checked to ensure the quality of water. In (post-)conflict situations, dead bodies contaminate wells and rivers.

Adequate shelter is important to protect people from the weather and provide some privacy. In some situations people can return to their existing houses but often these are damaged or need to be checked for booby traps. People may then need to stay in community halls until return is feasible, or they resettle elsewhere.

Coordination between the different actors is vital as the needs are large and well-intentioned actors fall over each other. Guidance is officially the role of the United Nations Organisation for Coordination of Humanitarian Affairs, but can prove to be difficult as relief organisations, donor agencies and military actors have different mandates, motives and identities.

Assistance should be provided impartially and based on needs rather than anything else. The military are interested in winning 'hearts and minds' to get stability, while other donors are interested in social and economic benefits. It is essential for the peacekeepers and the humanitarian and development officials working separately also to work in unison for the benefit of the population. The quality of the assistance needs to be ensured whereby the *minimum* standards of humanitarian relief in emergencies, as described by Sphere, can play a valuable role.[8]

From the start, long term development needs should be considered, to ensure sustainability. Often, many resources are offered by actors keen to be involved in the reconstruction of a country. This provides opportunities but also risks as donors and NGOs working independently can undermine the government or set up facilities which may not be appropriate. An example is the reconstruction of new health facilities without considering the population's anticipated priority needs and the required reforms of the health structure and recurrent costs to maintain investments.

Determining a national health plan facilitates a successful reconstruction of the health sector. The need for local ownership of this policy is evident. Ensuring the inclusion of women as well as different ethnic and vulnerable groups provides opportunities for the development of a health sector that will be culturally ensitive and accessible to all. The World Health Organisation WHO emphasizes a primary health care approach of prevention and early treatment. Such services should be affordable, close to the people, and based on community participation.

The rapid provision of basic services can help to legitimise the government and foreign organisations in the eyes of the people. If people see no real improvements, this creates tensions as were seen in East Timor and Afghanistan. The delivery of services related to health and education are particularly important as they affect every citizen and are a precondition for further peacebuilding and development.

All peacebuilding activities described hereafter can only win the hearts and minds of the population if their most pressing needs for survival are met. Food, drinking water, medicine, medical relief, shelter, heating, electricity and other emergency supplies, including building materials before winter falls, have to be distributed equitably. National and international donor organisations have to act as quickly as possible to address these needs. The first actor on the scene with the biggest transportation capacity is usually the military. Their role should be taken over as soon as possible by national authorities and domestic and international civilian relief bodies. The military are not always adequately trained to undertake relief work. Their first task is providing security, which requires military and police measures against those who break the peace.

Civilian relief workers generally do not like to work within or alongside military structures, as this may compromise their neutrality. Neutrality is most important when the war is still ongoing, as neutrality between opposing sides is what allows humanitarian agencies to negotiate access to areas still under control of opposing forces.

Donor governments and organisations which did not participate in the original military intervention, or even disagreed at the outset with this action, will not feel as responsible for emergency aid as those who took the original military action. The critics and watchers-on will be inclined to blame much of the suffering on those who undertook the military intervention. But apportioning blame does not stop bleeding or fill empty stomachs. The question is now: who can do what to help a population in need? The excuse for not supporting the relief and development effort because 'the military of country X, Y or Z are in charge' does not stand up to ethical scrutiny. At this stage the needs of the people should be the main priority, not 'who was right in the Security Council.' Experienced humanitarian relief institutions, like the International Committee of the Red Cross, have learned that only the needs of those who suffer should be taken into account.

4.4 FOREIGN AID WORKERS AND THE MILITARY

In peace operations, foreign aid workers find themselves working side-by-side with foreign military. Humanitarian organisations often find this uncomfortable, fearing it may undermine the image and effectiveness of their work. A study by the Dutch development aid organisation Cordaid distinguishes three attitudes: the neutral humanitarian position, the pragmatic, and the supporting attitude.

"Donor governments and military actors generally have welcomed and *encouraged closer collaboration* in the framework of their integrated policies. Important humanitarian and development actors, however, have raised concerns about compromising the humanitarian imperative and the associated humanitarian principles of impartiality, independence and neutrality. They also fear that aid will become subordinate to political and military objectives and logic. Finally, it has been argued that integrating military, humanitarian and development work will lead to a blurring of distinctions and thus endanger the safety of aid workers. Though the study critically reflects on these concerns, we observe that special caution is required when peacekeepers have no UN mandate, try to enforce a victor's peace or face significant resistance from local communities."[9]

Many non-governmental organisations, particularly their executives and boards, try to keep a distance from the military of international peace operations, to emphasise their humanitarian goals and political impartiality (neutrality). In practice in the field, aid workers of such organisations seem to establish quite easily good informal working relations. Both recognise that they need each other's work to succeed in their own tasks, improve their own working conditions, and serve the interests of the population.

The security of foreign aid workers is a major concern, particularly in countries where resistance to 'infidels', and 'western' political influence is high, or crime is rampant, especially where aid workers may be taken hostage. This is also a problem in places where aid workers are simply a source of ransom revenue, e.g. Colombia and the Democratic Republic of Congo.

In case of ill-advised policies or a pattern of misdemeanour of the military, the aid organisations should decide, of course, on the need and desirability of continued cooperation. In such cases, it may be advisable to keep a visible distance.

The approach of the British Military Provincial Reconstruction Teams in Northern Afghanistan is seen as ideal in the Cordaid study. The military play a small but important role in the background by focussing on security and stability. The military do not carry out reconstruction tasks but leave those to aid workers, who profit from the safety provided by the military. This study sees the US approach as less effective, however. The US military carry out quick impact projects to improve relations with the local population. At the same time, the US military approach is deemed 'heavy handed'. Such projects are a 'present' to the population or their leaders. But some gifts, however generous, may not encourage independent self-help by the local population.

Recently, it has become standard practice to add specialists in aid work to military teams to improve understanding of the work of the aid agencies. Closer interaction between military and civil actors (donors, international organisations, non-governmental organisations) is a logical consequence of current developments in the international arena. The reform of the United Nations (UN), the emergence of integrated approaches (which combine security, political and development instruments), the changing nature of warfare and peacekeeping, and the 'war on terror' all point in this direction of close coordination. Finally, the Cordaid report reflects some of the recent evolution in humanitarian and development intervention, such as the proliferation of multi-mandate organisations and 'conflict-sensitive' approaches.[10]

The Cordaid study observed that for the local population, it matters little who provides assistance. Strikingly, the peacekeepers are generally more popular than NGOs. People thank the soldiers for establishing security and disarming the combatants, and are grateful for the highly visible aid they deliver. Many NGOs, on the other hand, are censured for being uncommitted, untrustworthy and ineffective.[11]

"Given that many local communities are supportive of the military and quite critical of NGOs", the report notes, "aid agencies need to make more efforts to understand local perspectives and discourses." It concludes: "In a general sense, the dictum 'as civilian as possible, as military as necessary' is sound. Maximum use should be made of the abilities of each side."

4.5 TRANSITIONAL POLITICS

While emergency needs have to be satisfied, political decisions are also urgent, in order to lay the foundation for a future legal order. This is one of the critical tasks of 'transitional politics'.
Transitional politics involve the selection of suitable leaders who can negotiate continued peace, assume emergency powers for transitional security, and oversee the drafting of a new constitution, or improvement of an existing one.

The aim of transitional politics is to allow a new, stable and legitimate political order to crystallise, and kick-start the (re) building the rule of law. Transitional politics and transitional security are of course inseparable and cannot be considered or pursued in isolation.

Transitional politics need to focus on stabilisation and security rather than rapid elections. Politicians cannot run for democratic elections in a hailstorm of bullets. Democratic donor countries and media in many peaceful and highly developed countries are inclined to see elections as the only true hallmark of a new democracy. But if elections are not well-prepared by new democratic leadership of political parties, if the media are not yet free, and the electorate lacks basic security and daily needs, there is a grave risk that former war leaders and those supporting them, who fanned the flames of group hatred that incited the previous war, will again pop up, now legitimised by elections, only to block further democratisation should they be victorious in the elections. An example is the election of Charles Taylor as president of Liberia in 1997, who was arrested on international war crimes charges in 2006.

During the transitional political period, the temporary administration needs to first organise a population census and enable voter registration. A solid legal framework for political rights, elections, and an interim constitution are needed. International agencies like the UN's Office for Electoral Assistance, the Organization for Security and Cooperation in Europe (OSCE), the Institute for Democracy and Electoral Assistance (IDEA), and various other global and regional organisations and human rights institutions need to be involved to oversee proper procedures.

Foreign countries involved in ending a war generally push for rapid elections to allow them to bring their troops home under a banner of 'mission accomplished, democracy installed'. But haste makes waste; democracy needs a long time and great care to grow into a self supporting system.

The rule of law should ideally begin with restoring and maintaining public order based on *a new or interim constitution*. Writing a new or improved constitution

depends first of all on the political forces in the country. An interim agreement is a compromise document which regulates government power. In most cases the interests of those wrestling for power matters more than constitutional theory. Still, expert advice by constitutional specialists can help main leaders avoid mistakes and lay the basis for the rule of law and human rights.
Expertise centres for constitutional reform can be set up by a number of international organisations, which borrow at short notice from different academic and governmental institutions advisors with foreign assistance experience to assist the negotiators in their efforts.[12] A related recommendation is to formulate within the framework of the UN a number of constitutional models for pluralistic states with basic human rights, to be available for adaptation to national circumstances.

4.6 INTERNATIONAL ADMINISTRATION

When the political leaders in a war-torn country are not in a position to agree on a new constitution, and when the self-governing capacity of a country is still much too weak, the international community should give a mandate for *international interim administration* and state-building to assist the country to assume gradually the responsibilities of government and rule of law. The basis in international law can be laid through a resolution by the UN Security Council. This should be seen as temporary international guardianship to avoid anarchy and renewed violence. Several experiences since the 1960's have shown that this may be the best interim solution.

Sometimes, a country is so ill-prepared for sovereign self-government, self-administration and the rule of law, that international administration has to be continued for a considerable period. The Congo crisis since 1960 is a case in point. The UN withdrew due to political controversy and the death of the UN Secretary General. The Congo fell into the hands of a corrupt regime. The interim administration of Cambodia after the Khmer Rouge genocide is an example of a somewhat better experience. The Kosovo crisis since 1998 is a third example of the need for an interim administration, and East Timor a fourth. Haiti would have profited from prolonged international administration after the UN peace operation which started in 1995. But the US-led international community thought that a democratically elected president was the most important condition for reform. President Aristide was ineffective, however, and international support for peace-building dwindled after the peacekeeping phase. Increasing discontent led to renewed violence. The UN had to start all over again.

The old and by now dysfunctional mindset of decolonisation has made UN member states and political opinion leaders slow to recognise that in some countries there are simply not even the beginnings of effective government. In such cases, the only hope for the population is prolonged and intensive care by the international community. Many seriously ailing states, which become failed states in due course, and then fall into decades-long multi-party civil war, could greatly benefit from UN mandated international administration until they are ready for self-government as a sovereign independent country, or a state in a federation or confederation. The UN could prepare a standard schedule for interim administration which can be adapted to specific circumstances when the need arises. Such interim administration need not be implemented in all cases by the UN itself. It can also be delegated by the UN to regional organisations or coalitions on the basis of a UN mandate. These groups of states should, however, report regularly to the Security Council.

4.7 INTERNATIONAL COORDINATION

Ideally, the first phase of peacebuilding will be managed by an UN-based *peace implementation council (or a similar arrangement under a different name),* with representatives of the main post-conflict political actors and international aid donors. In cases where the UN Security Council is unable because of internal disagreement to manage this effectively, a peace implementation council has to be set up by a coalition of like-minded states under the leadership of at least one permanent member of the Security Council or a regionally leading power. Examples are the contact groups put together for Liberia and Sudan, where donor states engaged in the peace process try to push the agenda forward and remind the parties of their commitments.

The task of the peace implementation council is to bring political leaders, foreign donors and international organisations together and encourage fair *burden sharing* among participants. Most peacebuilding programmes suffer from very unequal burden sharing. It is not difficult for states to find reasons for not participating: 'our national interest does not include the situation in this foreign country'; the work had 'better be left to other, bigger countries'; the original peace operation or intervention was judged 'erroneous'; or: 'we have our own pressing, internal needs.' This last excuse is always valid, but of only relative value.

Most peacebuilding programmes are carried out by a small portion of the UN membership, aided by a large number of sometimes very small NGOs. Resources could be greatly increased by wider participation of states with the capacity to do so, as is shown in chapter 6 on mobilising resources.

In 2005, the UN established a Peacebuilding Commission (PBC) for improved peacebuilding in its most troubled states. This Peacebuilding Commission will have an overall Organizational Committee, which is tasked with setting the agenda and plotting general courses of action. Country specific committees are tailor-made and include relevant bilateral and multilateral partners for the country in question.
The Organizational Committee is made up of 31 member countries:
- seven members selected by the UN's Security Council;
- seven elected by the Economic and Social Council;

- five top providers of contributions to United Nations budgets and of voluntary contributions to the United Nations funds, programmes and agencies, including a standing peacebuilding fund;
- five top providers of military personnel and civilian police to United Nations missions;
- seven additional states elected by the General Assembly.

This Commission should fill a huge gap in the UN system. It will bring together all the major actors in a given situation to discuss and decide on a long-term peacebuilding strategy. As a result, money should be better spent. There will be a clear link between immediate post-conflict efforts and long-term recovery and development efforts.

The Peacebuilding Commission has little power, however, as it is an advisory body. Its recommendations will carry weight because of the diversity and relevance of all those participating. But what if the members are divided or not really interested?

While there is no specific mechanism to enforce/implement decisions, the Commission will be looked at as the primary body for disseminating advice on reconstruction. Its diverse composition of membership lends legitimacy to carry out this work.

The PBC has no mandate for conflict prevention measures. It can only act once a conflict has already broken out. The actual impact it may have will depend heavily on the five permanent members of the Security Council.

4.8 TRANSITIONAL 'JUSTICE' AND RECONCILIATION

It is difficult to complete the establishment of a peaceful order and make a good start on the road to the rule of law without taking measures against major war criminals.

The prosecution, arrest and trial of *war criminals* should begin as soon as possible after an end to hostilities, as their trial is a precondition for public trust in a new beginning and hope for national reconciliation. Most post-conflict states lack capacity to indict, arrest and put on trial suspects of war crimes. Since 1945, special international tribunals have been organized, starting with the Nuremberg and Tokyo tribunals. The UN Security Council established an international tribunal for war crimes committed in the former Yugoslavia since 1992 and a comparable tribunal for war crimes in Rwanda since 1993. For war crimes committed in Cambodia, a mixed national / international tribunal was established after several years of negotiations. The main suspect, Pol Pot, had died in the meantime. The International Criminal Court is presently investigating several war crimes committed in African countries, notably Sudan, Uganda and Congo.

Burundi The 8.4 million inhabitants are predominantly Hutu with significant Tutsi and smaller Twa and Baganwa minorities. This very poor country underwent several coups and changes of government since its independence in 1962. Rwagasore, leader of the multi-ethnic UPRONA movement, was assassinated after winning the 1961 elections. A coalition of mono-ethnic opposition parties came to power.

Ethnic violence became entrenched. In 1965, several thousand Hutus were slaughtered, including politicians and army members. Mass killings during the 1972 Hutu insurrection left thousands of Tutsis dead. In reprisal, Tutsis killed approximately 200,000 Hutus while many others fled.

During the late eighties, moderate Tutsi Buyoya released political prisoners and promised to bring Hutu elites into government. His initial hesitation led disappointed Hutus to assassinate several thousand Tutsis in 1988. The Tutsi ruled army responded with massacres, killing 20,000 Hutus. Approximately 60,000 citizens fled.

Buyoya eventually introduced state reforms safeguarding an equal distribution of power between Hutus and Tutsis. He freed the way to democratic elections.

Hutu parties won the 1993 elections. Fearful of a Hutu ordered genocide, Tutsis retained control over the army. Tensions exploded when Ndadaye was murdered four months after he had become president. During the subsequent years many Tutsis were slaughtered, which led to the genocide of Hutus. Over 150,000 people lost their lives.

In 1995, the UN Security Council investigated events leading to widespread killing. UN delegate Nyerere fled when Buyoya came to power through a military coup. International sanctions forced Buyoya to attend Nyerere's peace negotiations. Hutus and Tutsis jointly reached the Arusha Peace and Reconciliation Agreement in 2000, followed by the installation of a transitional government. Disarmament negotiations resulted in the Pretoria Protocol on Political Defence and Security Power Sharing in Burundi, improving national security significantly. In 2005, an elected government came to power.

The Arusha agreement tried to replace an emphasis on ethnic differences in politics by an attitude of inclusiveness and fair representation. Significant threats to political stability remain: ethnic divisions, civic distrust, corruption, extremism, regional instability, and local warfare. Perpetrators and victims are present in all layers of society, political parties and the state apparatus. Burundi mixes conventional and traditional mediation like Bashingantahe councils in justice and reconciliation. The peace can be easily disturbed. In 2006 Burundi was put on the agenda of the new UN Peace Building Committee to coordinate international assistance.

All war crimes tribunals which follow international legal standards have relatively high costs, large backlogs and a lack of resources. It is important to maintain credibility in the eyes of the affected populations, particularly when national or local tribunals are manipulated by political actors, as happened in Sierra Leone, where the selection of indicted persons was very controversial and was interpreted as an attempt by President Kabbah to corner political opposition. Of great importance to the future effectiveness of these courts is that the International Tribunal for war crimes committed in the Former Yugoslavia (ICTY) will be allowed to sentence the Serb suspects Mladic and Karadzic, before it is disbanded by the UN Security Council.

As international courts are only able to handle a limited number of indictments, while national courts are, for various reasons, generally very inadequate, many war crimes are left unpunished. To bridge the large gap between what should be done and can be achieved practically, the notion of *transitional justice* has gained attention.

Transitional justice denotes temporary justice mechanisms that are specific to the post-conflict setting inside a country. It is needed to deal, in the short term, with war criminals and their many collaborators. Transitional justice has become a common term but seems an internally contradictory notion. Is the goal lower or less just than non-transitional justice? Probably so, for practical reasons. The political will, legal basis, institutional arrangements, and human and financial resources in a war-torn country are often inadequate to really meet the international standards of justice. Transitional justice is a makeshift, provisional and inadequate effort to attain at least some degree of justice and begin the steps required to address the crimes of the past in a way that help achieve future reconciliation. The unsatisfactory qualities of transitional justice need to be improved by increasing international resources and qualified legal personnel.

The international expertise centre Transitional Justice, supported by private and public funds, is available to advise and assist national transitional justice programmes to deal with the large numbers of 'lesser' criminals. If suspects of war crimes are not properly tried, reconciliation falters too.

Reconciliation among former warring parties, population groups, victims of war crimes and suppression is an extremely complex socio-psychological task that generally takes more than a generation to complete. A failure is likely to lead to renewed bloodshed and oppression. Reconciliation is only possible if major political leaders, influential intellectuals, religious leaders, teachers and opinion leaders in the media actively pursue overcoming old hatreds and prejudices. Various civil society organisations need to encourage this patiently for decades. International, non-governmental organisations related to and supported by the world's religions and philosophies could provide additional services in this field, based on the experience which has been gained in a number of cases.

One should not assume, however, that religious leaders and their followers will always contribute to peacebuilding and reconciliation. Peace is preached, of course, but what is really meant? Peace for fellow believers, the own ethnic group, their own politicians? Everybody is in favour of peace, even the warmongers who want their enemies to stop resisting, in order that they can impose their view of peace, on their terms. There are many examples of religious leaders inciting group clashes or condoning violence. The question is not, who is for peace, but whose peace, and what kind of peace?

4.9 CRIMES AGAINST WOMEN AND GENDER ISSUES

In most post-conflict countries serious maltreatment and suppression of women and girls is endemic. In many contemporary conflicts, mass-rape, forced prostitution and other violent crimes have taken place. In recent years, the methods of warfare seem to have worsened and increasingly place women and girls at risk, as the conflicts in e.g. Liberia, Rwanda, and Congo have shown. Rape is used more and more systematically; as part of ethnic cleansing, to undermine communities and families, or to frighten adversaries. The fact that many of the fighting forces, especially in Africa, have a high HIV prevalence makes the consequences for women even greater. Yet, the true extent of women's ordeals in conflict situations will never be known, as many are too afraid to report such abuses. The gruesome nature and magnitude is often downplayed by military and political forces in the conflict.

Even if women try to flee the violence, they will not be out of harm's way as they may be required to exchange sex for safe passage or to obtain essential items like food. Or they can be targeted by traffickers, as recent Eastern European conflicts brought to the fore. Even when they arrive in camps they will be vulnerable if there is limited protection and if health services or psycho-social support are not available. Security is therefore at the essence and a proper camp lay-out and administration can assist in this. Reproductive health services are to be offered to ensure appropriate care for women, prevent and treat sexually transmitted infections and HIV and allow legal abortions, at least in the case of rape and serious health risks. Counselling for women who have experienced violence and rape is essential as is the assurance of their confidentiality. Women also need to be safe from abuse by those humanitarian actors whose role it is to protect and assist them; peacekeepers and humanitarian workers alike. In recent years, many of such incidents have come to light and continued tightening of procedures and zero-tolerance is required to prevent this.

Awareness needs to be raised of all actors involved in peacebuilding so they will better understand the way women are affected by conflict, different from men, and how women can contribute to peace. Increased deployment of female peacekeepers and police and judges is needed. International standards, such as UN Security Council Resolution 1325, already ask for more attention to protect women, assist survivors of sexual violence and to hold those who committed crimes against women accountable. To ensure this becomes reality, much more attention and resources are required. Reconciliation is generally not possible without trying the offenders. Providing free legal counselling and representation for women is important. Monitoring legal processes and training of those involved, can ensure that the rights of both the victim and the defendant are guaranteed. Training police and military forces how to deal with gender based violence to ensure women will feel better protected, can make a great difference. Legal reforms and the strengthening of the justice and security sector in post-conflict as well as refugee situations have to increase the protection of women by addressing issues like gender inequalities and abuse, not only in times of conflict but also during peace.

Actually, the transition from war to peace provides opportunities for change. Ensuring women are included in peace negotiations from the start, allows them to bring their perspectives to the fore and can provide means for continued inclusion in future decision making. Gender relations have often changed at times of conflict since women are left in charge of communities when their men and sons leave to fight, as shown by research undertaken by UNIFEM, the United Nations Development Fund for Women. Similarly, women and women's organisations were often found to play a significant role in peacebuilding at the grass root level. Their formal participation in peacebuilding can help to reduce the risk that inequalities are re-established in the post-conflict situation. Women's token presence in committees is not enough, since barriers to participation need to be broken down. Male mindsets need to be changed. This requires support, especially from NGO's, for empowerment, and personal security to be guaranteed by police and other security services, to allow women to raise their voice. Organisations like UNIFEM and OXFAM International, as well as governments and peacekeepers have an important role to play in this. This can lead the way for future political involvement and sustainable and equitable development to address the general problem of gender inequalities. These inequalities contribute to the fact that 70 percent of those who live below the poverty line are women and girls, while domestic violence is the main cause of injury and death to women globally, as emphasised by OXFAM. Ensuring that men and women will benefit equally from political, social and economic developments requires those who understand the gender relations in their specific context to be involved in its decision making.

Women need to be involved in peace negotiations not only because they are survivors and caretakers, but also because women will often have played a role in the pursuit of war by supporting or maintaining combatants, whether willingly or not. About 40 percent of the child soldiers are reported to be girls; most of them forced. Only focusing on the male combatant who hands in a gun is not doing justice to this reality. Disarmament, demobilisation and reintegration processes therefore need to pay attention to the different roles men, women and children have played during the conflict.[13]

Even when the active conflict is over, women resettling or returning to their community will need continued counselling and support to deal with the violence they experienced or sometimes participated in. Community education programs are necessary to reduce the potential stigma of these women, who may otherwise be rejected by their community. Similarly, specific attention needs to be given to prevent discrimination of female ex-combatants and women with disabilities. Support may need to be provided to those women who became the single head of a household because they lost their husband during the conflict. Women who are left to fend for their own in hopeless circumstances may see prostitution as the only means of survival for themselves and their children. Attention also needs to be given to the men returning from the war. Psycho-social care of male ex-combatants is needed as their traumas and inability to resolve conflicts in a non-violent matter usually results in increased violence to women.

Preventing gender-based violence in post-conflict situations requires the changing of power imbalances between men and women, to strengthen the inferior status of women. This means starting in schools to teach boys and girls how to behave, going into communities to particularly work with powerful male leaders aiming to change the beliefs and attitudes of especially men so they see the value of economic and social development of women. More research is needed of causes and possible solutions. Supporting and empowering women and female leaders, often through women organisations, will help to reduce subjugation and abuse. Safe houses to go to and other essential facilities where confidentiality is assured help them to stand up for themselves. It requires reform of police, to react on domestic violence, investigate rape, bring perpetrators to trial and reform discriminatory laws. Such changes are essential for peacebuilding that lasts.

4.10 REFUGEE ISSUES

Political violence leads people to vote with their feet: they seek refuge in less endangered areas, inside or outside their country. Often, refugees are driven together into areas that are far from safe, where they may be at the mercy of warring parties. Refugee camps can become fertile recruitment grounds or safe havens for warring parties. One example is the camps in eastern Congo and Tanzania in 1995-2005 where Rwandan Interahamwe fighters regrouped after the genocide. Another example is camps in Guinea where rebels and militia from Sierra Leone and Liberia recruited and trained fighters to join the insurgencies in both countries. After a war, peacebuilding activities may be especially difficult in or around refugee areas, because of strong group hatred and conflicts over personal and communal properties.

Refugees and internally displaced persons do not only flee out of fear of political violence, but also for fear of violent and other serious abuses by domestic, family, tribal, ethnic, cultural, criminal and religious persons. They are often subject to 'semi-political' violence, for instance where police gangs or security services abuse their mandate and terrorise groups for purposes of enrichment, group

Colombia. The nearly 45 million inhabitants are a colorful mix. The majority are mestizo, while whites and mulatto's form significant minorities. The original Amerindians form the smallest population.

The 1948 assassination of Liberal Party leader Gaitan resulted in a civil war between the Liberal and the Conservative Party. During 10 years of *La Violenca*, 200,000 citizens lost their lives. Formation of the National Front was the solution to the conflict. The political influence of both parties was equally distributed with alternating four year presidencies.

Most guerrillas disarmed after *La Violenca*. In 1964, remaining leftist guerrillas assembled in the National Liberation Army (ELN). In 1966, other leftist and communist fighters gathered in the Revolutionary Armed Forces of Colombia (FARC). Both groups adopted the 'foco' strategy involving small scale guerilla attacks to feed public discontent that would trigger insurrection. The government responded with US supported hunter-killer operations and civic action programs to improve living conditions.

During the 70's, the urban April 19th guerilla movement (M-19) gained public support. The government initiated counterinsurgencies against the M-19 and ELN activities.

Elections brought Betancur in 1982 to power to end the conflict. Negotiations resulted in a truce with the FARC and M-19. ELN refused to attend. Meanwhile, interests in cocaine trade had come to play a leading role. The government tried to fight the drug lords with assistance of US forces. Mutual distrust between the M-19 and the government abruptly ended the peace-process in 1985. Continued negotiations with the FARC resulted in a new political party, the Patriotic Union (UP).

In 1987, the cease-fire between the FARC and the government had fallen to pieces. The M-19 and smaller guerilla movements entered new peace negotiations. Elections followed and the Constituent Assembly of Colombia drafted a new constitution, adopted in 1991.

The FARC and ELN stepped up guerilla activities during the 90's. Larger parts of the rural population had grown to support the FARC against the government's war on drugs. Drug crops had become a major source of income for many Colombians. In response to brutal attacks, the government retreated from several areas. Paramilitary groups gathered in the United Self-defense Forces of Colombia (AUC) became a party to the conflict.

Peace talks were given up when president Uribe became president in 2002. His attempt to crush ELN, FARC and AUC improved security, but left many underlying causes unsolved. Corruption, drug cultivation, poverty, high unemployment, social inequality, absence of the government army in rural areas, guerilla attacks by the ELN and FARC, as well as attacks by the UAC continue this multifarious conflict. By proportion, Colombia counts an extremely high number of Internally Displaced Persons. It is one of the most complicated multiple civil wars which has been left unsolved.

hatred, sex or power. Often refugees suffering such abuse cannot prove the origin of the threat to themselves or their families. In some instances it stems from a lack of state monopoly on the use of force, and in others the state uses gangs or tribal militia as proxies for its own political ends (for example the Janjaweed in the Darfur region of Sudan).

Refugees and groups of internally displaced persons often live in insecure anarchy as gangs of criminals and (former) warring parties rule their lives. International aid agencies are quite powerless to stop this and curb misuse of aid materials. When international peacekeeping forces are present, they may be able to act against such abuse, depending on their mandate and their military capability. In many situations, refugee camps are left without any form of protection.

Host countries should be assisted with the organisation of police forces, temporary courts and detention facilities to curb crime in refugee camps in accordance with international law and the law of the country concerned, even though these legal systems may clash. Monitors, advisors and training experts could be made available from UN member states. A special international policing arrangement, to be implemented by UNHCR, could be made possible with a mandate from the UN Security Council. Improvement of police, temporary or mobile courts, and detention facilities in or near refugee camps would also

Sudan (South)

The population is estimated 39 million. It became independent in 1956 and was since then ruled by military regimes, some of them affiliated with political Islam. Sudan's rural population is mostly dependent on agriculture. Large oil exports, particularly to China, finance the regime and the booming capital.

Two civil wars between the North and the South have raged over Sudan in 1955-72 and 1983-2005. Ethnic and religious tensions between the Muslim Arab population of the North and the non-Muslim African population of the South date back to the colonial period. British rule administrated them as separate regions, but they merged when Sudan became independent.

This may have been a serious mistake of state design with grievous consequences. The South feared northern dominance and strived for more regional autonomy. Fights between the South and the North (supported by the government) killed 500,000 people. The Addis Ababa Agreement of March 1972 ended the first civil war. The South got a single administrative region with various defined powers.
In 1983, President Nimeiry intended to transform Sudan into a Muslim Arab state and imposed Sharia law. The non-Muslim South refused to obey. Under John Garang of the Sudan People's Liberation Army (SPLA) the fight for an independent South continued between 1983 and 2005. The war caused 2 million deaths and 4 million displacements. Peace negotiations

between the government of Sudan and the SPLA started in 1993, led by the Intergovernmental Authority on Development (IGAD) and supported by senior UN officials. Between 2002 and 2004, the parties agreed to various protocols that included arrangements about security, wealth sharing, and power sharing. In January 2005, the SPLA and the government signed the final Comprehensive Peace Agreement (CPA). It granted the South autonomy for six years, followed by a referendum on secession.

In March 2005, the Security Council established the UN mission (UMNIS) to support the implementation of the CPA, to provide humanitarian assistance, monitor protection of human rights and to support the African Union Mission in Sudan (AMIS) operating in Darfur. The authorized strength of UNMIS is 27,300 military personnel and 4,015 police.

The implementation of the CPA has been limited. Armed groups in the South that are not party of the agreement continue to use violence. The crisis in Darfur is complicating the situation. It remains uncertain if South Sudan will develop autonomously and overcome its serious poverty.

See box on Darfur in Chapter 8.

greatly facilitate the provision of effective relief and aid by non-governmental organisations.

At the end of a war, most governments want the refugees and IDP's to return rapidly to their home communities. But they return only if it seems safe, offers a better future, or if they are forced to return because they have no legal right or practical possibility to stay where they found shelter. Host governments often prompt refugees to return by reducing national and international assistance.

In refugee camps, crime often rules, as even the beginnings of law and order are absent. Camps are controlled by brute force, often exercised by gangs of young males. Women, children, elderly and members of tribes and families different from those exercising power suffer daily abuse. Many refugee camps remain in place for a long time even after the end of armed conflict. Its people live in limbo for half a generation or more. Law and order are formally the task of the host state, but this state is often not a rule-of-law state either. The most fundamental human rights, those to life, security of person, freedom from torture and freedom from arbitrary arrest and detention, are often not upheld.
Refugees fall under the jurisdiction of the host state, but the hosts often lack the interest and resources to implement this responsibility, leaving the refugees in a vacuum. UNHCR has stated that its officers should discourage the use of customs and traditional practices that violate basic human rights, but it has not been given the means, or the mandate to enforce these goals.

UNHCR did negotiate in Kenya for additional police presence in a refugee camp and paid incentives on top of Kenyan police salaries. In Kenya, mobile courts have sessions in refugee camps to make the state's justice system available for refugees.

The national, religious and customary law and practices of refugees often clash with the laws and practices of the host country. In general, neither of the two systems conform to international human rights standards. Often, the rights of women are particularly violated. There is usually no legal aid and representation of the accused. Quality and availability of translation services leave much to be desired. The lack of competent magistrates is widespread. Most prison conditions are life-threatening. Police and detention personnel are usually brutal and corrupt.

In most conflict areas, the capacity to re-integrate returning refugees is equally poor. The war has destroyed state structures and increased hatred between population groups. Homes, farms and other properties have often been seized by opponents or criminals. Lack of police, or the power of prejudiced police and local leaders, can encourage the rejection of returnees by the population. It may be very difficult for the returnees to prove their property rights when land and real estate registration is absent or faulty. Re-establishing rights can take many years of an uphill legal battle in poorly functioning courts.

Refugees who should but cannot return to their homes often become permanent refugees. For these people, new solutions have to be found. Resettlement in a different area of their country of origin, or migration to a third country, may be a more viable long-term solution. Many poor neighbouring countries receive large numbers of refugees and migrants who are difficult to absorb permanently and do not always meet the formal criteria for asylum as defined in international treaties and domestic legislation.

It is necessary to search for new solutions to the question of what to do for refugees who cannot return and also cannot be accepted permanently due to the legislation or the situation in the host country. A part of the solution may lie in resettlement programmes in a number of relatively under-populated areas in third countries in which perhaps new communities could be created with the agreement of the government in the area and aided by resettlement funds from other countries and international agencies. In the past, many refugees from Europe found a new future in North and South America, Australia and New Zealand. There are still undeveloped and under-populated areas in the world which could be developed into attractive resettlement territories if they were under good government, and if adequate international resources were made available to enable the refugees to build a new future there. Donor and recipient countries could negotiate with UNHCR such resettlement programmes and solve mutual problems together. This is, of course, not an easy solution, and will work only if conditions are right. Often, refugees and IDP's are reluctant to resettle far from their country. Moreover, tensions might arise between the resettlers and the original population in the area of resettlement. The natural environment may not allow additional settlers (e.g. for lack of water). There should be benefits to both to make it work. Such benefits can be provided by development assistance from the UN, EU, bilateral donors and NGOs.

4.11 PREPARATIONS FOR ELECTORAL DEMOCRACY

Elections are generally regarded as the ultimate way to settle the threat of new violent conflicts and lay the foundation for democratic government based on the rule of law. But one-time general elections are no miracle cure and do not suffice as a start of democracy. Elections need to be prepared carefully and have to be held not only at the national level for the chief executive and the legislative, but also at the regional, provincial or state level, as well as for municipalities. A whole series of successful elections, construction of stable electoral institutions and a free press are needed to make formal democracy function and survive nasty power struggles. Laws, attitudes and ethics have to be reformed to make democracy last.

After a violent conflict, domestic peace and basic security for the population are the most urgent. Before elections can be held, warring parties have to be demobilized, disarmed and re-integrated in society. Political parties need to be organized and free media have to be established. Electoral laws need to be enacted. Impartial technical international assistance is needed to newly emerging democracies. Electoral assistance aims at capacity building of indigenous electoral institutions, such as permanent independent electoral commissions. Ideally, elections are transparent to all observers and do not cause new violent conflicts. This requires constitutional reform in many states. Political parties themselves should be internally democratic and have enough administrative capacity to fight effectively for participatory democracy. Popular participation is the aim, especially of less influential and advantaged groups, women, the poor, indigenous peoples and suppressed minorities. To achieve this, parties have to be well-organized, well-funded with private and public funds, but not to make them dependent on specific elites. Parties should have various bonds to civil society organisations, be open to the media, and apply strict rules against corruptive influences. This is a daunting, never ending task even in established democracies.

In some countries, elections did not lead to lasting democratic government. An example is the election of Aristide as President of Haiti. His government did not solve the country's social, political and economic problems. International support for elections needs to be linked to steady progress in other areas. It is important to look beyond a single election and encourage a sustainable electoral process. This may take a generation, and even then, there is a risk of decline, as political parties can also hijack elections and establish less-democratic rule which abolishes certain human rights, change the constitution, and impose authoritarianism. Various examples, like the seemingly democratic elections in a number of Central Asian countries after the dissolution of the USSR since the early 1990s, leading to new but different authoritarian rule, are cases in point.

Since the 1980s, several providers of international technical assistance for electoral development have become active. The UN Secretariat established an Electoral Assistance Division EAD which has expanded its work to some 60 countries. Sweden started the International Institute for Electoral Assistance IDEA,

Haiti

Haiti declared its independence from France in 1804. The country has a history of instability and political violence. In the early twentieth century, the US invaded Haiti and occupied it between 1915 and 1934. The US centralized the government and urged industries to leave the provinces and settle in the capital. Nationalist rebels, the Cacos, engaged in guerrilla warfare. The US handed over control in 1934 to a Haitian minority.

The 1957 elections brought François Duvalier to power, nicknamed 'Papa Doc'. He remained in office till 1971. He controlled the population through repressive police named the Volunteers for National Security. His son Jean-Claude Duvalier, 'Baby Doc', succeeded him in 1971 and continued the atrocities. In 1986 'Baby Doc' was deposed and exiled to France. In 1991 the priest Aristide was elected president, but shortly after the elections, Cedras deposed him and took over control for three years. The second US intervention, this time under a United Nations Security Council mandate, put Aristide back in office. Aristide was succeeded by Préval as president. Both were assisted by UN peace operations which guided the development of a professional police force between 1994 and 2000.

During local elections in 2000, the political opposition turned on Aristide and his party, accusing them of election fraud. Aristide's controversial re-election in 2000 was marred by suspicions that he had threatened his opponents. In 2004, public upheaval and violent rebellion prevailed once again. Aristide was pressured into leaving the country. In 2004 about 8,000 peacekeepers from the UN Stabilization Mission arrived to maintain civil order. The 2006 elections brought Préval back to office. He promised to restore peace and order, though recent history tells us that the problems dividing Haitian society will probably resurface again after the UN leaves. Haiti remains extremely poor, civil society is very weak, and the country suffers from unemployment and environmental degradation.

We can learn from Haiti's experience that rapid exit of foreign troops and assistance can destroy initial success. Elections as a way of legitimizing the government, when there is no democratic system, can lead to premature withdrawal of the international community. Haiti has a long way to go in terms of building democratic institutions. Support of the international community is crucial for future peace and security in this unfortunate Caribbean half-island.

which is supported by many governments and NGOs. The UN Development Program became actively involved in technical election assistance since the 1990s. In 2006 the UN Democracy Fund became an important source of funds, providing support for civil society organizations.

The private International Foundation for Elections Systems (IFES) has worked in over 120 countries in the areas of elections, rule of law, civil society, and assistance to good governance. It is a leading NGO in the area of direct technical election assistance and works in tandem with other international organizations.[14]

Regional international organizations such as the European Union, the Council of Europe, the Organisation for Security and Cooperation in Europe, the Organization for American States, the African Union, the Office of Democratic Human Rights Initiatives (ODHIR), and the European Union also provide technical election assistance. Chapter 7 is devoted to the EU, as it is becoming the largest source of finance for these purposes. Other regional election networks also provide technical assistance, such as the Association of Central and Eastern European Election Officials (ACEEEO) in Budapest which represents elections officials from 22 countries from the former USSR and Warsaw Pact. This organization has offered technical help in Bosnia-Herzegovina, Georgia, Kosovo, and Palestine. Various national election commissions offer assistance, such as 'Elections Canada', the Indian Election Commission and the Federal Electoral Institute of Mexico.

There is also assistance for political party development. The US offers this through the National Democratic Institute and the International Republican Institute, which are part of the National Endowment for Democracy. Other examples are the German party assistance schemes of the Adenauer Foundation (CDU), Friedrich Ebert Foundation of the SPD, the Neumann Foundation of the Free Democratic Party and the Hans Seidel Foundation of the CSU. German party assistance helped, for instance, to democratize Portugal after the Spinola coup which abolished the Caetano government. Another example is the Netherlands Institute for Multiparty Democracy (NIMD) which carries out democratisation projects in a host of countries.[15]

Some examples of the 1990's show how not to provide electoral assistance: Angola, Cambodia and Haiti. Peacekeeping operations and electoral assistance were poorly coordinated. The UN overlooked electoral institution building as a strategy to build sustainable democratic systems. Elections can be used as a face-saving device by foreign countries which have sent peacekeepers, to get to the exit of difficult operations.

In fragile states the strength of electoral management bodies, and the respect they have earned, can make a great difference. Will the results of an election be respected, or will the opposing parties re-ignite hostilities? In Angola, the warring parties agreed in 1992 on putting down arms and participate in an election, but the parties were not yet demobilised and disarmed. Using its oil revenues, the Angolan government rebuffed offers of assistance by the UN and the IFES and contracted instead a large private firm to organize the elections. This undercut the Angolan Election Commission. When election disputes erupted between UNITA and the MLA, the contestants did not turn to the Election Commission to adjudicate their differences but took up arms again. The elections should have been postponed till demobilization had progressed further. The civil war lasted another decade and devastated Angolan society.

The Cambodian model is another example of poor implementation of international election support, even though the UN operations helped to avoid a return to civil war. From 1991 to 1993, the UN spent nearly three billion dollars to provide security, keep the country functioning and organize the country's first democratic elections. Cambodian citizens, NGOs and politicians did not get heavily involved in the process of running elections. The UN did not adequately encourage the Cambodians to develop an indigenous election management body that could continue for future elections. After the elections the UN withdrew; there was little local capacity to organize elections in the future.

At the outset of this paragraph, Haiti was mentioned as an example of how not to render international aid. Haiti may be a small part of the world, but its complex problems are a microcosm of what is wrong in many other, larger countries. After two hundred years of brutal, suppressive, and ineffective governments, the Haitian people badly need the kind of sustained international support that can build a lasting, functioning democracy. A serious weakness is the near-absence of civil society and domestic NGOs and the small size of the educated group of potential mid-level leaders.

The elections of 1990, which brought a promising priest to power, Aristide, were onducted by a Provisional Electoral Council, which received technical assistance from the United Nations, the OAS and IFES. These elections were successful largely because the provisional President of Haiti in 1990 appointed an electoral council composed of respected Haitians from across the political spectrum.

President Aristide and the Haitian Parliament that was elected in 1990 never completed the task of making the CEP permanent as was provided for in the Haitian Constitution. Corrupt, incapable government and instability has continued to plague Haiti, notwithstanding repeated and prolonged inter-

Angola counts 12 million people and is one of the poorest countries in the world: 70 percent of the population lives below the poverty line, and the life expectancy is only 38 years. Different ethnicities live in relative harmony with each other, including Ovimbundu (37%), Kimbundu (25%) and Bakongo minorities (13%). Increased oil production has caused a high economic growth rate in recent years.

After a long struggle for independence, the colonial power Portugal granted statehood in 1975. The Popular Movement for the Liberation of Angola (MPLA) and the National Union for the Total Independence of Angola (UNITA) then fought for control over the country and its rich oil and diamonds resources. The country became a cold war battleground: the Soviet Union and Cuba supported the Marxist MPLA, and the United States and South Africa supported the anti-communist UNITA. During the civil war, up to 1.5 million lives may have been lost and 4 million people were displaced.

In 1989, the UN initiated peace agreements and sent troops to monitor these: UNAVEM I, II, III and MONUA. In 1991, the MPLA and UNITA agreed to the Bicesse Accords which were intended to convert Angola from a one-party authoritarian government led by MPLA into a multi-party state with democratic elections in 1992. After claims of fraud in initial elections, a final run-off election did not take place and the civil war resumed.

There were four years of relative peace between 1994 and 1998, when the UN oversaw a new peace accord of Lusaka. In 1997 it was agreed that a coalition government with UNITA would be implemented. But UNITA violated the peace agreement by refusing to give up strongholds, by failing to demobilize and by retaking territory. As a result, the government suspended coalition rule in 1998, and the country plunged into civil war once more. The UN Security Council tried to stop the flow of diamond revenues to UNITA and oil to the MPLA. The UN retreated in 1999 for a variety of reasons, including absence of 'peace' to monitor, the shooting down of an UN-chartered aircraft and a general lack of confidence in the UN among Angolans.

In 2002, government troops killed UNITA leader Jonas Savimbi, and six weeks later, rebel leaders signed a cease-fire with the government. In this deal UNITA agreed to demobilize its soldiers and the MPLA pledged to provide food and shelter for the UNITA forces and relatives, who were cut off from basic supplies due to government action and UN sanctions. Some 5,000 UNITA forces were to be absorbed into the national military and approximately 40 into the national police.

After the end of a 27-year civil war, Angola is rebuilding its country since 2002. It is riddled by anti-personnel mines. Peace remains fragile, as separatist forces continue to fight over the control of natural resources

national electoral assistance. In 2004 and onwards, a new peacekeeping mission was needed to stop a groundswell of violence. International election assistance by the UN, OAS and IFES was not well coordinated and the elections held in the spring of 2006 were chaotic.

The organization of elections in Haiti since the 1990's has proven to be costly, difficult and chaotic due in large part to the highly ineffective way that the OAS and the UN provided technical assistance. The two organizations frequently left the Haitian CEP feeling confused and abandoned.

Fortunately, there are encouraging examples where the international donor community was effective, like in Nicaragua, where Presidential and Parliamentary Elections were held. Non-partisan assistance was provided by IFES, the OAS and the European Union to the Supreme Electoral Council.
In Iraq, the population went to the polls to vote in three elections in 2005, notwithstanding the threat of terrorist attacks. In 2003-5, the electoral process proved one of the few successes of post-war assistance. In 2005, the Independent Election Commission of Iraq conducted a parliamentary election for the interim government, a constitutional referendum, and a general election for the new government. The UN Election Assistance Division and IFES provided assistance under very threatening circumstances. As Iraq has fallen into civil war at the time of writing, this successful assistance to election preparation risks being lost in the internecine violence that is engulfing the country.

Bosnia-Herzegovina can be mentioned as a relative success story with better prospects. After the Dayton peace agreement, the OSCE and IFES helped organizing local, state and federal elections. A permanent and independent Central Election Commission was prepared by an Association for Free Elections of Bosnia-Herzegovina. This gained wide membership and became a multi-ethnic organization. Elections in Bosnia Herzegovina showed that international assistance can encourage former opponents to negotiate technical electoral and political party issues.

International donors should, of course, help designing or renewing the electoral systems in a transparent fashion that fits the political landscape of the recipient. Complex electoral systems as developed historically in some stable older democracies will often not be ready for export to another country. Foreign systems can exacerbate tensions.

The key choice is between majority-based or 'first past the post' systems such as used by the United Kingdom, India and the United States, or proportional representation systems, as in the Netherlands and Sweden, where candidates compete for seats in assemblies advocating party lists, led by major politicians, on the basis of different policy platforms. The advantage of majority systems is a clear result leading to a government majority, even though this may not precisely reflect popular majority in the country as a whole. The advantage of proportional representation is a higher democratic reflection of the views of the population, but a multi-party split may hamper clear majority formation which is needed for a stable executive. Mixed systems, such as the German since 1949, are a useful guidance in different situations. Representation with a part of the legislature elected nationally by proportion, and a part at the local level from single-member districts, can combine the advantages.

The nature of an electoral system and the preparation of parties for elections can not only reduce, but also increase ethnic and other tensions in a country. Electoral competition can encourage outbidding and populism with extremist rhetoric fostering polarisation rather than peaceful conflict settlement. Newly emerging democracies can benefit from impartial international expertise when they design new electoral systems.[16] Expert organisations offer advice based on comparative analysis of election laws, poll worker training, vote counting, adjudication of election disputes, voter education, use of election technology, and improving the role of free media for elections.

Mozambique has 19 million inhabitants of which 20-30 percent is Christian and 15-20 percent Muslim. The socialist liberation front FRELIMO started a war of liberation in the middle 1960s against Portuguese colonial rule and gained independence in 1975. A civil war between the FRELIMO government and the national resistance movement RENAMO, first supported by Rhodesia and South Africa during the apartheid regime, ravaged the country in the 1980s. The first president Samora Machel died in a suspicious plane crash in 1986. His successor Chissano allowed multiparty democracy in 1990. RENAMO changed into a political party. With the end of the Cold War and the abolishment of apartheid in South Africa, foreign intervention ceased, which contributed to the end of hostilities. The Roman Catholic Egidio order and the UN mediated a peace in 1992.

The war devastated the country and flooded Mozambique with land mines and small arms. The UN sent ONUMOZ to monitor the peace agreement. Five million internal and external refugees had to be resettled. ONUMOZ reached a strength of 7000 peacekeepers that protected humanitarian aid and assisted demobilizing 64,000 government troops and 23,000 RENAMO fighters. A new national army was formed. The UN sent 1100 international police officers but this force was not very qualified and remained ineffective in ending human rights violations. The UN trained 1600 people to prepare for elections in 1994, which were a victory for FRELIMO. Several elections have been held since.

Peace, political stability and economic aid have brought consistent growth since 1992. Crucial was the end of outside interference by countries which had fuelled the civil war, but now supported peace implementation. RENAMO's successful transformation to a political party was essential for peace. The UN postponed elections until demobilization was well under way (as opposed to Angola, were elections were held too early). Large development assistance from EU members helped to turn Mozambique in a successful peacebuilding operation. There is a fair degree of media freedom, but the justice and police systems need improvement.

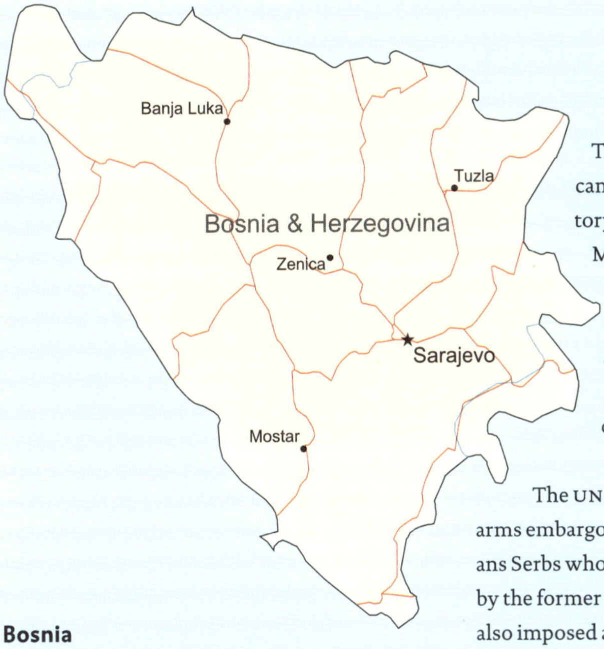

The Bosnian Croats started in 1993 a campaign to establish a Croat territory in areas bordering Croatia. In March 1994, the Washington Peace agreement established a cease-fire between the Bosnian Croats and Muslims. This did not end the war with the Serbs, which continued until the end of 1995.

The UN Security Council had imposed an arms embargo in 1991. This favoured the Bosnians Serbs who were well-armed and supported by the former federal Yugoslav army. The UN also imposed a no-fly zone. The UN protection force UNPROFOR, already present in Croatia, was expanded to Bosnia in 1992. Its mandate included monitoring the no-fly zone, supporting UNHCR to deliver humanitarian aid, and upholding 'safe areas' (including Sarajevo, Tuzla, Zepa, Goražde and Srebrenica).

UNPROFOR was neither mandated nor equipped to impose peace and engage in fighting enemy forces. Force was authorized by the UN only for self-defence of UN blue helmet soldiers. This mandate, which assumed impartiality and consent of the warring parties – which were still in full-swing civil war – seriously hindered the UN's effectiveness. The most disastrous failure of this mission was the conquest by Serb forces of the 'safe area' of Srebrenica in eastern Bosnia on July 11, 1995. Srebrenica counted about 40,000 Bosnian inhabitants and refugees, while 400 UN blue helmet soldiers from The Netherlands were stationed in the enclave. After their conquest, Serb military and militia killed about 7500 Bosnian men inside and outside the enclave and bulldozered the corpses into mass graves, which were revealed by US intelligence to the Security Council in August 1995.

Bosnia

Bosnia-Herzegovina formed a part of the former Yugoslavia between 1942 and 1992, together with Slovenia, Macedonia, Serbia, Kosovo, Montenegro and Croatia. Separatist sentiments increased after the death of President Tito, leading to independence of Slovenia and Croatia in 1991. The split-up affected Bosnia-Herzegovina (hereafter: Bosnia) the harshest. In 1990, Bosnia had included approximately 43 percent Bosnian Muslims, 31 percent Serbs, and 17 percent Croats. Bosnia declared itself independent from Yugoslavia (Serbia) in March 1992 after a referendum that was boycotted by Bosnian Serbs. They rejected the outcome.

In May 1992 the Bosnian Serbs had occupied 70 percent of the country. Serb leaders aimed at creating a larger Serbia, which would incorporate Serbian areas in northern and eastern Bosnia, including the city of Sarajevo. The Serb leader Karadzic and General Mladic, supported by Yugoslavia (Serbia), followed a policy of ethnic cleansing to expel Muslim and Croat minorities from what they considered Serb land. War raged over the country between 1992 and 1995. As a result, 200.000 people died and 1.8 million (almost half of the total population) fled.

Investigations by the UN, the Netherlands Institute for War Documentation (NIOD, 2002) and the Dutch Parliament later concluded, i.a., that although the blue-helmet UN mission was intended to uphold the enclave, located deep into enemy territory, it was militarily unable to defend it, which was mainly due to the small size and light arms of the UN force 'Dutchbat', while Serb artillery occupied the hills around the enclave. There was misplaced confidence in the readiness of UNPROFOR to timely deploy effective close air support if Serbs would attack. Earlier Dutch proposals for an air bridge to support the enclave had been rejected by key UN members. Previous proposals to evacuate the enclave preventively and resettle the refugees near Sarajevo had been rejected by the Bosnian government.

The fate of Srebrenica led to the end of the US policy not to support peacekeeping with ground troops in Bosnia. The US Congress forced the US government to take the lead in peace operations. This changed the Serb policy.

Directly after the fall of Srebrenica, the enclave Zepa had also been overrun by Serb forces, killing several thousand people. When another massacre threatened Goražde, NATO members issued on July 21, 1995 a deterrent warning that Serb targets would be attacked by air. This saved Goražde. When Serb attacks continued on Sarajevo, UK, French and Dutch military responded with air strikes and artillery against Serb military targets in September 1995. Meanwhile, the Croatian army had attacked Serb areas in the Krajina in August and expelled the population to Serbia.

The war ended with the Dayton Peace Agreement, mediated by the US, and signed in December 1995. It divided Bosnia-Herzegovina in the Republica Srpska and the Croat-Bosniak Federation. The blue-helmet UNPROFOR was replaced by 60.000 green-helmet troops of the NATO-led IFOR (later SFOR and EUFOR), which was responsible for enforcing the military aspects of the peace agreement.

Various international organizations were involved in the peacebuilding afterwards. The UN set up an International Police Task Force (IPTF) to oversee local police. UNHCR led the return of refugees; OSCE provided electoral support and monitored human rights. A High Representative received authority to monitor implementation of the peace agreement and coordinate the activities of foreign civilian agencies in Bosnia.

The Croat and Serb parts within Bosnia continued to act like independent states; both had police forces based on ethnic identities. Transforming the police into a neutral force was one of the most difficult parts of peacebuilding. The UN pulled out of police reform in 2003. A European Union Police Mission (EUPM) and peacekeeping forces of the EU (EUFOR) were still necessary to provide stability at the time of writing in 2007. No real reconciliation took place among the three populations. Ethnic violence might erupt again in Bosnia if these missions would leave.

The International Criminal Tribunal for the Former Yugoslavia (ICTY) in The Hague issued indictments against 161 individuals accused of committing war crimes. In mid 2007, 51 war criminals had received sentences for serious violations of international humanitarian law, but not yet the major suspects Mladic and Karadzic. In 2007, the International Court of Justice ruled that Serbia had been negligent in preventing genocide in Srebrenica.

The failing UN peacekeeping mission in the former Yugoslavia taught that it is impossible to have blue-helmet UN soldiers keep peace during an ongoing war without strong enforcement means, while the US, several NATO allies and other participants are deeply divided. The double key procedure for air support did not work. Refugee populations in enclaves should be protected with adequate green-helmet military forces or be moved preventively by UNHCR to safer areas, with military protection. The UN Security Council should determine clear mandates for its peacekeeping forces and provide for unified command.

Peacebuilding after cease-fire requires strong coordination, large resources, and international authority to break deadlocks caused by obstruction of former warring parties. The lessons of the UN's weak involvement in the civil war in the former Yugoslavia in 1991-5, while the veto-holding Great Powers of the Security Council were deeply divided, were that peace operations fail if there is no determined leadership by at least one of these Powers. NATO's role in enforcing the peace after the peace agreement showed the importance of deterrent power. Another historical lesson, learned once again, was that the break-up of a state containing many group identities usually leads to war, from which all parties heavily suffer, during many years, if not decades.

NOTES

1 Dobbins et al., *The Beginner's Guide to Nation-Building. Rand Corporation*, Santa Monica, 2007.

2 D.L. Philips, *Losing Iraq: Inside the Postwar Reconstruction Fiasco*, Westview Press, 2005.

3 UN Doc A/55/305.

4 D.A. Leurdijk, 'Robuuste Vredeshandhaving', *Internationale Spectator* 2006 nr. 7-8, p. 377. See UN S/Res./1296, 1289, 1313.

5 Thijs W. Brocades Zaalberg, *Soldiers and Civil Power: Supporting or Substituting Civil Authorities in Modern Peace Operations.* Amsterdam University Press, Amsterdam 2006.

6 Ibid, p. 11.

7 See UNSCR 1308 on HIV/AIDS and Peacekeepers. More info in *Guidelines for HIV/AIDS in emergency settings* (2003), IAS CTF. www.unfpa.org/upload/lib_pub_file/249_filename_guidelines-hiv-emer.pdf

8 *Humanitarian Charter and Minimum Standards in Disaster Response*, www.sphereproject.org.

9 *Cordaid, Principles and Pragmatism; Civil Military Action in Afghanistan and Liberia.* The Hague: May 2006.

10 Ibid.

11 Ibid.

12 Like the Venice Commission of the Council of Europe.

13 See UNIFEM (2004), *Getting it Right, Doing it Right: Gender and Disarmament, Demobilization and Reintegration,* for more information and ideas how to achieve this.

14 www.ifes.org. This section also draws on information provided by the President of IFES, R.Soudriette, 28 Nov.2006.

15 www.nimd.org.

16 www.aceproject.org forms an authoritative source in the field of election administration.

5 (RE) BUILDING THE RULE OF LAW

"We will spare no effort to (...) strengthen the rule of law"

UN Millennium Declaration, September 2000

The foundation for future rule of law is to be laid in the transitional phase, which was surveyed in the previous chapter. Transitional politics may have led to a provisional constitution or a basic agreement which will later on lead to a new constitution. Transitional 'justice' may have started purging the country of war criminals, war profiteers and serious collaborators with criminal political behaviour during the previous regime. Emergency laws may have facilitated the return of physical security. A beginning may have been made with disarmament, demobilisation and reform of the armed forces, the police and the intelligence services. A gradual return of public order may now enable efforts to lay the foundation for future rule of law. In the present chapter, the (re)building and reform of the legal and judicial sector will be briefly discussed.

5.1 THE ROLE AND RULE OF LAW

The 'role' of law is to settle conflicts equitably, to protect people's security and property, to restrain the use of political power by subjugating it to the law, and to guarantee basic human freedoms, in order to enable individuals and society to thrive. The first task of *public* law is to help provide basic human security and replace arbitrary rule, that is: achieve rule *by* law, which should in turn, develop further into the rule *of* law, in which the 'rulers', the administration and judicial and police system, are subject to the laws of the land as well as international law. We do not discuss here the role of *private* law, however important for peaceful life, reconstruction and development, as this study focuses on public policy in post-conflict peacebuilding.

The main elements of a complete rule-of-law system are:
- An independent judiciary;
- independent human rights institutions;
- government powers that are determined by laws;
- free and fair elections;
- transparent and accountable access to political power;
- police and detention systems whose powers are defined precisely by laws;
- military and security systems that function under the law;
- access to justice through competent and affordable lawyers, and no prohibitive levies or delays which discourage seeking justice.

The ultimate purpose of rule of law is to implement basic human rights as enshrined in advanced constitutions, which in turn reflect the international human rights treaties.

What exactly do we mean by 'the rule of law'? Next to the above-mentioned seven elements, one can also distinguish eight different functional requirements which have to be met:

- all laws are applied equally to all citizens, without discrimination based on legally irrelevant personal or group differences among the citizens;
- the right to fair trail is guaranteed to all;
- there is no arbitrary detention, no torture and cruel, inhumane treatment of detainees/prisoners;
- all laws are openly promulgated and can be scrutinised by the citizens and their legal aids;
- there is no retrospective application of penal laws;
- the judiciary is professional, intellectually independent and impartial;
- authorities derive their powers from laws; their decisions, policies and implementation are also under the law;
- all law enforcement agencies are given adequate means to perform their tasks.

These eight requirements form a broad set. The last element is, strictly speaking, more an element of good governance than rule-of-law, but the rule of law cannot function without it.

The standard of necessary elements and requirements for a complete rule of law system, as formulated above, is not met in more than one quarter of the UN member states. These standards are formulated, however, in many lofty UN declarations and policy memoranda. As ideals to be aspired to, they receive wide support. But reality is very different. It is impossible to attain all of these elements and requirements fully in the short time frame of international peacebuilding operations. The cultural, political, institutional and other conditions in most poor and middle income countries ravaged by war are not conducive to full human rights standards.

It is crucial to listen to the population: how they see their most pressing needs. Donor policies should follow these priorities. In countries that went through armed conflicts, the population sees basic needs for physical survival and some measure of law and order as their dominating priorities, often before the abstract notion of justice. Surviving the next weeks is the prime concern. This 'safety first' should be applied to international statecraft, too. That is why peacebuilding programmes should not be judged only by the high ideals and standards of OEDC type states, but by the desire of the population to be more secure than during the war period.

Establishing a functioning rule of law system takes many decades in most states. This is why peacebuilding operations should aim practically for a feasible improvement of the rule of law as it existed in the country concerned before the war. A government that keeps domestic peace and administers justice in a way which the population deems reasonably equitable and accessible is already a great improvement. This means that a complete overhaul of the judicial system is often beyond the realm of the possible in the period of international post-conflict peacebuilding assistance. Success in police and judicial reform is simply: having contributed to a more stable domestic order with greater personal security for the population, a lower level of violence, and a higher level of legal conflict settlement, meeting the basic rule of law standards of the population.

What is feasible? Recent studies by the Rand Corporation and the US Institute of Peace reviewed several county programmes to construct law and order after war.[1] These studies conclude that a new government and foreign supporters/peacekeepers have to set limited, practical targets. They cannot import a new state and deal with all obstacles to peace and development at once. For practical purposes it is often impossible and imprudent to avoid involving traditional authority structures. The dilemma is that the 'old' can severely compromise the new state building by reliance on power holders who violated basic human rights. This is a dilemma between short-term stability with limited resources, and international standards of good governance and basic rights. Brushing aside all local chieftains, or dismantling the state, leads to anarchy and renewed violence, particularly of a criminal nature. The choice of the donors is not between the bad old and the good new, but between different levels of what might be feasible and meets minimum standards of the population. What can be attained depends, of course, on the starting position, the desire of the population and its leaders, the time and the available resources. In the practical short run, there are choices and trade-offs between stability and justice, between stability and democracy, between local authority and good government, between leaving the country soon with 'unfinished business', or long term involvement leading to an unsustainable task for the donors.

The rule of law that has been attained in most Western societies is the result of a long historical development with ups and downs. It is assumed by many theorists and historians that the rule of law is related to a strong middle class, to a well developed civil society, and to the existence of a 'democratic' political system with elaborate power sharing arrangements and counter weights against abuse of political power. The rule of law is also often seen as strongly related to economic freedom and liberal market economics with free access. Such freedoms prevent long term material domination by a ruling class over a poor citizenry, while economic collectivism, dominated by a state which owns crucial sectors or even the entire productive apparatus, generally leads to authoritarian rule. In such authoritarian economic systems, the law is not above the rulers, but the rulers use the law to control the population and national resources in the interests and ideology of the ruling 'elite'.

The rule of law is sometimes seen by Western observers as closely linked to the values which prevail in Western society. Individualism, liberalism, personal responsibility and ambition (achievement orientation) are seen as crucial for an OECD type of country and high economic development. If such values and conditions would be necessary preconditions for establishing the rule of law, efforts to import rule of law in non-Western societies, or impose a 'Western' rule of law system, would be short-lived and fail after external actors leave. In this view, it might not be possible to start rule of law systems in non-Western authoritarian, religiously and ethnically divided countries with weak institutions, dominated by political patronage and clientelism. This view is not supported by evidence of rule of law systems in non-Western societies with different cultures, values and beliefs, such as Japan, South Korea, India, Singapore, Taiwan, and South Africa, which have to varying degrees relatively independent judiciaries. The same may hold true for a number of Islamic societies, as there are reformist Muslim countries with relatively impartial judiciaries, such as Kuwait, Tunisia, Turkey, Indonesia, and Jordan. The aspiration of almost all governments to improve human rights standards and their subscribing to the international treaties on human rights indicate that the wide gap between words and deeds is not first of all a gap of principle but foremost of implementation. We return to this in section 5.13.

5.2 RULE-OF-LAW ASSISTANCE AND DEVELOPMENT COOPERATION

Traditional development assistance, which has been provided to poor countries since the 1960's, was originally aimed at economic growth and poverty reduction. This economic assistance has remained partially unsuccessful, especially in parts of Africa and the Middle East where many recipient countries have seen not just a lack of economic improvement but also a decline in the quality of human life of the urban and rural masses, for various internal and external reasons. Traditionally, many development assistance donors steered clear of questions of poor or bad government in recipient countries. Where aid was given on the condition that the recipient government should make economic policy improvements, this conditionality was sometimes ineffective or even counterproductive. Often recipient governments found easy ways to circumvent conditions after paying lip service to the international advice and demands.
Only in the last fifteen years have donor countries and institutions introduced legal reform and assistance programmes to their development cooperation. Many recipient countries have remained less than enthusiastic about such contributions to their legal sector.

The political will inside a country to reform and develop the rule of law can be encouraged, but it cannot be imposed from outside. If there is a clear will in a country to improve the rule of law, but a lack of resources and expertise slows down progress, the country will be a grateful object of assistance. In such a case, the choices a donor has to make are relatively easy.

If the bottleneck is not resource scarcity but the lack of will to reform the legal and judicial sector, donors have little leverage. They will meet open resistance from the leadership, or softer, diplomatic and bureaucratic tactics against improvements. In such cases, it may be better to focus on persons and segments of institutions which appear receptive to assistance for professionalisation, as well as non-governmental programmes for rights awareness and education, training of defence lawyers, setting up legal-aid shops in local communities, encouraging a free press, advising civil society, encouraging women's and human rights organisations, and so on. Encouraging the rule of law and reduction of arbitrary decisions and corruption may also benefit from projects to improve the professionalism of the state's administrative organs, but this can also be counterproductive. A more professional civil service which serves not the population but the needs of a criminal regime, can be worse for the people than an ineffective civil service.

In countries that are in ruins due to (civil) war or dictatorship, the question is, of course, what measures can encourage (new) rulers to accept limits to their rule? They are inclined to strengthen, not weaken, their grip. If the ruler needs tax income from wealthy citizens who demand a say in the ruler's policies, he will have to give in to some of their demands. Strange as it may sound, this is the way the preparation for a number of wars in Europe in the sixteenth and seventeenth century helped to bring monarchs under laws enacted by beginning parliaments. But this doesn't work in Africa, if the ruler gets his pay from a foreign diamond or oil company.

If there are neither strong civil society organisations nor an influential entrepreneurial class, who will force the ruler to behave? Can foreign aid donors achieve this? They can to some extent, but only if the ruling elite is really dependent on these donors and if they impose precise conditions with performance benchmarks on aid, if performance is monitored and if donors apply effective sanctions. If the ruling elite are not dependent and if various donors follow very different policies that undercut each other's efforts to encourage good government, sanctions and aid conditionality will not change the government much for the better. In such situations, it may still be possible to identify hopeful agents of future change in the government and encourage and strengthen these.

It is certainly in the interest of developed democracies that are rule-of-law states, to encourage the rule of law and democracy in states with serious shortcomings in maintaining the domestic rule of law. Juridical cooperation, development cooperation and general foreign policy of advanced countries can and should contribute to the growth of rule of law elsewhere.[2]

High-income rule-of-law states are, however, small in number. Most of the 192 UN members are not rule-of-law states. Aid donors of legal development aid have to set priorities. They cannot help all needy countries equally at the same time. Difficult choices have to be made as to whom to help, with which programs and to what level of achievement. This question, how to allocate limited aid means most effectively, will be discussed in chapter 6.

In countries that are not rule-of-law states, the legal and judicial system, security services, armed services, police and both the local and the highest courts do not serve justice in the abstract. They serve the dominant order and the interests of the power elite. The power elite define what the national interest is, and that is usually not the same as the interest of the population; it may at times be the opposite. The security and armed services purport to defend the country against threats to national security from foreign aggressors or domestic rebels, but in reality these military, police and intelligence organisations mainly serve regime security, that is, the security of the regime against threats that might arise from the population itself. This explains the often high defence and police costs in poor countries, even in those against which external aggression seems very unlikely.

International assistance for legal sector reform started to grow only in the 1990s. The urgency of legal reform in communist countries that had changed overnight to liberal politics highlighted the pressing need to develop effective mechanisms for reform. Abolishing communist regimes did not instantly create functioning social market economies, but in many cases led instead to a plundering form of privatisation, to abuse of unregulated market power, and to a surge in crime. A new awareness arose – or rather, an old truth was rediscovered – about the importance of good governance, strong institutions and clear, well-administered laws. This awareness increased further after the poor results became clear of military interventions for humanitarian reasons in states that had collapsed due to war or other forms of political violence.

The United Nations Development Programme (UNDP) was among the first to call 'Justice and Security Sector Reform' a condition for human development, and rightly so. This admission, that it is not economic policy that alone pushes development forward, was a big step forward in UN thinking, away from the focus of UN organisations and international financial institutions on economic growth. The UN and the Bretton Woods institutions had steered a wide berth around key political questions such as gross suppression of human rights or aggression towards neighbouring countries.

Nevertheless, reform of the legal and justice system proved to be no miracle cure transforming an appalling lawless state into a neat, rich, rule-of-law country. Legal reform can only contribute to real respect for human rights after the security system has been reformed, which will happen only once the main political forces have agreed on power sharing and the building of a rule-of-law state.

International assistance for judicial reform or, more generally, legal sector reform, aims at improving the fairness and efficiency of a national legal system. The legal system is the constitution, laws, other regulations, customary law, international obligations, and all institutions and persons charged with creating and maintaining the law: the legislature, courts, public prosecutors, defenders, police and prison systems, paralegal institutions, alternative dispute resolution bodies, war crimes tribunals and ombudsmen. The legal sector also includes legal education, legal aid and advice and information. This system comprises public institutions and non-governmental organisations, and both officials and private individuals.

All rule-of-law assistance to reform has to start with the prevailing legal systems of the country concerned. Their legal system may consist of:
- Common law (generally seen as of British origin or type, predominant in the US and Commonwealth countries. For a list of Commonwealth countries, see the chart in chapter 6);
- civil law countries with continental European legal systems, also found in Latin America and individual developing countries that do not belong to the Commonwealth;
- religious law (Christian, Islamic, Jewish, etc.);
- socialist law from the communist period in Eastern Europe, China, Vietnam and Cuba;
- international law with its various components.

Often, elements of several legal systems apply at the same time in a country, in a rather unique mix. The mix is often different depending on the legal sub-sector; that is, public law or civil law.[3] Often, some legal elements and areas in a national legal system are modernised, while others are absent, old-fashioned or ill-developed.

5.3 ASPECTS OF LEGAL REFORM

The justice and legal system in need of reform in the framework of peacebuilding comprise both the police, local and higher courts, all penitentiary and other corrections institutions, the ministry of justice and its services, the legislative systems, and the legal education, training and research institutions.

A first question is, of course, which legal system prevails in the country at hand. The elements of law in need of reform are often grouped according to their application to a particular sector: trade law, property law, financial (institutions) law, environmental law, educational law, health sector law, etc. Commercial law often receives priority from the government and business due to interest in economic growth and foreign investment. Transition from communism to a market economy also leads to priority for commercial law. Assistance and advice from different donors can cause an illogical mix of legal systems, such as US-inspired commercial law next to other civil law derived from the Roman system, or elements of religious and customary local law.

Ideally, legal reform should start with constitutional reform, as this determines the state structure and forms the framework for the legal and judicial order. It improves the delineation of government power, settles power conflicts among groups and regions, improves the courts' mandates, creates or strengthens judicial independence and enshrines citizens' basic rights. But in practice, governments tend to focus on limited modernisations which do not undermine their power base. Most governments are more interested in commercial law reform, as they want to attract foreign and domestic investment and improve export earnings, rather than improving power-sharing and political reform.

The failing of a state and its collapse into violence and anarchy is usually due to a failing government in a wrongly designed state structure. In such a case both the capability and policies of the government (political leaders and/or the organs of the state) were not up to the challenges of good governance. The state was a creation by domestic, coercive force and international power configurations which did not really, or not at all, reflect the solidarity of the peoples involved. The causes of such ill-design of states are varied: in some cases the original establishment of the state (through military events, monarchic inheritance, rebellion, secession, international diplomacy or other origins), its frontiers and constitution (often made during decolonisation) did not fit the social, tribal, and economic fabric of society. In others, the state apparatus may have been captured by individuals who used it for private gain, tribal rule over other ethnic entities, or political leaders who tried to impose an oppressive ideology.

As far as state failure is due to original, structural flaws in the make-up of the state, failed states are really in need of careful restructuring in order to achieve effective, stable, good and possibly democratic governance, in accordance with internationally accepted norms and treaties. In several failed states, this restructuring may require federalisation and regional autonomy to reflect the variety of the populations in the state and their desire for self-government. The restructuring of an ill-designed state is usually a very painful, bloody process which may lead to civil war. There is also a risk that the outcome of the struggle is worse than the original situation. There are only a few situations of states which were redesigned or divided peacefully after elections and negotiation, like the split-up of Czechoslovakia. An encouraging example of the opposite, free reunification of a population divided by outside forces, is the unification of Germany in the early 1990's. The spit-up of the Union of Soviet Socialist Republics in the early 1990's is also a case in point which shows that redesigning is possible without prolonged civil war. These examples are positive exceptions to what is probably a more general rule in political history, that split-ups, secessions, the redesigning of main power relations, and achievement of autonomy or near-independent statehood within a (federal) state frequently risks violent clashes if not civil war. This seems to be the case particularly in regions whose state structures were imposed by foreign powers, like in the periods of colonisation and decolonisation by West European powers, and expansion and contraction of other foreign empires, like tsarist Russia and the USSR.

As constitutional redesign is a touchy, if not an explosive subject; it is often impossible for foreign aid donors to bring real improvements. Outside advisors generally have to work within the existing power system. Not being able to help correct the structural faults in the system, does not mean that all assistance is doomed to failure. Improvement of civil and penal law and procedural as well as administrative law may in due course lead to improvements in more sensitive, constitutional areas. Assistance in these less politicised subjects may not be recognized as a threat to those in power, at least not in the short run, but offer the power elite some economic and reputation advantages of modernisation.

When constitutional reform is not possible or not urgent, improvement of the courts system is usually needed urgently. This is discussed in section 5.6.

5.4 (RE) BUILDING POLICE AND PRISON SYSTEMS

We saw in the previous chapter, that rapid establishment of some basic law and order, if necessary as temporary martial law, and a speedy transition to civilian policing, as well as a fair beginning of the public prosecution and court system, is crucial to the success of the first phase of post-conflict reconstruction, when the population expects personal security. Once this beginning is made, the police system should start with thorough reforms.[4]

With the word police, we also refer to related institutions like the ministries of Justice, Police, or the Interior, i.e. whatever department is responsible for police. We also include different police services like federal, national, state, provincial, municipal and country-police, gendarmerie-type police services, border police and special police forces against drugs, as well as police intelligence services.

There is not one prototype for an ideal, new police organisation. The best system depends on the constitutional structure of the country, its history, culture, sociology and legal system. It may be wise to start reconstruction and reform on the basis of available domestic structures. This is not recommended, however, if the police is seen by the population as very brutal and suppressive and one of the causes of the war to begin with. Then, new names and faces, new structures and uniforms help to engender hope and trust.

Police reform tries to establish civilian, professional, accountable, non-partisan police under the law, respecting basic human rights. Police should be purged soon after the war, in order to gain trust of the population. International monitors, advisers and trainers are needed. A major step is employing many women and members of suppressed ethnic and religious groups in the new police. Merit criteria should govern hiring and promotion.

Inclusion of formerly opposing people in an entirely new police might be easier than making former enemy police organisations work together. In the Bosnian federation, integration became a façade, as Croats continued to report to Croat superiors, etc.

In the beginning after a cease-fire, and for a longer time if spoilers remain in positions of power, the police task of maintaining public order can only be carried out with military backing. Ideally, this should take place under international surveillance, such as UN observers and peacekeeping personnel.

The Rand Corporation made an analysis of many police operations in post-conflict countries and concluded in 2007 that, by an large, *at least* 10,000 international soldiers are needed per 10 million inhabitants in light peace operations with the consent of the parties to guarantee success in establishing post-war security, and about 1000 international police officers.[5] The domestic police should be built up to at least 20,000 per 10 million inhabitants within 5 years. Furthermore, international financial assistance should be at least $ 125 per inhabitant per year in the first two years to pay for peacekeeping and police forces, training domestic police, (re)building their infrastructure and providing equipment.

The assistance should not last less than 5 years, as rebuilding improved police and security services cannot be done instantly. (Re)building the justice system even takes much longer. Such requirements have been overlooked in the design of many peacebuilding operations in the 1990's and early twenty-first century.

Usually, combat operations are well-planned, while post-combat establishment of public order is neglected. Post conflict (re)establishment of internal security takes as much planning, preparation and intelligence operations as planning a military intervention.
There is often a very serious public order gap and police deployment delay after military interventions. The 'shock and awe' of successful US military operations in Iraq and Afghanistan were followed by paralysing deployment delays in police and justice reform measures.

The domestic security gap between a cease-fire and post war (re)construction of a stable state requires immediate application of international constabulary forces (well armed police trained to work in a hostile environment). Donor countries and international organisations would do well to set up arrangements that enable them to rapidly mobilise such police and justice assistance to countries in need. This requires prior selection and training of personnel, and making arrangements for fast dispatching from other (regular career) positions to send these people on foreign missions.

For success, police assistance programs also require detailed police intelligence information on the country concerned. It is sometimes overlooked that police operations need even more detailed intelligence than military operations. It is prudent to make arrangements for such intelligence gathering and analysis, prior to an intervention.

Joint exercises are also needed to train military, military police, constabulary forces, civilian police, justice reform advisors, and emergency aid specialist to think, communicate and act with greater mutual understanding of each other's professions, views and attitudes during peacebuilding operations.

Guatemala

Mayan civilization flourished between the fourth and eleventh century. Guatemala became a colony of Spain between 1523 and 1821, and gained independence in 1840. A mixture of civilian and military governments ruled during the 21st century. In 1954 the US supported local actors in their overthrow of President Jacobo Arbenz Guzmán. The decades that followed were marked by military coups and fraudulent elections. This triggered the rise of various left-wing revolutionary movements. The Guatemalan regime responded with a brutal counter-insurgency and worked with right-wing militias including the White Hand (Mano Blanca) and the Anticommunist Secret Army (ESA) to repress opposition. Gross income inequality, poverty, and political inequality continued to fuel the rebellion, and a 36-year war raged from 1960 until 1996, taking the lives of 100,000 people and causing 1 million refugees.

The violence reached its highest levels in the early 80s when General Efraín Rios Montt came to power. Although the Guatemalan National Revolutionary Unity (URNG) was the official target of counter-insurgency, thousands of civilians were also killed. Official reports show that government forces militias were responsible for over 93 percent of the violence between 1960 and 1996.

The UN mediated efforts between URNG and the government. The UN verified the Comprehensive Agreement on Human Rights of 1994 (MINUGUA). 250 Human rights monitors, legal

experts, indigenous specialists and police officers were employed. Following the Agreement on the Ceasefire of 1996, the UN extended its mission in January 1997 to include verification of cessation of hostilities, the separation and concentration of the forces, and disarmament and demobilization of URNG combatants.
In May 1997, 155 military observers completed this mission.

Although democratic elections have taken place, major politicians are accused of corruption. Governments suppress opposition. Since 2001, the number of assassinations, lynchings, kidnappings, theft, drug trafficking, and prison uprisings have all increased. Income inequality remains very high and 56 percent of the population lives below the poverty line. In part, this is caused by extreme land inequality. In 2001, only 1.5 percent of the population owned nearly two-thirds of the land.

In many failed and post-conflict states, police actions are not restricted to upholding the law, as police are rarely impartial in the political conflicts that require attention. As a result the police can acquire a reputation for brutality and excessive violence amongst the public. It is important to attach international monitors, advisors and trainers to police forces. In most post-conflict situations, there is a great lack of such international personnel. It is even scarcer than military peacekeeping forces. A new code of conduct for the (new) police will help, particularly if new laws are required while no legislature is yet in place. This code of conduct can be formulated by new police authorities with the assistance of international police monitors or advisors.

To check against human rights abuses committed by the police, priority in international oversight should be given to prevention of physical abuse, arbitrary detention and gross corruption. The UN High Commissioner for Human Rights has produced manuals that can be used for training and to guide monitors.[6]

Figure 5.1 Main factors improving basic security

Peace agreement
Power sharing agreement
Legitimate government
Guarantees to parties who lost the war
Functioning military services
International military peace forces
International observers
Emergency assistance (food, water, health, housing)
Basic services (energy, water, sanitation)
Public works absorbing unemployed ex-combatants
Effective police services
International constabulary forces
International police monitors, trainers, advisors
Care of refugees and IDP's, protection and resettlement; return of property

Police reform should not just be a part of general security sector reform, along with reform of the military and other security organisations.[7] The focus of police in post-conflict societies is often only on regime security, and not on the safety of individuals. During the war, the police have often been an instrument of oppression. The objective of police reform should be to create a force capable of upholding the law and help enforce basic human rights that can be recognised by the citizens as a force for internal peace rather than regime security. The police are the most visible manifestation of the rule of law in daily civilian life. In the UN's peace operation in El Salvador, for instance, the reformed police became a source of citizens' confidence in the state's ability to provide security, in part thanks to reform programmes supported by external donors.

For donors, the behaviour of the police is a good measure for assessing the government's compliance with human rights standards. Foreign monitors of the country's police inhibit violations and instill some confidence among the population. One might widen this observation and infer that international monitoring of police brutality and corruption would give a good indication of how countries develop into rule-of-law states, or revert to oppression. Such monitoring restrains abuse and contributes to peacebuilding. Advisory, training and monitoring missions of international police officers encourage domestic police to improve professional standards and to respect human rights.

Police are the most frequent interface between citizens and the state. A set of five studies of policing in East African countries showed that there is a pattern of illegitimate political interference and partiality, prompted by the government and by personal preferences of policemen.[8] Excessive use of force, brutality, torture, corruption of police officers, impunity of misdeeds because of secrecy and lack of accountability, are all hallmarks of oppressive systems.

Reform of the police and legal sector also requires penal reform. In many places, squalid, overcrowded prisons keep many people behind bars without fair trials. Most poor and middle-income countries do not meet basic standards. Unhygienic conditions and poor medical help breed diseases. Most prisoners are young urban males who leave prison in a much worse mental and physical condition than when they were first incarcerated. Suspects are often detained for long periods before their trials, together with convicted criminals. An inefficient and unjust penal law system, large backlogs in the courts and overcrowded, squalid prisons multiply the injustices committed by the organs of the state.

As prisons usually do not re-socialise detainees, but make them even less adapted to society, alternative sanctions other than prison sentences are needed. This will also serve to avoid overcrowding.

Monitoring, advice and training of prison guards and managers have to be provided by donor agencies. Standard minimum rules for the treatment of prisoners have been formulated by the UN.[9] Organisations like Penal Reform Inter-

El Salvador

El Salvador became independent in 1839. It has 7 million people. In the 21st century it went through a wide range of military dictatorships. The root causes of the civil war during 1980-1992 can be found in worsening social circumstances in the 1970s, which increased opposition against the governments of Colonel Molina and General Romero. They retained power by manipulating elections and brutally repressing opposition forces.

A group of military officers, supported by the US, overthrew the regime in 1979. José Napoleón Duarte of the Christian Democratic Party (PDC) headed a provisional right-wing government. Harsh suppression of opposition groups continued, including frequent killings by death squads. Infamous was the murder of a critic of the government, Archbishop Romero, in 1980. Following this, a major military resistance organization, FMLN, was formed. Civil war erupted between government forces and the FMLN, causing at least 75,000 deaths between 1980 and 1992.

The UN Secretary-General assisted in peace negotiations. The parties reached their first agreement in 1990 by deciding to ensure respect for human rights. The Security Council authorized an UN Observer Mission in El Salvador (UNOSAL) in 1991 to monitor this. The peace agreement of Chapultepec (1992) included a ceasefire, reform and reduction of the armed forces, establishment of a new civilian police, and reform of the judicial and electoral system. UNOSAL monitored and assisted in the implementation. The UN also observed the presidential and legislative elections in 1994. When the mandate was completed in 1995, a smaller civilian mission (MINUSAL) continued until 1997.

El Salvador could avoid renewed civil war since 1992. The ceasefire held and most reform plans were implemented. The United Nations played a central role. Of great importance was successful police reform. With the help of the international community, El Salvador seems to have succeeded in creating a relatively stable post-conflict state.[9]

national based in London can assist countries and donors with expert advice. The need of such oversight and advice was once more clearly demonstrated by the Abu Graib prison scandal in Iraq during US operations in 2004.

Prisoners of war are protected under the Geneva Conventions. International oversight of POW's by the Red Cross and human rights organisations (like Human Rights Watch and Amnesty International) is crucial. In the fight against terrorist networks, which are non-state actors, a new type of 'POW' has emerged that does not fit neatly into established international legal standards and, as a result, could end up being denied basic human rights. This makes oversight by human rights and humanitarian aid organisations all the more important.

Reform programs of the police, penitentiary institutions and the courts system should be integrated in the wider Judicial and Security Sector reform (JSSR).[10] After an armistice or peace, the population expects immediate peace and security. But instead, many people may experience an increase of insecurity. During the war, violence may have been very brutal and intense, but after war, new forms of violent insecurity arise. Post-war violence undermines reconstruction, state institutions, political settlement, foreign investment and economic progress. Personal insecurity seriously threatens refugees, women and children. The violence of the war is now supplanted by criminal social, economic, ethnic, religious, political and other violence. Only in case a post-war government rapidly imposes some reasonably just order which, under the circumstances, is considered acceptable by the population, with a monopoly of armed force for the state (if necessary with temporary military rule), can a post-conflict crime wave be curtailed or even avoided.

Crucial to an effective secure order after combat ceases, is also that the political settlement underlying the cease-fire offers realistic hope to the defeated parties that they will be able to participate in a new future of the country. Magnanimity towards defeated parties, but from a position of strength, is the key to peace. If former warring parties that have lost the war, now feel very insecure, they will act as spoilers of the peace and try to win back political power through violence or even terrorism. Such political violence now undermines (new) state institutions and the government. Sometimes this political struggle is transformed into an ethnic or religious struggle. Part of this post-conflict violence may also be vengeance killings.

Next to continued political violence, economic violence threatens peace and state building. Robbery, looting, kidnappings, trafficking in drugs, weapons and people, and also white collar crime, robbing state institutions (enterprises) of their capital, like in post-communist states, will seriously undermine public trust in new authorities and foreign peacebuilders. This economic violence is often mixed with political violence. In most cases studied by Call et al., homicides, kidnappings and robberies surged in the first 2-3 years after an armistice or peace agreement and then 'stabilized' at a high level for about two or three years before declining.

In addition, social violence tends to rise, partly as attempts to strengthen or protect group identity, when a minority feels endangered by the new 'order'. Another form of social violence is common crime and youth gang violence. Unemployed, young males, broken social networks and displacement foster this crime wave. Family violence, especially against women and children, also increases after war due to demobilised, home-coming soldiers, who are unemployed, frustrated, traumatized and inclined to anti-social behaviour. Of particular concern are brainwashed demobilized child soldiers.

The conclusion is: after war, tough police measures, with large-scale military back up, are needed to halt the probable crime rise. If reliable police is not available, the policing will have to be done by military ground forces. If there is no functioning government in place, temporary military rule will be needed. International organisations and aid donors have to take into account that law and order is an overwhelming top priority for the population and a condition for reconstruction.

5.5 WIDER SECURITY SECTOR REFORM

Reform of the old security sector (police, armed forces, intelligence) is needed to get effective maintenance of the law and basic security. Demobilizing warring parties, disarming them, and reintegrating soldiers and military into a functioning economy, or recruiting them for reformed police and defence forces, is a huge and urgent task. This DDR (demobilisation, disarmament and reintegration) has become a standard component of peace building. Demobilized soldiers may join irregular private armies or crime syndicates. A large part of the demobilized male labour supply should be absorbed by reformed police forces, legally regulated private security services, and the construction and transportation sectors.

The armed services, police, detention and intelligence services require a program of professionalism, purges (vetting), and pluriformity (to lessen dominance by certain ethnic or religious groups). Especially the police forces and the prison guards need basic human rights training, as we saw in section 5.4.

Reform of intelligence services restricts their activities, puts them under strict legal obligations and civilian/political/legal supervision, and makes them professional, politically neutral and not involved in repression. They have to obey the (new) constitution and human rights standards.

In small countries, and when there is relatively large donor assistance, it may be feasible to create *new* armed services. In larger countries, and in case of little donor support, it will be better to purge only the war criminals and reintegrate the military by using as much as possible existing personnel. In all cases, the forces should be made accountable.
Security Sector Reform clarifies the mission and changes the size, organisation and civilian supervision of the services. Successful reform also requires a new budget. The laws applying to the services need to be modernized. All services

Rwanda The 9.9 million Rwandans are predominantly Hutu with a significant Tutsi and small Twa minority. Ethnic tensions date back to the colonial and pre-colonial era. Belgians had appointed Tutsis in large numbers to influential governmental positions. They resisted the Belgian policy shift towards enhancing the position of hitherto subordinated Hutus. Hutus responded to Tutsi opposition with massacres and forced mass departures.

The Hutu party PARMENTHU won the 1961 elections and Kayibanda was voted president. Rwanda gained independence from the Belgium-administered UN trusteeship in 1962. Kabiyana executed several thousand Tutsis and educated Hutus during his rule. In 1972, Kayibanda initiated an exodus of Tutsis in response to Burundi's president Micombero's Hutu suppression.

In 1973, the Hutu Habyarimana overthrew Kabiyana in a military coup and established the Second Republic. The one-party state expulsed, detained and tortured opponents without trial. Uganda responded by forcing 600,000 refugees back into Rwanda. Rwandan forces withstood their return and exiles remained in Uganda. Rapidly deteriorating living conditions resulted in a call for political reform.

Reform negotiations commenced in 1990 with the Franco-African summit.

The Tutsi militia Rwanda Patriotic Front (RPF) meanwhile invaded the country. Hutus, united in *le réseau zero*, propagated civil violence against Tutsis and moderate Hutus. The 1993 Arusha Peace Accords created a formal ceasefire and required a transitional government.

Inability to establish a government of national unity, and the shooting of Habyarimana's airplane unleashed the gruesome '100 days' of Rwandan genocide. Ten percent of the population, perhaps up to a million Tutsis and moderate Hutus, were slaughtered by army forces and civilians. The small UN Assistance Mission for Rwanda was unable to keep the peace. Under Kagame's leadership, the RPF took over Rwanda and 2 million Hutus fled the country. He turned the country into a one-party state and holds the presidency to date. Kagame's fight against Hutu militants led him to take a leading part in the wars in Congo. Rwandan troops retreated after the signing of a peace agreement in 2002.

Peace negotiations resulted in agreements emphasising inclusiveness and representation. Justice and reconciliation is supported by the International Criminal Tribunal for Rwanda, traditional Gacaca 'courts', and the National Unity and Reconciliation commission.

Peace and stability remain precarious. The inclusion of Hutus is limited under Kagame's rule. The Institute for Justice and Reconciliation identifies several future challenges: a lingering genocidal ideology, better reconstruction of institutions, public security, and scarce resources. Rwanda experiences high population pressure. The genocide demonstrated that UN interventions are ineffective when improperly funded and early warnings by experts on the ground are not taken seriously.

have to come under legitimate political superiors. Incorporating and merging former enemies, downsizing the forces, purging the worst elements, and training the remainder to behave more professionally takes much time and large resources. In some small and externally safe states, it has even been possible to entirely abolish military forces: Costa Rica, Panama and Haiti.

When a national army was able to entirely defeat opposing forces, military reform is likely to be limited, as the forces start with a strong position in the new era. Armies of rebel forces that have been victorious are likely to impose their structure and political vision on the new emerging state. When a war is ended by intervention by foreign peacekeeping forces, it is difficult to merge the standing opposing forces into new services, as neither side was victorious. Both may silently wait for the international peace forces to leave and keep their weapons and adherents, even informally and secretly, to wait for a new chance to change the map of the peace agreement, or start the war all over again.

When security, police and judiciary leaders representing the old system are very recalcitrant, political leaders often choose to just reshuffle bureaucracies and adopt new rules without practical consequences for abusive and corrupt personnel. International training courses for the old, wrong persons have little effect in such cases.

5.6 COURT REFORM

Court reform enhances the integrity, independence, impartiality, responsiveness and efficiency of the courts, improves the professionalism of judges and clerks through training, reduces bureaucracy, simplifies procedures, improves libraries, information systems and court administrations, the budget process, buildings, equipment, and so on. A wider but related notion is improvement of judicial administration, which also includes public prosecutors, defence lawyers, legal aid and pro-bono legal assistance for the poor. Court reform can also be seen as a threat to the power elite, particularly if the elite have to fear independent verdicts against corruption and oppression. In such a situation, assistance to improving procedural law or other smaller steps may sow some seeds for future progress.

The independence and professionalism of legal officers, especially judges, is increased not only by training, but particularly by financial autonomy; better procedures for selection and appointment; strict rules on fixed terms, retirement ages or 'life' tenure; discipline and impeachment rules and all other measures to shield them from the pressure of corruption, politics, media and momentary public emotions.

Improvement of the legal profession is also achieved through professional training and the strengthening of law societies, bar associations and information systems. Particularly important are human rights courses and training on gender issues (especially the rights of women).

Access to the law is improved by lowering the often very high mental, social, political and financial barriers for the population. It is usually necessary to raise the public's awareness of individual rights, particularly after long periods of oppression. Alternative dispute resolution procedures, ombudsmen and simple local courts with easy access are important to raise confidence in the legal sector. Training defence lawyers, encouraging basic, low-cost legal aid institutions ('law shops') and training paralegals can be a meaningful beginning of legal reform. It increases the demand from the population for better administration of justice, and exerts a reformist pressure on ineffective, authoritarian systems.[11]

Fair trial requires independent professional courts, a mechanism to clearly advise the defendant on the charges against him and the right to legal defence and representation (if necessary, pro bono). The defendant's other rights, such as an interpreter, appeal to a higher court at least in penal cases, and public trial (with certain exceptions), should also be upheld.[12]

Focussing only on the formal legal system to the exclusion of customary law and forms of dispute settlement embedded in the culture of the population decreases the likelihood of success. Traditional forms of conflict resolution by village elders, lay judges and arbiters should not be disregarded as not meeting international standards. Due to the poverty and culture of a country, it may still take decades of development before there is professional justice comparable to OECD standards.

The purpose of assisting other countries with building a legal order should, of course, not be to 'impose' such OECD government standards, but to assist the population in achieving its own aspirations of (legal) well-being (insofar as these desires are not inconsistent with international law and human rights). The legal system should not be imposed from the outside, but should aim to reflect the consensus of the population on their most urgent needs: their most basic rights to life and freedom of expression.

In most poor countries or countries in transition from authoritarianism to modernity, not only the coercive forces but also the judiciary have been guilty of appalling human rights violations. International and national civilian oversight encourages improvements and reform. Human rights ombudspersons will help. Police oversight offices are needed. Just setting up separate human rights advocacy institutions is not enough, as they may get little grip on corrupt organisations. Very important is independent journalism with help of foreign media and aid foundations, as the media stimulate investigations into police misconduct and judicial corruption.

Gender equality and reduction of abusive practices have to be tackled via various avenues. Not only politics and old laws prove difficult to change, but culture and religion are especially stubborn. International pressure, advocacy, and domestic women groups will help to change practices gradually. Muslim countries are most resistant to employing women as police and judicial officers. Female foreign legal experts who act respectfully can help to change attitudes.

Most court systems are severely understaffed and many legal officers are poorly educated, prone to corruption, and not impartial in the political and ethnic/ religious disputes. It takes a long time to reform and retrain sitting judges. It may be hard to discharge hopeless cases due to judiciary independence. Legal independence can be a road block against legal impartiality. In that case, international judges are needed in appellate courts to stop serious violations of human rights by lower courts. In Kosovo it was even necessary to allow the UN head of mission to revoke judicial decisions which discriminated the Serb minority. The ideal of separation of powers can work in practice *against* human rights and peace, when crucial offices are abused. It is vital to prevent such clashes between principles in practice by putting the judiciary system as soon as possible under new oversight committees composed of reformist domestic functionaries and international judges. Very helpful for reform is training new *female* judges, as many abuses relate to suppression of women and gender inequality.

Police, judicial and prison reforms are a 'tripod'. If one leg remains very weak, the system will not stand up. In his study, Call shows that most cases of post-conflict judicial reform have been very inadequate, and even harder to do than police reform. UNDP concluded in 2002 that justice reform was a blatantly missed opportunity in Bosnia.[13] "Excessive emphasis on constitutions, laws, and formal authority is misplaced. Legal reforms are insufficient without institutions that can guarantee rights, protect citizens, and enforce laws"[14] Written guarantees often do little to protect endangered groups in practice. Legal reforms can be hampered by legal personnel trained in the old system, clinging to their own political and ethnic or religious views, privileges and old habits.

Reforming police, other security organisations, and legal personnel is not just a matter of pushing recruits through courses or inviting judges to a donor country to see how things should be done Western style. Recruit training and retraining of vetted personnel will not have lasting results if there is no continued mentoring, supervision, and further training, at multiple levels, during several years. Not just law books and knowledge, but skills, attitudes, mindsets and values have to be improved.

5.7 MAJOR CRIMINALS AND WAR CRIMES

After the war, the new authorities are likely to be challenged by political and military war criminals, as well as various other adversaries which do not accept the cease-fire, such as terrorists. There is also likely to be very virulent crime that is not political in motivation. The 'criminal sector' has to be fought fiercely to bring back normality, stability and order. Emergency powers are needed to stamp it out. 'Transitional justice' and rehabilitation of the legal order can only develop well after criminal profiteers of chaos under control.

In civil wars, state order is not only attacked by warring parties for political reasons. Non-political criminals use the chaos of war to loot, murder and rape, and to grab high positions in the government or in state-run companies. In a number of wars, political leaders have let criminal gangs free to murder, loot and rape, as the leaders gambled that such destruction would serve their own purposes. These criminal gangs are not so much motivated by nationalism, ideology or religion, but by the opportunities that the chaos of war and the destruction of the state (or tribal) order offer for criminal enrichment. Violent hooligans use war to widen their repertoire of crimes, often posing as 'militia'. An example is the Arkan Tigers in the war in the former Yugoslavia. They portrayed themselves as a nationalist militia but avoided military combat against professional soldiers. Their prime purpose was to loot, rape and kill weak civilians. Such groups are also found in African wars and in the Middle East. So-called nationalism is then replaced by extremist tribalism or violent religious fundamentalism to fool observers into believing these 'fighters' have some sort of ideology to motivate them. The mandate of professional military peace enforcers should include protecting the population from such thugs and hunt them down without undue respect for their 'political' or 'religious' ideology. Otherwise, they undercut the entire peacebuilding program.

Most, but not all, of such criminals *during* war were already criminals *before* the war. During the war they grabbed ample opportunities for violent crime.

But also regular, disciplined bureaucrats and military officers can turn into the most serious war criminals, some of them 'white collar' or 'clean hands' mass murderers who 'only' gave implicit instructions, or allowed 'proxy killers' to run rampant, or followed and delegated orders from above.

It is particularly bitter to the population if war criminals are given amnesty as part of a cease-fire agreement or peace deal. This is one of the harshest examples of the trade-off between peace and justice. This is sometimes hard to avoid. Distant theoreticians believe that peace and justice are basically the same. Making such compromises is one of the hardest tasks of the diplomatic mediators, political leaders and peacemakers, which often get them into trouble afterwards, once the situation has stabilised.

In this respect it is worth noting that Call et al. did not find a clear relation between, on the one hand, the degree to which war crimes and past human rights abuses were dealt with by the courts after an armistice, and on the other, the confidence of the population in the post war legal/judiciary system.[15]

In some cases, amnesty as part of a peace agreement did not block legal and judicial reform. In others, lack of justice regarding past crimes undermined confidence in the future, as could be expected. The eight cases analyzed by Call failed to establish a clear connection between justice for past crimes and the quality of the justice reform. This needs to be further investigated in other case studies.

5.8 TERRORISTS

Terrorism can seriously disturb peacebuilding and rule-of-law assistance, particularly in the early phase, when the constitution, main institutions and confidence of the population in a new future are still very vulnerable. Terrorism is usually the small-scale use of indiscriminate violence against mostly civilian targets, with the purpose of getting wide media attention to spread fear everywhere and create chaos. The circle of fear is many times larger than the actual number of victims. Terrorism counts on world-wide media exposure to spread the fear and demoralise domestic and foreign audiences.

The ideological motivation of terrorism varies from secular ethnicism and nationalism to religious and ideological extremism. Terrorism can also thrive without much ideological or religious motivation[16] for non-political, non-religious, non-ethnic but economic gains that are expected by those who threaten disaster to civilians if the authorities or other governments do not give in to financial demands.

Even though terrorism is clearly recognised by the public and media, it is sometimes argued that it is difficult to define. It is said that one man's terrorist is another man's freedom fighter. This is a common error of thought. Terrorism was clearly defined by the UN Security Council in 2004:
(Terrorism consists of)

> "criminal acts (...) committed with the intent to cause death or serious bodily injury, or taking of hostages, with the purpose to provoke a state of terror in the general public or in a group of persons (...) intimidate a population or compel a government or an international organisation to do or to abstain from doing any act, which constitute offences within the scope of and as defined in the international conventions and protocols relating to terrorism ..."[17]

Terrorism and transnational crime go hand in hand, as many terrorist networks also engage in other criminal activities to finance their operations.

For the new interim authorities of a post-conflict country, fighting terrorism is a major task that can easily compromise reconstruction. A comparison with a medical approach to serious disease may clarify the point: heavy radiation treatment or chemotherapy is used against metastasised aberrant cells in an organism that is already extremely weak from other diseases. If the therapy is too strong and broad, it damages healthy tissue and changes its DNA in such a manner that different cancers spread even more rapidly. The cure lies in precision, but the quandary is how to pinpoint and remove the terrorist cells. As this survey is not a study in counterterrorism, we have to leave this important question[18] and move on to other subjects.

5.9 PRIVATE SECURITY FIRMS

States, private companies and other organisations often hire non-state forces, i.e., private security services, private soldiers, early retired military and soldiers from other states who seek gainful employment on their own. This 'outsourcing' or privatisation of police and military tasks is age-old. A newer form is represented by private security companies, which are serving across the globe. Their tasks range from logistic support, training personnel, running prisons, removing mines, protection of officials, even advising combatant officers during hostilities, to actively fighting terrorists and participating in war operations in Africa and the Persian Gulf area on behalf of governments or oil and mining companies. In the US-led operations in Iraq, private security organisations were given a major role, engaging tens of thousands of personnel from a wide range of countries. These companies act as contractors and subcontractors of governments, to help solve the lack of government personnel.

The questions are: under whose legal powers do private security companies work, and what is their status under national and international law? Who is accountable for possible crimes? Who is responsible when personnel are taken prisoner, wounded or killed? The legal status can be clear if the UN, other official organisations or governments enter into legal contracts (for instance, for de-mining of roads, or guarding officials and offices). Then, official responsibility is taken, and rules of engagement for legitimate use of arms are determined.

5.10 CORRUPTION

A prevalent threat against the rule of law, undermining many states, is corruption. Resources are channelled away from use for public well-being into private pockets. It seriously distorts decisions which government officials have to make, as well as the daily actions of police, the verdicts pronounced by courts, the maintenance of rules in prisons, etc. Corruption is a transnational, global phenomenon. Illicit acquisition of personal wealth and other advantages damages democratic institutions, socio-economic progress, the rule of law, and human rights. Corruption is often seen as an endemic problem in recipient countries. It is, of course, also a serious weakness among many donor institutions. Sub-contracting many peacebuilding activities to private bodies or governmental units without strict oversight causes an unknown percentage of available peacebuilding funds to be lost.

Prevention and eradication of corruption is a responsibility of all states, non-governmental institutions, private companies and citizens. The UN convention against corruption of 2003 was signed by 140 states and entered info force in 2005, after ratification by at least 30.
The treaty introduces codes of conduct for civil servants, rules for public spending, auditing of the public and private sector, measures against money laundering and rules for the finances of political parties.

Sri Lanka became independent from the British in 1948. Its 21 million inhabitants are 75 percent Sinhalese Buddhist in the South and Centre, 12 percent Tamil Hindu's mostly in the North and East, and 7 percent Muslim. The country has reached a high literacy. Yet poverty is widespread and economic inequality is high. It is ravaged by an ethnic conflict since 1983 which caused more than 70,000 deaths and at least 200,000 displaced.

Democratic elections after independence resulted in a Sinhalese majority government which ignored the demands of Tamil parties for language rights and autonomy. Government policies to reduce access for Tamils to universities and government jobs and colonisation of the East with Sinhalese furthered Tamil radicalism, striving for an independent Eelam homeland. The Liberation Tigers of Tamil Eelam (LTTE) became the main movement. In 1987, an Indian Peace Keeping Force was brought into the North East. The Sinhalese saw India, with its large Tamil population in the South, as a threat and forced India to depart, leaving the LTTE in control, which created a 'de facto' state in the North. Violent attacks on Sinhalese forces, killing hundreds of policemen and using suicide bombers to target political leaders, branded all Tamil resistance as terrorism. The Sri Lankan government also committed serious abuse with extra-judicial killings and disappearances of many Tamils.

A 2002 ceasefire between the LTTE and government, facilitated by Norway, saw some relative peace during four years, but was broken. A Sri Lankan Monitoring Mission, of mainly Scandinavians, records violations. Subsequent peace talks failed as the demands by the LTTE for an Eelam would require a constitutional change that the Sinhalese nationalists in parliament refuse to approve. Excluding key Sinhalese political leaders weakens the peace process as there are many internal divisions among the Tamil and Sinhalese groups. The LTTE withdrew from the peace process in 2003. Tamil forces split in 2004 between Tamils in the North and the East. The peace process also caused a crisis in the government.

A tsunami hit Sri Lanka in 2004, killing about 35,000 people. Hope that this disaster would help to build peace faded as the government was blamed for distributing more aid to the Sinhalese than to the Tamils.

The 2005 presidential elections were won by Sinhalese nationalists but were boycotted by the LTTE. Most Tamils may be satisfied with autonomy to give peace and stability. The current Sinhalese government may be aiming for a military victory on the LTTE rather than a political solution. The LTTE may not give in on its demands for an independent Eelam. The international community seems frustrated with the return to violence. Economic incentives used by donors in the recent peace process remained without the desired effect.

The treaty is a big step forwards as it brings corrupt actions under international penal law and regulates recovery from other countries and restitution of assets which have been acquired by corruption. It works, of course, only to the extent various states and their legal systems will apply the treaty vigorously in practice.

5.11 INTERNATIONAL ORGANISATIONS

The codes of conduct, manuals and policies for legal sector reform mentioned above show how large the involvement is of various international organisations in promotion of the rule of law. The UN Secretariat and its related institutions, however, lack adequate numbers of personnel and external experts to carry out many necessary reforms. Judges, prosecutors, police experts, defence lawyers, prison experts, constitutional lawyers, civil and criminal law advisors and managers with international experience to organise these activities are in short supply. They have to be recruited for their knowledge of different legal systems, cultures, languages, attitudes towards other populations and social skills. (In the state-building operation in Iraq, the US contracted many inexperienced young professionals who followed US standards without understanding the country they were working in.)

Experienced international experts are often needed at short notice but have to be sent on rather long missions. It is difficult to meet all these criteria at once. Rapidly deployable legal reform experts should ideally be made available by legal and judicial institutions and academic and research institutes for various brief and, if need be, reiterating missions abroad. Their missions can be organized by national and international legal reform organisations. They can also employ suitable persons who have just entered (early) retirement, even though such experts may lose effectiveness after a few years.

The UN Secretary-General made some general proposals in 2004 to the Security Council to strengthen the role of the UN in peacebuilding and legal reform.[19] Finland, Germany and Jordan tried to specify these proposals further, noting that the UN Secretariat's work in this area was fragmented over eleven divisions and agencies. The three countries aimed to concentrate capacity in one unit managed by an Under-Secretary-General. The UN Summit of 2005 established a Peacebuilding Commission to strengthen the efforts of the UN, major international organisations, and the policies of many member states contributing to peacebuilding (See section 2.4).

The main source of finance for development aid used for peacebuilding is, however, not the UN Secretariat, but the European Union and its members. Chapter 7 deals with EU policies and programmes for these purposes. A small but rising portion is devoted to improving respect for human rights and reforming domestic legal systems in third countries. The EU has the means and policies to grow into the main donor of legal reform aid.

Since the second half of the 1990's, several other international organisations have added peacebuilding to their programmes. The UN Development Programme, the World Bank Group, and other important sources of development finance have widened their lending policies to finance institutional development, which may reduce the risks that countries fall back into violent conflict. Some of these peacebuilding programmes also finance legal reform projects.

The European Commission published in 2003 its *Handbook on Promoting Good Governance*,[20] with tools to design rule of law assistance for specific cases. Many NGOs are also active in this area. The Vera Institute designed the Global Guide to Performance Indicators across the Justice Sector, which helps to measure the state of affairs in various countries.[21]

The International Centre for Transitional Justice[22] in New York and Cape Town can help countries where massive human rights abuses have taken place. It gives training courses and publishes advice for various post-conflict situations.
It assists countries to account for past atrocities and prosecute perpetrators by documenting massive human rights abuses, establishing truth commissions and advising on reform of corrupted institutions. This centre also facilitates reconciliation. It is financed by official national and international as well as private donor institutions. The Centre's activities and budget are still very small in comparison to the needs.

The UN and the International Association of Prosecutors have produced handbooks intended to guide the reconstruction of a public prosecution service after hostilities have ended.[23]
An international Code of Conduct for Law Enforcement officers was already set by the UN in 1979.[24] The Basic Principles on the Independence of the Judiciary and Human Rights in the Administration of Justice were formulated in 1985.[25] In 1984, the Convention against Torture and other Cruel, Inhuman and Degrading Treatment or Punishment was adopted.[26]

5.12 THE CHANCE OF SUCCESS OF LEGAL REFORM

The ultimate success of legal reform depends on the answers to several questions:
- Is legal reform encouraged by the government?
- Is it demanded and driven by leading persons within the legal system?
- To what extent does the reform reflect the wishes, norms and values of the population?
- Do the reforms aim to gradually approach internationally accepted standards of justice?
- Are international donors willing to continue adequate support in the long run?

The pattern of answers differs of course by country.

Legal sector reform can be an analysed in terms of supply and demand as discussed in section 3.4: Who comprises the demand side – the leaders, institutions and population of the country under reform? Or is reform being pushed (demanded) from the outside by influential donors who are also the suppliers? If domestic demand is low but foreign supply is high, legal reform is given little value by the country concerned and does not take root. In Latin America, there is considerable domestic demand for legal reform. In Africa, legal reform is urged mainly by international donors. In many Asian countries which emphasize economic growth, domestic demand is strongest for modernisation of commercial law, but less so for other areas.

Fragmented, individual and short-term activities of donors lead to a lot of waste and little lasting return on aid activities. It is important to arrange meetings of the recipient institutions with all relevant bilateral donors, international organisations and NGO's. Such coordination meetings should outline priorities, set the agenda and divide the tasks among those present. The meetings should be chaired by the UN, the EU, a regional organisation like the African Union, the Organization of American States or the Association of South East Asian Nations (ASEAN), or an important NGO, like a professional international legal organisation. Donor coordination is often best designed in a practical manner by the countries most involved in the particular case. An example is the joint effort of Danish, German and Dutch embassies in Uganda, which rotated the chairing of such legal and judicial reform assistance for several years in the early 21st century in agreement with the Ugandan Justice, Law and Order Secretariat.

A well-functioning legal system might be depicted as a series of interconnected barrels with liquids streaming from one to the other. The capacity of the system is determined by the holes in the various barrels and the leaks in the pipes. Clever reform starts with an analysis of the entire system and fixes the lowest cracks first. Frequently, legal reform projects try with little effect to remove a very visible bottleneck, but the system leaks badly elsewhere. Improving police investigative capacity to the point where a very weak public prosecutor's office is overburdened with cases makes little sense. Enacting magnificent modern laws while the judges are corrupt will not greatly improve the administration of justice. Effective reform starts with a precise diagnosis of the most urgent leaks and bottlenecks.

Success or failure in establishing secure order and rule of law after violent conflict can be estimated by measuring some indicators.[27] The success of the military tasks in securing order can be indicated by periodical reports on insurgency casualties, domestic and foreign troop casualties, political violence incidents, and the perception by the public of national interior security. Success of police tasks is indicated by violent crime rates and estimates of trafficking in drugs, people, weapons, and burglaries, as well as police casualties, and reporting by international police monitors. Crucial is the perception by the public of a decrease of street violence.

Success of justice reforms is measurable in terms of increasing access to legal advice and to local courts, larger numbers of verdicts, shorter pre-trial detention, shorter waiting periods, larger numbers of prosecutors, judges and court clerks, less corruption, and various improvements in the penal and corrective institutions.

As we noted at the beginning of this chapter, there is an optimal time frame or 'window of opportunity' of several weeks to months to get a country on track. The population is hopeful. Defeated war leaders and black marketeers are in hiding or on the run. Spoilers of the peace may need some time to lick their wounds and regroup before they can disturb peacebuilding. If the forces of peacebuilding are slow to arrive, this 'golden hour' to get the country on track may be lost. Later on, it will be difficult to get the cooperation of all parties for a better re-start of the country's future.

5.13 HUMAN RIGHTS AND STATE BUILDING

The ultimate purpose of building up rule of law is respect for human rights. The universality of human rights has been reconfirmed many times by the UN member states. Five human rights conventions have been signed by most of the 192 UN members since the world organisation was formed in 1945.

The UN's Universal Declaration of Human Rights of 1948 was not binding, but declared human rights to be universal indeed. The later International Covenants on Economic, Social and Cultural Rights of 1966, and the Covenant on Civil and Political Rights of the same year, are based on the same conviction, which is elaborated in these treaties. Universality was reconfirmed at world-wide UN conferences in Tehran (1968) and Vienna (1993). In 2005, the UN members reaffirmed:

> "that all human rights are universal, indivisible, interrelated, interdependent and mutually reinforcing (...) While the significance of national and regional particularities and various historical, cultural and religious backgrounds must be borne in mind, all states, regardless of their political, economic and cultural systems, have the duty to promote and protect all human rights and fundamental freedoms."[28]

So much is clear. But the institutions to enforce human rights on a global level are a faint reflection of these ideals.

In 2005, the UN abolished its Human Rights Commission because its work was deemed ineffective. Membership of countries which were frequent abusers of human rights made the Commission a political battleground where many members tried to soften reports critical of their own actions.

The new UN Human Rights Council, set up to replace and improve on the Commission in 2006, is composed of 47 member states. Its work began in late

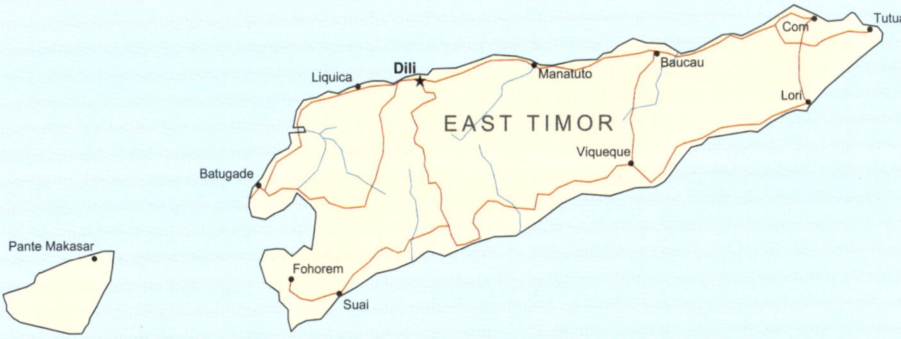

East Timor Located in Southeast Asia, this half-island was a colony of Portugal. In 1975, it was invaded by the Indonesian army and incorporated as a province. Gross human rights violations took place. The number of deaths is estimated between 100,000 and 250,000. The United Nations condemned the occupation by Indonesia as illegal, but took no action to free the country.

In a referendum held in 1999, an overwhelming majority of East Timor voted for independence. The Indonesian army and militias did not accept this and launched a violent campaign, causing thousands of deaths, displacements of more than three quarters of the population and destruction of the infrastructure.

The UN Mission in East Timor (UNAMET), established to oversee the referendum, lacked the mandate to stop this. An international military force led by Australia (INTERFET) was authorized by the UN Security Council in September 1999 to provide security to the population. Following this intervention, the UN started a peacebuilding mission to encourage institutions for a viable state. The United Nations Transitional Administration in East Timor (UNTAET) was empowered to exercise all legislative and executive authority between 1999 and 2002.

East Timor became an independent state. The UN did not depart but continued to provide assistance to core administrative structures, and sent extra civilian advisers, police advisers and human rights officers to East Timor.

UNTAET was seen as one of the most far-reaching peacebuilding missions in the history of the United Nations. Its mandate included establishment of law and order; setting up an effective administration; assisting in the development of civil and social services; coordination and delivery of humanitarian aid; rehabilitation and development assistance; supporting capacity-building for self-government; and encouraging conditions for sustainable development. This mission ended in 2002.

East Timor was widely regarded as a very successful peacebuilding operation. International assistance was large compared to other cases. The absence of a judiciary system hampered the UN in the beginning. After completion of the UN peacebuilding operation, violence erupted again in 2006 when disgruntled military revolted. After 37 casualties and after 155,000 people had been driven from their homes, a second intervention led by Australia ('Operation Astute') was necessary to stabilize the country and its democratically elected government. New elections held in 2007 led to a loss of the leading party Fretilin and gave a majority to an alliance of opposition parties. About 10 percent of the population was still living in refugee conditions.

2006. Members are elected by a majority vote from the UN General Assembly. Membership lasts 3 years. A country can serve two consecutive terms. Compared to the previous Human Rights Commission, this council will meet more frequently and will be able to discuss urgent questions sooner.

The General Assembly will take the track record of countries which are candidates for membership into account. Candidates have to state their own agenda for improvement. This will reduce the opportunities for notorious regimes that serve on the Council to block meaningful action against their own violations. Many such regimes served on the Human Rights Commission in the past, and some even chaired it during periods of gross violations in their own states, undermining the credibility of the UN.

All new members will now undergo a periodical review of their own human rights record during their period on the council. The UN General Assembly can remove a member with a 2/3 majority in case of serious, lasting violations of the human rights treaties. On the downside, however, it should be noted that a membership of 47 countries is too large to be very effective. There is no clear, new sanctions mechanism which the Council can use against serious perpetrators of mass suppression. Among the first members, there are again several notorious violators of the UN's basic human rights treaties. Still, the new Council offers a new chance to improve international respect for human rights. This respect is essential for the future of peacebuilding and legal reform.

As there is no world state with an effective global legal order that is enforced by a 'world police' and effective global courts, human rights for all the world's peoples remain an abstract ideal, far removed from the daily life of many of the world's billions of poor and oppressed people.

Human rights can be enforced by national courts in developed nation-states and by regional international systems that are part of strong international legal regimes. The best example is the European Court of Human Rights in Strasbourg. It has legal power over the member governments for as far as they have ratified the applicable treaty provisions and have surrendered these sovereign powers to this court.

It is often believed that human rights are a 'natural right', a condition that is owed to people by virtue of their mere existence. It is a sobering thought that the level of respect for human rights in most OECD member states is historically and geographically quite exceptional. Most of these rights are violated massively in other countries outside the OECD area by non-democratic or outright criminal governments.

Human rights do not descend from the heavens upon all human beings as 'natural law' or transcendental rights. Upholding human rights is the work of strong institutions that are part of effective states. Historically, most peoples have not enjoyed many rights. Citizens' rights have grown only slowly, along with the growth of the legal order within modern, highly developed states. It is perhaps arbitrary to point out historical developments that signify the birth of 'the' modern state, such as the often-mentioned peace of Westphalia (1648).

Supremacy of law to curtail arbitrariness of rulers was historically achieved by strong middle classes (feudal and patrician) that demanded stability, property rules and legal certainty, limited taxes and influence on the appointment of rulers. The influence of commercial patricians led to the end of feudalism in a number of countries and to a separation and balancing of different powers according to the 'trias politica'.

This was a West European development that has been followed in many but not all OECD countries. The question remains whether this state model and the 'universal' human rights that follow from it, can find universal application in very different societies.

States evolved historically under the influence of a multitude of physical and immaterial factors. The idea that without the state there is a war of every man against every man (Hobbes) is a thought that does not reflect reality, however. Even in very violent civil wars, the large majority of the population is not engaged in violence and tries to eke out a living while shielding itself as much as possible from the war that it did not want at all. It is the younger males, recruited by older leaders, who fight the war and do the killing.
Most humans in a 'stateless state' are not 'wolves unto themselves,' i.e. animals living in small packs, constantly attacking each other; they evolved as social beings in small societies that were usually rather peaceful within themselves, but defensive if not aggressive against others.

Social contract theory (Rousseau, Rawls) which also leads to a strong state with full human rights is a set of ideas which encourages rational thought about justice, but it is not a reflection of historical reality, as humans do not freely choose the society they live in (except, to a very limited extent, free migrants). Humans are after all simply born into a society, which teaches and imposes its existing rules, whether they are just or unjust from a philosophical point of view.

The rule of law is a highly developed legal order, and legal order is an aspect of social order, which is based on a stable and legitimate power order. The origins of social order can be found in the ways in which groups of animals live together and maintain their internal and external security in order to survive. The relatively simple state of nature, or natural state for humans with little education and civilisation, evolved slowly, originally probably from groups of a few dozens to hundreds of human beings living together.

In such small group societies, the institutions of social order were visible and concrete: the chief, the group of elders, clan heads, patriarchs or matriarchs. There were clear unwritten rules about human relations and personal and communal property rights. People can identify easily with this 'state', which is personified by important people, ceremonial events and chiefs who uphold the political, social and religious rules often at the same time.

Larger, more complex societies of several thousands of people developed from the small tribal ones, and perhaps about 10,000 years ago the first societies developed with more complex institutions to maintain the agricultural and complex irrigation systems, constructing large cities with urban civilisations, serving also the rulers' desires for cultural glory and political expansion.

The modern state with strong bureaucracies is by itself not an inherently good achievement. Examples abound of strong modern states with extensive legal systems, committing heinous ('barbarian') acts of aggression against other states and suppressing or murdering millions of their own inhabitants.

State-building, therefore, should not be an aim in itself, as organs of states can commit atrocious acts. Our interest is only in state institutions that can contribute to a high quality of human life, as measured by peace, security, justice and other aspects of human civilisation.

An OECD-quality legal system embracing the rule of law is a condition for achieving a high respect for all human rights, both the political freedoms and the rights to fulfilment of a high level of social, economic and cultural well-being. By itself, a modern legal system is not enough to turn this expected well-being into reality. Examples are those wealthy OECD countries that still have relatively widespread poverty, corruption and crime.

The modern OECD type of state is a complex set of institutions, rules and values that are required to enable human beings to live well according to modern human aspirations. The modern state is a highly technological, literally artificial (man-made), 'civilised', very differentiated and structured society so complex and abstract that the solidarity of inhabitants with the state and its institutions, and the acceptance of the democratic political class, is increasingly called into question by at least part of the non-voting electorate, as well as those who vote not according to their policy preferences but who follow a gut feeling of general opposition and malaise.

These reflections, at the end of this chapter on (re)constructing justice after war, are not meant to diminish the impetus of democracies, legal and human rights organisations to spread the rule of law, human rights, and democracy. There is the strong persuasion that human rights are inherently good, needing no further justification. Moreover, states in which human rights are highly respected are much less frequently at war with each other than non-democratic states. Fully grown human rights states appear not to experience civil war, although this cannot be excluded entirely as a possibility. As human rights states also enjoy a much higher standard of citizen well-being, as indicated by the human development index measured annually by UNDP, it is not difficult to make a plausible argument that the encouragement of human rights in other states is not just an idealistic task. It is a matter of enlightened self-interest, as other human rights states around one's own and the region will help to serve the national interest in well-being and security. The more human-rights states, the better.

Aceh This autonomous Indonesian province of over 4 million Islamic people is located on the northern tip of Sumatra. Aceh has rich natural resources. It struggled for independence already during the Dutch colonial rule. The Japanese invasion of Indonesia in 1942 ended Dutch occupation but continued the suppression. The Association of All Aceh Ulema'a (PUSA) opposed the Japanese occupation.

Indonesia gained independence in 1949. The regimes by Sukarno and Suharto amalgamated the provinces Aceh and North Sumatra. Ethnic differences between the predominantly Christian North Sumatran population and Islamic Achenese triggered rebellion. The Indonesian government initially defied the rebellion but finally granted Aceh autonomy with 'special territory' status.

The Indonesian government commenced mass exploitation of Aceh's national resources in the 70's. Presence of the military of Indonesia (TNI) reduced Aceh's autonomy and increased social strife. Deteriorated living conditions led Di Tiro to unite Acehnese with a desire for an Islamic state in the Aceh-Sumatra National Liberation Front (ASNLF). Support for independence movements grew vastly due to TNI repression, changed social circumstances and feelings of economic injustice.

In 1989, under the name Free Aceh Movement (GAM), the ASNLF intensified the struggle for independence. The government responded by declaring Aceh a Military Operation Zone (DOM). Nine years of violence and grave human rights violations followed. Circumstances improved temporarily when president Wahid came to power. In august 1998, the government lifted the DOM status. The Joint Understanding on a Humanitarian Pause officially ended the battles for three months in 2000.

A referendum on independence never came about. War criminals were not prosecuted and humanitarian aid did not reach Aceh.
The GAM intensified its terror campaign and the TNI remained present. Aceh officially gained more autonomy and adopted the Sharia law in 2003. Government repression meanwhile increased.

In 2004, the tsunami cost over 45,000 lives and left half a million homeless. The urgency of emergency aid, reconstruction and changes in leadership enabled peace talks between the government and GAM. A memorandum of understanding brought an end to 29 years of fighting.

Peace has a chance of becoming sustainable when Aceh is granted fair economic rights and autonomy. Indonesia's dependence on Aceh's natural resources complicates this. Additional challenges are human rights violations by Aceh's authorities.

NOTES

1 Jones, S.Q. et al., *Establishing Law and Order after Conflict* (Rand Corporation, Santa Monica, 2005) Hereafter referred to as Rand 2005. Charles T. Call, ed., *Constructing Justice and Security after War*. US Institute of Peace, Washington DC, 2007.

2 WRR, *The future of the National Constitutional State*, Report 63, The Hague, 2003.

3 Civil law concerns the private sector, relates to legal and natural persons and family, commercial law and many related areas. Public law consists of constitutional law, criminal law, administrative law, international public law and human rights law.

4 Call, Op Cit, chapters I and II, and Rand 2005, chapters 2, 6 and 7.

5 *Nation Building*, Rand 2007, pp. xxvi-xxvii. Note: these figures vary greatly according to the nature of the country and the heaviness of the needed UN intervention.

6 *Human Rights and Law Enforcement*. www.unhchr.org.

7 Holm and Eide, eds,: *Peacebuilding and Police Reform*, London: Frank Cass, 2000, pp. 41, 65 et passim.

8 Published by the Commonwealth Human Rights Initiative and the East Africa Law Society. soros@topica.email-publisher.com, June 13, 2006.

9 ECOSOC Resolutions 663 C and 2076.

10 Charles T. Call, ed., *Constructing Justice and Security after War*, US Institute of Peace, Washington DC, 2007, chapter 11.

11 Grass-roots demand for easy access to the judicial system is encouraged by the concept of micro-justice, comparable to micro-credits which encourage small entrepreneurship. www.microjustice.org.

12 *Amnesty International Fair Trials Handbook* (1998) www.amnesty.org.

13 Call, pp. 395-396.

14 Ibid., pp. 396-397.

15 Ibid., pp. 397-398.

16 Jessica Stern, *Terror in the Name of God*, Ecco/Harper Collins, 2003; *The Ultimate Terrorists*. Harvard University Press, 1999.

17 UNSC Resolution 1566 (2004), par. 3.

18 See e.g. F. Bolz, K.J. Dudonis and D.P. Schulz, *The Counterterrorism Handbook*, CRC Press/IPTS, Andover Hants (UK) 2005.

19 S/2004/616.

20 Europe Aid 2003.

21 www.vera.org/indicators.

22 www.ictj.org.

23 www.unhchr.ch.

24 UNGA, Res. 34/169.

25 UN Res. 40/32 and 40/146.

26 UN Res. 37/94.

27 Rand 2005, chapter 6.

28 UN Doc.A/Res./60/1, 24 Oct. 2005, par. 121.

6 RESOURCES AND COSTS

"Everyone has duties to the community in which alone the free and full development of his personality is possible."

Article 29, Universal Declaration of Human Rights 1948

In this chapter, we will look at the means which are potentially available for peacebuilding operations and rule-of-law assistance. What matters most is how to encourage the *domestic capabilities* for peacebuilding and the rule of law in a country. Foreign aid can be very important; it can encourage but cannot entirely replace for long an absent domestic demand for improvement of the legal order.

6.1 INTERNAL RESOURCES

In all countries plagued by war, there is strong demand for peace and justice. The former war leaders may or may not heed these desires, but the population is usually sick and tired of the war and longs for a new future. In most wars, a relatively small percentage of the population was actively engaged in the fighting, while those who did the suffering formed the great majority.

The basic needs, of all people everywhere, are safety of oneself, one's family and friends; safe drinking water, food, shelter, medical help, and a glimmer of hope that an unbearable life will get better. It is important to hold objective opinion polls in the country to measure and show what people want, as this may encourage the leadership to change policies, once confronted with the outcome. If the leadership does not pay attention, polls might still encourage advocates of reform to continue their work and not give up.

Those interested in reform have to identify potential, respected persons who may become leading agents of change. The human resources for a new future are always there, but they need to be marshalled and led in the right direction. They may even form a considerable but not yet organised segment of the population, particularly suppressed, educated persons, returning refugees, the many who kept silent during the past but now see chances to exert some positive influence; all those who were waiting for new, promising leadership. All countries, also the poorest and least endowed, have human and natural resources and comparative advantages that can be exploited more fairly and effectively, to the benefit of the population.

Mobilising people and institutions for reform is the task of a leader. New leadership has to arise from the population after a war. Reformists can be supported by foreign NGOs. Foreign governments or international business companies (often of an extractive nature) may be supporting other leadership that they deem more promising from their point of view. Even small NGOs can make a crucial difference by supporting key moral and new political leadership in order to make new voices heard.

As long as there is no able and firm new leadership in charge of the country, interim administration by the international community may be the only viable solution, as was discussed in section 4.6. Such interim administration has to identify and encourage promising new leaders at different levels of government and administration. Only once this leadership is strong enough and supported by an adequate civil service, it will be possible for the international administration to pull out gradually, without causing a collapse of the new beginning.

In many post-conflict countries, women's organisations foster dialogue for peace, the rule of law and equal rights. These may be women who lost family members, women who were born and raised in families of the 'opposite' ethnic or religious group who married men of the group which is now 'the enemy', and women who want to open the political system to new representatives and leaders. These women, once organised, can exert a strong influence in support of human rights.

Interfaith councils can exert similar influence, which helps to weaken the grip of former warlords and old-style politicians on the future of the country. The contribution made by religious leaders depends, of course, on the political nature and effect of their views. Although most religions (and also secular ideologies like communism) preach peace and justice for all, religious and ideological leaders are as fallible as all other human beings. Some Orthodox priests in Serbia blessed in 1995 criminal militia groups that were to participate in the mass killings of Bosnians. There were Roman Catholic priests in Rwanda who encouraged the genocide in 1994. Certain Islamic mullahs preach self-sacrifice through terrorist acts, killing countless civilian Muslims and others. In fact, most religions and secular ideologies have been involved actively or passively in gross atrocities at different times in history, also against people of their own group. Interfaith councils, however, generally consist of religious leaders who are keen to listen to each other. We may assume that they will exhibit tolerance, and share a preference for peaceful conflict settlement and reconciliation. Multi-religious institutions are likely to play a positive role in peacebuilding and reconciliation.

Local and regional individuals of influence and eminent national figures can persuade other opinion leaders, politicians and warlords to change old-style government, abolish wrong attitudes and overcome organised group hatred. Such contributions can be made by modern sports heroes, television, music and movie stars as well as traditional clan heads or village elders. It is essential for foreign donors to elicit support for peacebuilding from all these kinds of opinion leaders.

6.2 INTERNATIONAL RIGHTS AND DUTIES OF STATES

As the quote on top of this chapter emphasises, the individual and his rights do not exist in a vacuum, but in a community from which these rights derive. Rights exist because there are also duties to respect these same rights by others, and obligations to contribute to the well-being of the community. It is everybody's responsibility to contribute according to capacity to the possibility of enjoyment of these rights by everyone. Implementing these responsibilities gives rights their substance. Rights create duties, and duties rights.

As much as the development of the individual requires the development of the community with its institutions, and ultimately the human-rights state, the development of the state requires the development of an international community. But if these statements are truisms, it follows also that states have not only rights but also legal and ethical duties to each other and to each others' citizens, even if some of these ethical duties are not yet clearly defined legal rights that are subject to enforcement. The further development of the international order will need to specify these duties of states to the international community and to citizens of the states that form it. International human rights treaties create clear rights, but the enforcement system is as weak as the international governance system. In the following sections, we will attempt to look into the possibilities that might flow from these responsibilities for further peacebuilding.

6.3 DEVELOPMENT ASSISTANCE

First, *the present development cooperation funds* can be used, and increased, for peacebuilding and encouragement of the rule of law. The international standard for developed states is to contribute 0.7 percent of Gross National Product to development cooperation. Many larger countries contribute proportionally much less than smaller ones, which shows that the low aid performers still have unutilised possibilities. The 2005 agreement of the EU that all members should implement the aid target (set in the 1960s by the UN) of 0.7 percent of GNP, will lead to a considerable increase, if implemented. *If other OECD countries follow this pace of increase, vast additional resources will become available.*
This is illustrated in tables 6.1 and 6.2.

Total development aid from OECD countries was $107 billion in 2005, which was one third of one percent of their GNP. About 23 percent of this flows through multilateral organisations like the World Bank Group, the European Union and UNDP.

If all OECD countries would implement the internationally agreed goal of 0.70 percent of GNP, aid would more than double. An additional $120 billion would become available.

It should be observed that many non-OECD countries, which used to be 'developing countries', have similar capabilities once they reach a per capita annual income of, say, € 5000. There is no economic or objective political reason to apply the UN donor target of 0.7 percent of national income (GNP) only to so-called Western industrialised countries. Other countries also have aid possibilities that are proportional to their wealth.

Table 6.1 Ten lowest development aid performers in 2005 among OECD members

Net Official Development Aid as % of GNP	
Greece	0.17
Portugal	0.21
US	0.22
Australia	0.25
New Zealand	0.27
Spain	0.27
Japan	0.28
Italy	0.29
Canada	0.34
Germany	0.36
Average of DAC OECD members:	0.33

Source: OECD, DAC, February 2007
www.sourceoecd.org

Table 6.2 Ten largest donor countries of net official development assistance in 2005 in billion USD

US	28
Japan	13
UK	11
Germany	10
France	10
Netherlands	5
Italy	5
Canada	4
Sweden	3
Spain	3

Source: OECD, DAC, February 2007
www.sourceoecd.org

In addition to the usual donors of foreign assistance (member states of the OECD), it would be wise to widen the circle of donors of both financial and personal resources to many non-Western states. The low level of international assistance by non-Western middle income countries is not in accordance with the oft-repeated calls of the international community for stronger action to improve development efforts and peacebuilding. Large Asian economies have considerable means and very appropriate expertise to render assistance to less fortunate states and populations. The Conference of Islamic States and the Arab League can mobilise significant financial and expert resources for the development of the rule of Islamic law in many states in need, where the population demands improvement of its own legal system, rather than introduction of OECD type legislation. A stronger participation of these countries in international peacebuilding programs and judicial reform, particularly by those states which attempt to translate international human rights norms gradually into domestic legislation and jurisprudence, should be welcomed strongly.

Similarly, developing countries which have experience in building democracy, like a large state as India, could be encouraged to assume a larger role in the advocacy and advising of democratisation in other non-Western states. Peacebuilding and rule-of law reform which would turn into another self-appointed 'white man's burden' would certainly not be successful. It is a universal responsibility, if UN declarations and binding global treaties on human rights are to be implemented. Engaging states and NGOs from all over the multifarious world would vastly improve possibilities.

Financial resources for international assistance can also be rapidly increased by charging a small fee on suitable, frequent economic activities, particularly relating to energy and raw material use. For instance, a small levy on every airplane ticket or other easily taxable international transaction can help finance a UN or EU peacebuilding fund. This could yield vast resources.

Of course, the most crucial factor is not finance, but professional, experienced people who can be motivated to contribute to peacebuilding. Expert personnel for legal advice, interim management and administration, monitoring and training in peacebuilding countries can be recruited not only from academia and existing government services, but also from among early retirees with suitable experience. There is a vast reserve of experience in the 50-plus generation, which has relatively low additional income needs and is easier to rapidly send on missions abroad than less experienced younger professionals (with families).

Next to an increase in development aid funds, it is possible to devote a large share of presently available funds to peacebuilding and rule-of-law support. There is considerable room for *re-allocation* of existing development funds and budgets, as only a small portion is presently devoted to peacebuilding and rule-of-law assistance. It is clear that countries governed by law and strong institutions develop much better economically than those that are not. The causes of this relationship are obvious. It follows that investment in improved rule of law has generally high returns in economic growth, market expansion, social peace, and political stability, apart from the values of and interest in human rights and democracy in and of themselves. Economic progress financed by foreign aid is often very vulnerable to political instability and corruption. From this, it follows that shifts of expenditure towards rule of law projects would be very rewarding in economic terms. Such additional expenses can be financed by changing priorities away from pure economic assistance to institution building and training.

6.4 DEFENCE ORGANISATIONS

The contributions of donor countries and international organisations for post-conflict peacebuilding and rule of law assistance can already be improved without major increases in government expenditure. Defence budgets, which total over € 900 billion per year,[1] finance capabilities that could be used in part for peacebuilding as long as armed forces are not engaged in actual war. Armed forces often have, by the nature of their special tasks in case of war, a large excess capacity in peacetime, and military peacekeeping personnel are widely available from standing armed forces of dozens of countries. See table 6.3.

It should be noted that the number of active troops per 1000 inhabitants varies greatly between a high of 49 in North Korea (the most militarised state) and 0 in the 24 countries without armies. For comparison: Russia has 7.24, the US 4.76, China 1.71, and India 1.20 military personnel per 1000 people.
Of course, troops of some nations cannot be engaged in a number of peace operations, either because of their regime, policies or quality, or because their governments do not have enough objective distance from the operation, and participation might complicate rather than solve problems. Even when this is taken into account, the table indicates there are large unused capabilities for participation in peace operations abroad. Some armies are overstretched (like the US army) while others do not participate at all.

Only a small percentage of active troop strength is actually employed in peace operations. While some countries are heavily involved, others participate with small proportions or decline to participate altogether. Not only soldiers, but military police, gendarmerie and other personnel with mixed military/police training are also very suitable for the first phase of peacebuilding activities, when physical security and public order are top-priorities. Here, too, burden sharing is uneven.

Only a few percent of the UN member states' military personnel are deployed abroad. Some countries are close to their capabilities for military peace operations (the smaller North-West European nations) and have a high ratio of personnel deployed abroad in relation to population size (like the UK). The US armed forces are presently overstressed with unfortunate operations in Iraq and in Afghanistan. Others, particularly the more populous European nations France, Germany, Italy and others, have a low ratio of participation. This applies even more strongly to Japan, even taking into account that this populous nation, which still is the number two economy in the world, has only recently formed a Department of Defence. Its self-defence forces are already considerable. So is its interest in international stability and the rule of law.
If the reorganisation of armed forces, which started after the end of the Cold War and is not yet completed in most UN member states, were sped up and completed, to enlarge the expeditionary capacity for peacekeeping and peace-building, there would be vast additional means.

Table 6.3 Largest Armies in the World, 2006

Active troops in 1000[2]

China	2,255
US	1,423
North-Korea	1,325
India	1,106
Russia	1,037
South-Korea	687
Pakistan	619
Iran	545
Turkey	515
Vietnam	484
Egypt	450
Myanmar	428
Ukraine	361
Indonesia	316
Thailand	307
Syria	296
Taiwan	290
Brazil	287
Germany	285
France	259
Japan	239
Italy	230
Colombia	207
Eritrea	202
Saudi Arabia	200
Morocco	196
Mexico	193
United Kingdom	188
Ethiopia	183
Iraq	180
Spain	178
Greece	178
Israel	168
Poland	163
Sri Lanka	158

One way to estimate the potential for peace operations is the personnel of UN and other peace operations divided by the total number of military personnel in the world. In mid 2007, the UN engaged 71,000 troops in peace operations. NATO had 52,000 troops mainly in Afghanistan (36,000) and Kosovo (16,000). The US and its coalition forces had 176,000 in Iraq. The UN and NATO total, including Iraq, was 300,000.[3] The total military strength in the world in 2006 was more than

20 million, measuring only active troops and not reserves and paramilitary.[4] This means that *only 1.5 percent of active military troop strength in the world was engaged in peace operations.*

6.5 REDUCING CORRUPTION

It is estimated that many billions of euros are lost every year through corruption.[5] Fighting corruption by strengthening the rule of law and independent media has a very high financial return, even though the exact amounts are not easily quantifiable. The UN Convention against Corruption (2003), mentioned in section 5.10, specifies the varied character of corruption, from demanding money for a judge's verdict, to donations to 'development funds' that enrich a ruler's family. The common feature is abuse of public and private power for private gain. Corruption is rampant in post-conflict societies as war typically leads to war profiteering, and warlords become local, regional or national rulers.

Donors have to be very alert; most corrupt officials are very wily in designing ways to nullify counter-corruption measures. Foreign admonishments, dialogue, diplomacy, patience, 'change of attitudes' and paper changes of regulations often have little effect. It is important to strengthen domestic deterrents against corruption, such as free media, independent judges and professional prosecutors. Transparency International has developed a National Integrity System to assess and fight corruption. Prosecution of corrupt acts, exposure in the media, and severe legal penalties are essential to make corruption a 'high risk low return' activity.

6.6 INTERNATIONAL DIVISION OF TASKS

As individual donor countries, non-governmental organisations and international institutions cannot address and take on all questions of rule-of-law assistance everywhere in the world equally and at the same time, it is efficient to ensure an *international division of donor tasks* with different countries specialising on various fields of assistance. This has to evolve on the basis of multilateral cooperation, taking comparative expertise and national advantages into account. (In section 8.2.2, some remarks are made on the comparative advantages of different countries).

An international division of tasks should, of course, lead to a greater focus and more momentum of certain donors in a particular set of countries, but not to a rigid and thoughtless division among donors of countries in need. It is not healthy if recipient countries become very dependent on just one or two donors, while others turn a blind eye to what may go wrong or is neglected. The allocation of assistance never starts from scratch in a theoretical situation, but begins with an existing pattern of needs, abilities to help, and available networks which have already been built up. It is comparable to investment analysis: in which parts of a portfolio can one expect the most progress? Which are the weakest spots that need to be strengthened? The crucial question is: where can the highest marginal returns be made for the recipient? This leads to a certain specialisation on areas and sectors or subjects of emphasis.

Countries with strong, expeditionary armed forces and much persuasive political and military power (deterrence) would do well to take the lead in the military aspects of peace enforcement, peacekeeping, arresting war criminals and the demobilisation and disarmament of former warring parties, as well as assisting in the fight against remaining pockets of armed resistance and terrorism. Smaller well-established democracies with no particular foreign policy axe to grind, would do well to focus more on assistance that is most politically sensitive in recipient countries. This includes constitutional advice, police reform, security sector reform, transitional justice, training prosecutors and judges, support for independent media and gender equity programmes.

6.7 ALLOCATION AND COUNTRY CHOICE

In the previous sections, it was shown that the means for peacebuilding and assistance for the rule of law could be vastly increased if governments are prepared to make this choice. The next question concerns how the volume of aid should be allocated to various purposes and countries. After determining a given volume of aid, the question is to which countries and subject matters these means should be devoted, and in which order of priorities.

Country selection and allocation can take place by using a number of criteria, related to the enlightened or narrow national interest of the donor, the donor's national values, membership of organisations and national comparative advantages.

One could use the following list of questions to find the best allocation of resources for peacebuilding. These questions are not a list of independent criteria, but a guide to arrive at an optimal use of resources, with the highest marginal returns. This list might also help to limit the risk of failure.

- What is the actual or possible *mandate under international law* for the peacebuilding operation in question? Is there a UN Security Council mandate?
- Which countries needing post-conflict rule of law assistance are indicated as priority states, of interest to the *national foreign policy goals*, and the goals of crucial international organisations? For instance, which countries are most important to the EU's Common Foreign and Security Policy, for various reasons such as proximity, refugees, cultural or historical bonds and strategic importance?
- Which countries have *organisational links* to the EU and deserve, as a result of those links, special attention? The same question is relevant for NATO, the OSCE and the Council of Europe. Which countries are participants in the Partnership for Peace programme of NATO? Which are members of the OSCE? See chart 6.4 for the concentric rectangles of memberships. It makes sense that, if other factors are equal, members and applicant countries of organisa-

tions like the EU, NATO and OSCE deserve special attention when assistance is needed. For instance, the entry of Romania, Bulgaria and the expected accession of Croatia and perhaps other Balkan states like Bosnia, Macedonia, Albania, Montenegro and perhaps a reformed Serbia in the EU in the foreseeable future makes them especially interesting to other EU members as candidates for legal reform assistance. As we note in Chapter 7 on the EU, the interest of countries to attain membership gives the EU a reformist influence on these countries, which reinforces potential effects of police and legal sector reform.

- In which countries is the donor government already participating in *military peacekeeping* operations and would it also like to contribute to a lasting result in civilian peacebuilding?
- With which countries does the government already have ties of *development cooperation* where it can attain synergy and use some leverage by devoting more attention to the legal sector?
- What contributions can be expected from *other donors*; which cases are neglected but important, and where can one make a real difference? Neglected cases pose a hard choice: they have a high need, but the tasks may be huge and the risk of failure is great, since others are not pitching in. This multiplies negligence, particularly of the worst failing states.
- What is the donor's national or institutional *comparative advantage*? If other countries and organisations specialise as well, what is the area on which one should concentrate? Or to put it in plain English: what are we best at, in comparison to other states, and where can we make the most of our efforts, given what others will be doing? We will elaborate on this in section 8.2.2.
- Is there a lead organisation or *lead country* to which we can attach our contribution to gain leverage and impact, not only in the recipient country, but also with respect to the policies of this leading donor? Is this main donor likely to continue its efforts for a number of years to achieve results, or is it inclined to leave after a quick fix, which might soon disintegrate after departure?
- Which human and financial *resources* are probably *available from all donors* for this mission, and for how long? Will other countries agree to rotate with our personnel once we run out of resources? If not, devotion to the tasks for a brief period might be in vain.
- Can we count on *political and military support from other countries* if our own contribution, especially our peacebuilding experts are threatened or endangered?
- What is the *risk* that peacebuilding and rule of law support will fall to pieces due to *domestic developments in the recipient country*? What is the risk of a return to war and the risk of the (new) government becoming obstructionist or even more corrupt than it is already? The risk of war returning depends on external threats that may upset the domestic peace and on the degree of internal acceptance of the new domestic order as reasonably just and hopeful. Small but violent groups can disturb the new order that would be otherwise accepted by most of the population.

Table 6.4 Membership of main international organisations

UN

Afghanistan
Algeria
Angola
Antigua and Barbuda
Argentina
Bahamas*
Bahrain
Bangladesh*
Barbados*
Belize*
Benin
Bhutan
Bolivia
Botswana*
Brazil
Brunei*
Burkina Faso
Burma
Burundi
Cambodia
Cameroon *
Cape Verde
Central African Republic
Chad
Chile
CHINA
Colombia
Comorus
Congo
Congo (DR)
Costa Rica
Cuba
Dijbouti
Dominica*
Dominican Republic
East Timor
Ecuador
Egypt
El Salvador
Equatorial Guinea
Eritrea
Ethiopia
Fiji*
Gabon
Gambia*
Ghana*
Grenada*
Guatemala
Guinea
Guinea-Bissau
Guyana*
Haiti
Honduras

India*
Indonesia
Iran
Iraq
Israel
Ivory Coast
Jamaica*
Jordan
Kenya*
Kiribati*
Kuwait
Laos
Lebanon
Lesotho*
Liberia
Libya
Madagascar
Malawi*
Malaysia*
Maldives*
Mali
Marshall Islands
Maurtania
Mauritius*
Micronesia
Mongolia
Morocco
Mozambique*
Namibia*
Nauru*
Nepal
Nicaragua
Niger
Nigeria*
North Korea
Oman
Pakistan*
Palau
Panama
Papua New Guinea*
Paraguay
Peru
Philippines
Qatar
Rwanda
Samoa*
Sao Toino and Principe
Saudi Arabia
Senegal
Seychelles*
Sierra Leone*
Singapore*
Solomon Islands*

Somalia
South Africa*
St Kitts and Nevis*
St Lueia*
St Vincent and the Grenadines*
Sri Lanka*
Sudan
Suriname
Swaziland*

Syria
Tanzania*
Thailand
Togo
Tonga*
Trinidad and Tobago*
Tunisia
Tuvalu*
UAE

Uganda*
Uruguay
Vanuatu*
Venezuela
Vietnam
Yemen
Zambia*
Zimbabwe*

OECD

Australia*
Japan ▲
Mexico
New Zealand*
South Korea

Switzerland

Holy See

NATO

Canada ▲
Iceland
Norway
Turkey
UNITED STATES ▲

Belgium
Denmark
FRANCE ▲
Germany ▲
Greece
Italy ▲
Luxembourg
Netherlands
Portugal
Spain
UNITED KINGDOM ▲
Czech Republic
Hungary
Poland
Bulgaria
Romania
Slovakia

EU

Austria
Finland
Ireland
Sweden

Estonia
Latvia
Lithuania
Slovenia

Cyprus*
Malta*

Albania
Andorra
Armenia
Azerbaijan
Belarus
Bosnia and Herzegovina
Croatia
Georgia

Kazakhstan
Kyrgyzstan
Liechtenstein
Macedonia
Moldova
Monaco
M ontenegro
RUSSIA ▲

San Marino
Serbia
Tajikistan
Turkmenistan
Ukraine
Uzbekistan

OSCE

* = Commonwealth Coutries ▲ = G8 Countries **Bold** Capital Type - Permanent Members of the UN Security Counsil

Adapted from: UK Department of Foreign and Common wealth Affairs, 2004

137

6.8 PRELIMINARY COST ESTIMATES

Peace operations are costly. But wars are far costlier in killed and traumatised people, refugees, destruction of the country, its nature, environment, cultural heritage, and so much more. Peace building is an extremely rewarding investment in well-being and socio-economic progress. One (civil) war can destroy hundreds of thousands of lives, traumatize millions, destroy billions of euros and set back a country and its neighbours in their development for decades.

It is useful to roughly estimate what peace building operations might cost. There is no systematic and complete picture. Only parts of the puzzle are available: military costs of some operations, economic aid expenses in some countries, and casualties. The Rand Corporation made calculations based on a number of country cases.[6] The Rand study drew lessons from many case studies by a team of country experts and analysts of peace operations. Only a handful of these have been accounted for financially. It is, however, the most informative and practically relevant study we have seen so far.

Rand emphasizes that such calculations are only of indicative value, as all cases are different. For the present study, we have adapted Rand's estimates, first to account for inflation and exchange rate changes.[7] We also adapted Rand's figures to fit operations in a hypothetical country of presumably 10 million inhabitants. We added an estimated number of years of the duration of separate elements like police support and judiciary reform. These changes may make it easier for the reader to apply these figures to specific future cases as 'rule of thumb' first estimates. We refer to the many assumptions and caveats in Rand's estimates. The figures that follow only indicate the orders of magnitude that have to be considered when decisions are made about operations. They may be way off the actual costs in specific operations. For instance, operations in Iraq and Afghanistan are very expensive, but those in El Salvador, Mozambique and Guatemala were relatively cheap.

The first cost model represents a 'standard' UN operation in a poor country (income per capita $ 500 which is about € 375). It is assumed that the former warring parties agree with the UN operation. There is no widespread resistance among the population. Some domestic capacity for security, order and government remains. The operation starts with blue-helmet peacekeeping and includes police reform, rule of law reform, humanitarian aid, governance reconstruction, infrastructure, economic stabilization and development, and assistance for democratization. Most of the UN soldiers come from other UN members than OECD countries, as NATO and OECD country soldiers are expensive and cost about € 150,000 per person per year. We added assumptions about the duration of separate elements and assume that inflation and exchange rate changes even each other out. In the first years, the costs of 16,000 blue helmet troops and 2000 international police dominate the picture, but in later years the focus is on reform and development. See table 6.5. The total amounts to about € 18 billion, which is

Liberia Americo-Liberians (mostly freed slaves) established the republic in 1847. Liberia was a largely peaceful one-party state until 1980, when Samuel Doe came to power.

Rebels led by Charles Taylor of the National Patriotic Front of Liberia (NPFL) took up arms in December 1989 against the government of Samuel Doe. The rebels split up in a faction led by Charles Taylor (associated with Mano tribes) and a faction led by Prince Johnson (associated with Gio tribes). These three armed groups became involved in a power struggle. This civil war between 1989 and 1996 left 150,000 dead and caused 850,000 refugees.
The Economic Community of West African States (ECOWAS) mediated peace talks and established a military observer group ECOMOG in 1990. The UN Security Council imposed an arms embargo and provided humanitarian assistance. In 1993, the Cotonou Peace Agreement was signed; the UN authorized the observer mission UNOMIL to support ECOMOG. The fighting parties continued, however. In 1994 1.8 million people needed humanitarian assistance.
An amended peace agreement and expanded mandates of ECOMOG and UNOMIL created stability for elections in 1997.
Charles Taylor was elected president. The UN left immediately after the elections in 1997 in Liberia. Serious abuses of human rights continued and political opponents were excluded.

No security sector reform had taken place. In 1999, the Liberians United for Reconciliation and Democracy (LURD) took control over the north. The Movement for Democracy in Liberia (MODEL) was based in the south.

A Comprehensive Peace Agreement was signed in 2003. The UN sent a peacekeeping force of 15,000 military and 1115 UN police officers (UNMIL). This mission disarmed more than 100,000 combatants, of which 65,000 benefited from reintegration. Organized repatriation helped 67,000 refugees.

Taylor was exiled in 2003. The transitional government was unable to curb corruption. In 2005, Taylor was arrested for trial of war crimes.

The case of Liberia highlights that when former warlords become president, their election can kill a beginning of democracy. The UN made new elections possible in 2005. Ellen Johnson-Sirleaf was elected president, started an anti-corruption program and installed a Truth and Reconciliation Commission.

€ 1800 per inhabitant, or € 180 per person per year during 10 years, equalling almost one-half of the per capita income of the country concerned. Many peace operations have cost much less, but we prefer to err on the high side.

Table 6.5 International costs of light peacebuilding operations in a country of 10 million inhabitants

Items	Persons	€ mln.	Years	€ total mln.
UN blue-helmet military	16,000	720	5	3,600
Local troops paid by donors	30,000	100	5	500
UN police	2,000	140	5	700
Local police paid by donors	22,000	36	5	180
Legal assistance		36	10	360
Humanitarian aid		340	2	680
Governance asst.		520	5	2,600
Democratisation		100	10	1,000
Infrastructure and econ. development		840	10	8,400
Rounded off total				**18 billion**

The second type is a heavy and extremely difficult peace building operation, which starts against the will of one or more warring parties. One could imagine this as an operation which is driven by the new conviction in the UN that there is a 'responsibility to protect'.[8] It concerns a seriously endangered population group in a country with either a very weak and incapable government, or its opposite, a violent, suppressive and genocidal government. In this heavy peace-building model, one or more major UN members, with the support of a coalition of other states, have to force their entry and impose a UN Security Council resolution (or a decision of another organization – which would have less than universal legitimacy[9] and might be more difficult). At least part of the population is presumed to be hostile or much divided. The war which is being ended left very little domestic capacity for security and governance. This type we call *heavy peace building with enforcement*. It is assumed that 130,000 green-helmet soldiers of NATO and OECD quality and equipment, and 16,000 international police officers, are deployed in a country of 10 million people. See table 6.6. This operation totals € 157 billion, or € 1570 per inhabitant per year, which is 4 times the income per capita of the country concerned.

Striking in these tables are the heavy costs of the international military, particularly of NATO-quality, and the relatively low cost of police and legal assistance items.

The differences between the standard and heavy operations are not only in the requirements for foreign troops (numbers, qualification, equipment, salary) and foreign police. Non-military assistance is assumed by Rand to be equal for both

Table 6.6 International costs of heavy peacebuilding operations in a country of 10 million inhabitants

Items	Persons	€ mln.	Years	€ total mln.
Foreign soldiers	130,000	26,000	5	130,000
Local soldiers	30,000	100	5	500
Foreign police	16,000	2,500	5	12,500
Local police	22,000	36	5	180
Legal assistance		72	10	720
Humanitarian aid		680	2	1,360
Governance asst.		520	5	2,600
Democratisation		100	10	1,000
Infrastructure and econ. Development		840	10	8,400
Rounded off total				**157 billion**

types, but that may be rather optimistic. We have changed this in our calculations, assuming some costs to be double in the heavy, difficult operation as compared to the light version, erring again on the safe side. Expenses for infrastructure and development are assumed to be the same in both types.

An important difference, not shown in the tables, is that the costs of the standard operation are usually spread among the UN members, as they are paid from the budget and special peacekeeping funds to which many countries make contributions, also those not sending personnel. Generally, enforced operations are more controversial among the UN membership, as they impinge on state sovereignty, and are supported only by a coalition of willing states, e.g. a lead nation like the US and a number of NATO members, which pay for their own troops and the development assistance costs.

Even the enforced peace building operation assumes that the intervention comes at the time that warring parties suffer from war-fatigue but need to be pushed into a cease-fire. Imposing peace from the outside on a country that is in an early phase of a full-swing civil war, may require such high foreign troop numbers, expected battle casualties and high expenses that foreign donors are simply not prepared to accept the burdens. (This was, for instance, the case in 1991-5, when the US and other NATO members were not willing to enforce peace on the former Yugoslavia.)

For police and judiciary assistance it is assumed that the light peacebuilding operation in a poor country of 10 million inhabitants might require about 600 local judges, 600 local prosecutors, 4200 local corrections staff for 40 correctional institutions, with altogether about 120 international advisors. Domestic costs of the entire rule of law system are estimated at € 26 million p.a. and international costs of reform at € 17 million p.a.[10] It is assumed that of the total of € 43 million, a substantial share of the local expenses is also paid for by foreign donors, and their bill will be about € 36. In the heavy peacebuilding operation, this is doubled to € 72 million p.a.

Let us now assume that in a particular year the UN is responsible for peace operations in ten countries that total 100 million inhabitants. One of those countries had a hopeless regime and was engaged in genocidal campaigns. Many outside powers could not bear watching mass murder to continue and decided to undertake a heavy peacebuilding operation, starting with a forced military entry, and followed by a 10 year peace building program. This might cost € 157 billion for the total of 10 years, based on assumptions shown in table 6.6.

Let us also assume that nine light peace building operations are carried out during these ten years. This would cost € 180 billion, based on table 6.5. The sum of one heavy and 9 light would cost € 34 billion per year (Euros of 2007).

These amounts seem very high. But are they really? The annual military expenditures in the world amounted to € 903 billion in 2006.[11] Annual development assistance from OECD-countries was € 107 billion[12]. Their sum was € 1010 billion p.a. *One heavy peacebuilding operation and 9 light operations in different stages would average just over 3 percent of the global military and development aid expenses.*

This expense would be a sound investment in human security. These calculations, though imprecise, show that these are within the realm of the possible. This is not to say that all such expenses are prudent; the US and UK expenses for regime change in Iraq are extremely high and have not improved security in the world, but probably worsened it. UN peace operations in Cyprus, Sierra Leone, Ivory Coast, El Salvador, Cambodia, East Timor, Mozambique and many other forms of peacebuilding with the consent of the parties are deemed by most observers to be relative successes that improved the fate of the population and their neighbours over what might have happened without such outside help.

These preliminary estimates show, that the UN, NATO, EU and other international organizations and donor agencies need not refrain from necessary and feasible peacebuilding operations for lack of financial or military resources. Available economic and military means suffice to implement several peacebuilding operations in various countries in turmoil. What matters most is not lack of resources, but poor national and international decision-making, serious waste of resources in wrongly designed interventions, and uneven burden sharing. With large resources available, money is another word for priority. Priorities are set by governments, opinion leaders and the electorates, which shape each other.

NOTES

1 SIPRI Yearbook 2007, Oxford University Press, 2007.
2 En.wikipedia.org based on 231 national and international sources, accessed July 12, 2007. The table is limited to armies larger than 150,000 troops.
3 Sources: UN.org; NATO.int; en.wikipedia.org, accessed July 12, 2007.
4 Calculated from en.wikipedia.org, based on 231 national and international sources, accessed July 12, 2007.
5 www.transparency.org.
6 Dobbins, J. et. al. *The Beginners guide to Nation-Building* Rand Corporation, Santa Monica, 2007. Hereafter referred to as Rand 2007.
7 We added 25% inflation given that Rand's figures relate to the first years of the 21st century and changed dollars to euros at the rate of 0.75.
8 International Commission on Intervention and State Sovereignty, *The Responsibility to Protect.* Ottawa, International Development Research Centre, 2001.
9 UN Security Council resolutions have the highest level of legitimacy based on the UN Charter. A decision by a regional organisation like the Organisation of American States, the African Union the Association of South East Asian Nations, the European Union or the North Atlantic Treaty Organisation could also legitimise the use of force, depending on the Security Council, the relation of the country of operation to the regional organisation, the position of the government of that country, and other factors determining the legality of the use of force.
10 Rand 2007, p. 106-7.
11 SIPRI Yearbook 2007, Oxford University Press, 2007.
12 www.oecd.org/dac, accessed 18-06-07.

Iraq

Iraq became independent in 1932. Its population is estimated at 27.5 million and contains an Arab majority (75-80%) of Sji'ite and Sunni Muslims, a large Kurdish minority (15-20%) and many smaller minorities.

The Baath party of mainly Sunni Muslims came to power by a coup in 1963. Saddam Hussein gained leadership of this party in 1979. His dictatorship ruled Iraq until 2003. Territorial disputes and the Sji'ite revolution in Iran tempted Saddam to invade its neighbour in 1980. An eight-year war between Iran and Iraq (1980-88) took the lives of 1 million people. Chemical weapons were used widely against Iranian troops, and also killed 5000 Kurds in an attack at Halabja in 1988. Iraq gained no territory in this bloody war.

In August 1990, Iraq invaded Kuwait. The UN Security Council imposed economic sanctions. Iraq did not pull out on the deadline of 16 January 1991. The UN mandated its members to take all necessary steps to end the occupation.

A coalition of 26 UN members, led by the US, Great Britain and France, attacked Iraqi forces in Operation Desert Storm. Air campaigns and ground offensives quickly drove Iraq from Kuwait. The US decided at the time not to push on to Baghdad and not to topple the Saddam Hussein regime, fearing this would cause great instability in Iraq and the region. Later events proved this to be a wise decision.
The ceasefire agreement included a call for the elimination of Iraq's weapons of mass destruction, ballistic missiles and related arms production. A verification system was set up. Iraq refused to cooperate with the UN and the International Atomic Energy Agency between 1991 and 2003, despite stiff economic sanctions. Saddam violently suppressed a Sji'ite uprising in the south and attempts to topple him.

The US and UK considered the supposed development of weapons of mass destruction by Iraq a threat to international security. In February 2003 these countries asked the UN Security Council to authorize the use of force against Iraq. France, Germany and Russia opposed this.
A coalition led by the US and UK decided to intervene in Iraq without UN authorization. The main stated reason was Saddam's refusal to cooperate with the UN and remove all weapons of mass destruction. Other reasons to topple Saddam were the violent repression of the population, suspected links with the terrorist organization al-Qaeda, and a belief that Iraq could be reformed into a pro-Western democracy. This would have a beneficial effect on the Middle East, it was thought. A pro-Western Iraq might also improve the world oil market.
On March 19 2003 the first troops were sent. The regime of Iraq was overthrown by a brief 'shock and awe' campaign with much military force of high technology.

The Baath party and the Iraqi army were disbanded by the Coalition Provisional Authority (CPA), which ruled until June 2004 when sovereignty was returned to the Iraqi interim government. Legislative elections held in January 2005 were followed by a new constitution. Most Sunni Arabs boycotted the December 2005 elections, but a high turnout of 70 percent and low levels of violence made the elections successful. A Sji'ite dominated coalition of four parties took office six months later. The UN Assistance Mission for Iraq (UNAMI) supported this political process.

In other aspects, the intervention in Iraq was much less successful. The coalition troops failed to bring stability in 2003-7. Various insurgency forces launched terrorist attacks against the opulation, coalition troops, the CPA and the new Iraqi government. Opponents included former members of the army and police, Saddam Hussein loyalists, Sunni Muslims, Sji'ite Muslims, Al-Qaeda, and others using chaos to further their aims. Many Iraqis died in internecine violence. Tensions between Sunni and Sji'ite Muslims escalated since 2006 to a civil war.

Rebuilding an Iraqi police force, army and a judicial system proved to be very difficult. The disbanding of the Iraqi army left 2.5 million jobless without re-integration programs. NATO got involved in training, equipping, and technical assistance of a new security force. The removal of 30,000 civil servants of the Baath-regime, including teachers, town administrators and doctors, slowed down the reconstruction process.

A special tribunal was set up for Saddam Hussein, who was hanged in December 2006.

The continued insecurity and the worsening humanitarian situation led to 1.8 million internally displaced people and 2 million refugees in neighbouring countries in 2007. Official numbers of civilian deaths are lacking; estimates of independent organizations range between 70,000 and 650,000.

As of June 2007, the number of mainly US troops in Iraq increased to 176,000. The estimated costs between 2003 and mid-2007 are 500 billion dollars. The operation has led to 3500 killed US soldiers and 25,000 wounded US and UK soldiers.

This intervention remains extremely controversial in the US and UK and across the world. Much echoed criticism includes incorrect interpretation of intelligence information about the threat of weapons of mass destruction, a failure to provide post-combat security in Iraq; poor preparation for the reconstruction phase; wrongly disbanding the Iraqi armed forces and underestimating terrorist insurgence after initial military victory. The US accuses Iran and Syria of stirring up violence and resistance. Iran may encourage a Sji'ite South Iraq.

At the time of writing, the northern Kurdish state seems all but independent. The southern Sji'ite part of Iraq may develop into a separate state. The Sunni middle, and parts of Baghdad and other cities are subject to violent internecine strife which the US appears unable to stop.

Some lessons of the intervention in Iraq are: do not intervene if there is no urgent threat to regional security; if there is no mandate under international law; do not underestimate the opportunities for terrorist resistance; plan not only for the military campaign but prepare in advance for the restoration of public security; and use domestic authority structures and allegiance patterns to restore order. From a humanitarian point of view, this intervention was counterproductive. It also appears to have destabilized the Persian Gulf region. The likely outcome seems not in the interest of the intervening countries and has weakened US leadership in world politics.

7 THE EUROPEAN UNION AND POST-CONFLICT PEACEBUILDING

"We are committed to the peaceful resolution of conflicts in the world and to ensuring that people do not become victims of war, terrorism and violence. The European Union wants to promote freedom and development in the world. We want to drive back poverty, hunger and disease. We want to continue to take a leading role in that fight."

Berlin Declaration of the European Union Heads of State and Government, 2007

7.1 INTRODUCTION

After the exploration of peacebuilding in the previous chapters, it is useful to look specifically at the policies and instruments of the European Union. It may be the largest source of assistance for rule-of-law support activities in the foreseeable future. The European Union and its members have already become the largest source of bilateral and multilateral assistance in the world for development, humanitarian, emergency and peacebuilding programmes.

This chapter explores how its members have empowered the EU to play a role in peacebuilding since the 1990s. Even though the EU and its members form the main source of funds, their activities are still fragmented. The EU and many of its members still lack much influence on peacebuilding in recipient states, because of the weakness of the Common Foreign and Security Policy (CFSP) of the EU and a lack of coherence of the activities of individual member states in some recipient countries.

7.2 POLICY AND INSTITUTIONS

7.2.1 THE ESTABLISHMENT OF A COMMON FOREIGN AND SECURITY POLICY

The member states of the European Union (EU) have aspired to coordinate elements of their foreign policies since the 1970s. The first efforts in the 1970's and 80's were motivated particularly by the wish to play a role in the conflicts among Israel, the Palestinians and Arab countries, as well as a desire to reduce dependence of EU countries on the US. But it was not until the early 1990s – when Germany had just been unified and the Soviet bloc had collapsed – that coordination of foreign policies became more than just an aspiration. Members desired a common foreign and security policy in particular to help guide the developments in Central and Eastern Europe. Even though the EU was not very successful in this area in the 1990's, the tasks ahead encouraged further cooperation. Since the US presidency of G.W. Bush and the intervention of the US and Britain in Iraq, the desire of the EU members for more intense EU foreign policy cooperation has grown further.

Albania Most of its 3.5 million citizens are Albanian; minorities are predominantly Greek. Albania was occupied by Romans, Byzantines and eventually Ottomans until 1912. The Italian occupation in 1939 annexed territory and created an ethnic Albania. In 1944, communist resistance came to power and established a repressive collectivist system under Enver Hoxa. His rule isolated the country.

Shortly after the Berlin wall collapsed, Albania tried to connect with the West. Initial elections were corrupt, but democratic parties eventually came to power. Economic liberalization did not put the country on track, as it lacked institutions to manage markets. In 1997, accessibility of weapons, civic unrest caused by poverty and a corrupt savings fund led to riots. Militias took hold of cities and southern parts of the country. Neighbouring Italy led a UN peacekeeping force of 7000 UN troops (Operation Alba) to restore order. Large numbers of refugees entered from Kosovo in 1998-1999. The short-lived governments suffered from internal disputes and corruption scandals. After the 2005 elections, democratic parties returned to power. In 2006, Albania signed the stabilization and association agreement with the EU taking the first step towards accession.

Albania struggles with its poor economic position. A large share of the working age population migrated to wealthier countries. Political parties remain unstable. There is much organized crime.

The goal of EU-membership gives a drive for reform. Under EU guidance, Albania is creating stability by developing its economy and redistributing wealth more equally among the population.

The Common Foreign and Security Policy (CFSP) was already introduced in the Maastricht Treaty of the European Union (TEU), which came into force in 1993. 'CFSP' was set up as a separate, second pillar of the European Union, to ensure the intergovernmental nature of the policy, meaning the countries did not want to be bound by majority decisions. Five overlapping goals were set out in the treaty: (1) to safeguard the common values and fundamental interests of the union, (2) to strengthen the security of the union, (3) to preserve peace and strengthen international security, (4) to promote international cooperation, and (5) to develop democracy and the rule of law, including human rights.[1] Setting these goals opened the door for joint post-conflict peacebuilding activities.

The leading institution in the European foreign and security policy is the Council of the European Union and its Secretariat. The European Commission and the European Parliament have a less pronounced role in this area. The member state governments regard foreign affairs as an area where they should keep the initiative and not lose national control.

7.2.2 POLICIES

The treaty of Maastricht distinguishes common positions and joint actions. Common positions require the member states to implement national policies that comply with the position defined by the union on a particular issue.[2] For instance, the Council adopted a common position in 2001 on combating illicit traffic in conflict diamonds for areas in armed conflict, as a contribution to prevention and settlement of conflicts. It stated that it would "support and contribute to the efforts of the international community to break the link between conflict diamonds and the financing of armed conflict" in countries such as Liberia, Sierra Leone and Angola.

Joint actions are activities by the member states under the auspices of the CFSP.[3] An example of this is the Council Joint Action on a European assistance programme to support the Palestinian Authority in its efforts to counter terrorist activities emanating from the territories under its control.[4] Another example is the Joint Action on the European Union Integrated Rule of Law Mission for Iraq (EUJUST LEX), in which the council declared its intention "to address the urgent needs in the Iraqi criminal justice system through providing training for high and mid level officials in senior management and criminal investigation".[5]

Although the establishment of the CFSP, especially its security element, was a step forward, the policy often remained declaratory, slow and weak.[6] The Council often only came together to discuss an issue at the moment when an international crisis was already acute. Every member state had then already made its own analysis, which resulted in months of arguing to reach a common diagnosis. To solve this problem, the Amsterdam Treaty, which came into force in 1999, established a Policy Planning and Early Warning Unit in the General Secretariat of the Council – which would pool information and provide analysis of international issues for more effective and united policy responses. The tasks of the unit are to monitor and analyse developments in areas relevant to the CFSP, to provide assessments of the EU's interests, and to write policy papers with options for the Council. In practice, however, the unit became more preoccupied with the day-to-day policy of the CFSP than with planning and early analyses.[7]

The treaty also launched 'common strategies' for areas in which the member states have important interests in common. These strategies specify the objectives, duration and the means to be made available by the union and the member states. The first was the Common Strategy on Russia, in which the European Council declared the EU would support Russia's transformation to a stable, open and pluralistic democracy.[8]

7.2.3 INSTITUTIONS

It is important to stress that it is the Council of the European Union, particularly the General Affairs and External Relations Council of the Ministers of Foreign Affairs, as well as the European Council of the Heads of State or Government, which are the prime actors in European foreign and security policy. These policies are part of the so-called second pillar of the EU.

In the first pillar,[9] which is focussed on the common market and external trade policies, it is the European Commission that most often has the initiative. Some elements of this first pillar are also very relevant for the second pillar (common foreign and security policy). These are: common trade policy, boycott and sanction decisions, development assistance and cooperation with the African, Caribbean and Pacific countries regulated in separate treaties. The institutional set-up of the EU therefore requires good cooperation between the first and second pillar to reach an effective external policy in various peacebuilding tasks.

Council decisions on the CFSP require unanimity. This downgrades the decisions to what is acceptable to the most reserved member. The Amsterdam Treaty did not change this. As a result, decision making on post-conflict peacebuilding activities is generally not forceful. There is a possibility of 'constructive abstention', meaning members abstain without blocking a decision. Moreover, deciding by qualified majority is possible for decisions applying a common strategy defined by the European Council, as well as for any decisions implementing a joint action or common position already adopted by the council. This opens up new possibilities. There is, however, a safeguard clause, enabling states to block qualified majority voting for important reasons of national policy.

The Nice Treaty opened the possibility of 'Enhanced Cooperation' in the common foreign and security policy, to safeguard the values and serve the interests of the Union. But the Treaty limits enhanced cooperation to joint actions and common positions and stipulates that this enhanced cooperation shall not relate to matters with military or defence implications.

Cyprus, south of Turkey, has nearly 800,000 inhabitants, who are predominantly Greek orthodox. In the North there are mostly Turkish Muslims. Cyprus became independent from Britain in 1960 after years of resistance by the Greek Cypriot EOKA party that strived to be united with Greece. The new constitution allocated three out of ten minister positions, 30 percent of parliamentary seats and public service jobs, and 40 percent of army positions to the Turkish minority, which constituted 18 percent of the population.

Greek Cypriots proposed amendments to the constitution to reduce Turkish Cypriots influence. Three years after the independence these tensions became a violent conflict. The UN tried to encourage peace in 1964, but riots continued throughout the peacekeeping intervention. The UN Peacekeeping Force in Cyprus (UNFICYP) was unable to stop the violence that drove Turkish Cypriots into enclaves.

The conflict intensified when in 1974 the Greek military government attempted to take control of the island. In response, the Turkish army took control over vast areas of Northern Cyprus. UN peace talks failed and peacekeepers were sent to Cyprus to prevent a civil war. The country was divided into a northern area controlled by Turkish Cypriots, an area to the South under Greek Cypriot control, in the middle a UN buffer zone, and two British Sovereign Base Areas.

In 1983 the Turkish Republic of Northern Cyprus (TRNC) was declared. It was recognised by Turkey but other countries did not. Between 1992 and 1995, UN led peace talks failed to end the separation. The Greek part of Cyprus strove for entry in the EU.

A new round of UN peace talks resulted in the partial opening of the buffer zone. The Annan Plan tried to create a loose federation of the Greek Cypriot and the Turkish Cypriot parts. When 75 percent of the Greek Cypriots voted against it in the reunification referendum, while 65 percent of the Turkish Cypriots supported the plan, re-unification was blocked by the Greeks.

In 2004, Cyprus joined the EU. The southern section became part of the EU, whereas areas occupied by the Turkish community were not.

Both parties are to date unwilling to compromise. UN blue-helmet peacekeeping was successful in that it prevented renewed war since 1964, but UN peace talks failed due to intransigence of the parties and their parent states Greece and Turkey. Even the EU accession procedure was unable to bring the two parts together. Still, the EU may be able in due course to unite both parts.

The Nice treaty, in force since 2003, did make decisions of the Council somewhat easier. It states that if no members object to or call for a unanimous decision in the European Council (the so-called emergency brake), enhanced cooperation is adopted in the Council by a qualified majority, with a threshold of only eight member states. This provision is, however, rarely used.

An improvement already introduced with the Amsterdam Treaty is the appointment of a senior official to personify the CFSP. It was decided that the Secretary-General of the Council would also fulfil the role of 'High Representative' for the CFSP. Javier Solana Madariaga was the first to take up this post. His task is to improve the visibility and consistency of the CFSP, and lead the Policy Planning and Early Warning Unit. At the request of the presidency, he enters into political dialogues with third parties.

The Nice Treaty introduced qualified majority voting to appoint the Secretary-General of the Council (High Representative for the common foreign and security policy) and the deputy.[10]

The previous Amsterdam Treaty had already introduced the possibility for the Council to appoint special representatives for certain political issues. These representatives support the work of the High Representative by representing the EU in trouble spots. In 2006 there were Special Representatives for nine conflict regions: (1) Bosnia and Herzegovina, (2) the Former Yugoslav Republic of Macedonia (FYROM), (3) Central Asia, (4) Sudan, (5) Moldova, (6) the Middle East peace process, (7) the South Caucasus, (8) Afghanistan, and (9) the African Great Lakes Region. There was also a representative for the negotiations on the future status of Kosovo and a Special Coordinator for the Stability Pact for South-Eastern Europe.

7.2.4 SECURITY AND DEFENCE

The development of a European Security and Defence Policy (ESDP) within the common foreign policy CFSP is probably the most significant element of the post-conflict peacebuilding activities of the EU. The Maastricht Treaty had already determined that the CFSP would encompass all EU security issues, including "the eventual framing of a common defence policy" which could "in time lead to a common defence".[11] For the elaboration and implementation of decisions and actions, however, the EU needed to request action by the West European Union (WEU), which was determined to be an integral part of the development of the EU.

The Amsterdam Treaty went a step further by incorporating the so-called Petersberg tasks.[12] The Petersberg tasks were "humanitarian and rescue tasks, peacekeeping tasks, and tasks of combat forces in crisis management, including peacemaking".[13] They had been formulated during the 1992 conference of the ministers of Foreign Affairs and Defence of the WEU member states in the Petersberg Hotel near Bonn. The task of conflict prevention was added later.

Macedonia was a nation within the Republic of Yugoslavia. In 1991, Macedonia gained independence peacefully and entered the UN as the former Yugoslav Republic of Macedonia. A naming dispute with Greece continues as yet. The 2 million inhabitants are predominantly Macedonian with a substantial Albanian minority and smaller Turkish, Roma and Serbian ones.

Governed by socialist parties, Macedonia was not actively involved in the Yugoslav wars that took place in the nineties. The UN Preventive Deployment UNPREDEP of some 800 soldiers on the border with Serbia kept it out of the war. Ethnic tensions between Macedonians and Albanian citizens exacerbated when Macedonian nationalist parties came to power in 1998. In 1999, the country housed over 300,000 Kosovar Albanian refugees. The refugees returned to their homes after the Kosovo war.
In 1999, the ethnic Albanian National Liberation Army (NLA) targeted Macedonian security forces near the border of Kosovo, capturing small areas to the North and West. Ethnic Macedonians protested in the streets and attacked Albanian villages and the Muslim minority.
The Ohrid Agreement in June established a ceasefire. Albanian rebels agreed to give up separatist demands, disarm, and respect Macedonian government institutions in return for decentralization, increased participation in the government, police force and army, and acknowledgement of the Albanian language. The NATO and Macedonian army cooperated in the 30-day operation 'Essential Harvest' to retrieve weapons from the rebels. After a few shooting incidents, the ethnic war ended in 2002.
Macedonians were confronted by atrocities, but both sides managed to keep them relatively small. Macedonia was able to recover from this ethnic war, because the Ohrid agreement addressed the problem of ethnic inequality. Macedonia also proved that preventive involvement of a UN peace force can avoid war. International involvement remained limited to NATO's assistance in arms recollection. As Macedonia wants to become a member of the EU and NATO, both organizations had considerable positive influence on the Macedonian leadership to encourage it to award the Albanian minority its share of decision-making in government.

After a summit in Saint Malo in 1998 – which took place in the midst of the Kosovo crisis – France and Great Britain declared for the first time that the EU should have "the capacity for autonomous action, backed up by credible military forces, the means to decide to use them, and a readiness to do so, in order to respond to international crises".[14] This statement was endorsed during the European Council held in Cologne in June 1999 – immediately after the Kosovo war – and was included in a common declaration.

At the Helsinki European Council in December 1999, the member states set themselves the goal of being able to deploy rapidly [within sixty days] and then sustain [for at least one year] forces capable of the full range of Petersberg tasks as set out in the Amsterdam Treaty, including the most demanding, in operations up to army corps level (up to 15 brigades, or 50,000-60,000 military) by the year 2003.[15] The purpose of this European Rapid Reaction Force (ERRF) is "to intervene in crises before they become full-scale wars, and to release NATO from participating in some military interventions".[16] The ERRF undertook its first military mission on 31 March 2003 in Macedonia and was officially declared ready for action in May 2003.

The European Rapid Reaction Force can be used both separately and together with other international organisations. It can deploy at the request of the Organization for Security and Cooperation in Europe (OSCE) and the United Nations (UN). It can share expertise and resources with NATO, but it cannot deploy at the sole request of this alliance.[17] A Capabilities Development Mechanism (CDM) was created to avoid duplication between the EU and NATO and enhance communication between the two organisations. EU and NATO were already cooperating in Kosovo and in the Former Yugoslav Republic of Macedonia.

The Political and Security Committee (PSC) was established to manage the ESDP. This committee has to keep track of international developments, define policies and to monitor implementation[18]. It is assisted by (1) the Politico-Military Group, which examines the political-military aspects of all proposals within the framework of the CFSP, (2) the Civilian Crisis Management Committee, which is established to improve relations between military and civilian components, (3) the European Union Military Committee EUMC, which gives military advice to the PSC as well as to the High Representative for the CFSP, and (4) the EU Military Staff EUMS, which is part of the Secretariat of the Council and is responsible for early warning, strategy planning and situation assessment.

As civilian aspects have often been neglected by the international community in peace operations, an EU civilian crisis management capability has been developed. At the Göteborg European Council of 2001 four instruments for this civilian management capability were launched: (1) police action, (2) rule of law, (3) civil administration, and (4) civil protection.[19] With regard to police action, the objective is to create the possibility of providing up to 5000 policemen – including 1000 within 30 days – for various tasks, ranging from restoring order in cooperation with a military force to the training of local police. With respect to the rule of law, the EU attempts to be able to contribute up to 200 officials – judges, prosecutors and other specialists – to supplement police in the criminal justice process. In the field of civilian administration, the aim is to dispose of a pool of experts – capable of deployment within a short timeframe – who can offer their expertise in the field of civil registration, taxation, education, water supply, etc. Regarding civil protection, the objective is to be able to assist humanitarian actors through emergency operations. Here the EU is expected to be capable of providing two or three assessment and/or coordination teams consisting of ten experts that can be dispatched within three to seven hours, as well as civil protection intervention teams consisting of up to 2000 persons at short notice.

The Göteborg European Council paid special attention to cooperation with other international organisations in civilian aspects of crisis management. Guidelines were set to ensure that the EU should add to the work of other international organisations in conflict prevention and crisis management.[20] It should learn from their experiences and make sure that its work will be compatible with those other organisations. EU action is expected, however, to be visible as EU contributions, also when the EU only adds to the work of others. The EU can also be tasked to take the lead in an international peace support operation.[21]

In late 2003, the European Council held in Brussels adopted for the first time a European Security Strategy. This strategy states that the member states aim to tackle their security priorities in a framework that emphasises multilateral institutions and the rule of law. Since the EU only has limited military power itself, the strategy highlights that priority security objectives should be addressed through effective 'multilateralism', whatever form that may take.

7.2.5 EUROPEAN AGENCY FOR RECONSTRUCTION

The European Agency for Reconstruction (EAR) was established in February 2000 as the main reconstruction arm of the European Union in Kosovo. The ongoing activities of the agency were formally confirmed and expanded to Serbia and Montenegro in December 2000.[22] At that time, a general legal framework for EC assistance for Albania, Bosnia and Herzegovina, Croatia, the then Federal Republic of Yugoslavia and the Former Yugoslav Republic of Macedonia was established by the so-called Community Assistance for Reconstruction, Development and Stabilisations (CARDS) Regulation.[23] The European Agency for Reconstruction would manage the majority of CARDS activities in the two areas that it covered. In December 2001, the agency's activities were extended to the Former Yugoslav Republic of Macedonia.[24]

The EAR built on the experiences of the European Commission Task Force for the Reconstruction of Kosovo (EC TAFKO) – a temporary task force that was set up in the summer of 1999 to implement emergency programmes in Kosovo – and took over the completion of this task force as part of its 2000 programme.[25] The head-

Kosovo is located in the south of Serbia. Its population of 2 million is predominantly Albanian; the Serb minority is shrinking. Serbia and Kosovo used to be part of Yugoslavia. In 1989, Milosevic became president and abolished Kosovo's autonomy. Kosovo's Albanian leaders have been striving for independence since 1990.

The Republic of Yugoslavia fell apart in violent conflict as of 1991. Slovenia, Croatia, and Macedonia were the first to leave Yugoslavia. Bosnia declared independence in 1992. Milosevic attempted to strengthen with violent means Serbians living in adjacent territories.
In 1998, the insurgency of the Kosovo Liberation Army (KLA) provoked a counterinsurgency by Serbian forces. This caused many refugees and deaths. UN resolutions condemned the violence and urged a solution that respected the FRY's territorial integrity but restored Kosovo's autonomy. After the 1999 Rambouillet negotiations failed and the Serb forces continued violent practices, NATO initiated a 78-day bombing campaign against Serb military and infrastructural targets.

Subsequently, Kosovo's governance was taken over by the UN administration Mission in Kosovo (UNMIK) and the NATO-led KFOR troops to provide security. Kosovo developed governing institutions and witnessed its first parliamentary elections. In September 2000, Milosevic lost the FRY elections and Kostunica became president. Later that year the reformist Democratic Opposition of Serbia (DOS) won the Serb elections.
Montenegro declared independence from Serbia in 2006 after a referendum. Serbia then adopted a new constitution which assumes continued membership of Kosovo.

State-building in Kosovo is guided by the UN, the EU and OSCE. Suspects of war crimes appear for the International Criminal Tribunal for the former Yugoslavia. Many in the international community argue for Kosovo's independence under international tutelage, as suggested by the mediation report by Athisaari, but Serbia remains unwilling to grant independence. Kosovo's future is left in the hands of the divided UN Security Council.

The case of Kosovo shows that a humanitarian intervention can lead to secession, which requires long-term support to a weak, new state. Secession risks encouraging other secessions elsewhere. The second lesson is that the primary oppressing party (Serbs) can become an oppressed minority after external intervention. The international community should guarantee the rights of all to avoid reverse ethnic cleansing. A third lesson is that immediate deployment of a police and criminal justice assistance is needed after cease-fire.

quarters of the agency are in Thessaloniki in Greece, but there are operational centres in Pristina, Belgrade, Podgorica and Skopje.

The EAR is an independent agency of the European Union; it is accountable to the Council and the Parliament and is overseen by a Governing Board – which is composed of representatives of the 25 member states of the EU and the commission. The agency has managed a total of about € 2.6 billion since 2005. The EAR programmes are designed to support good governance, institution building and the rule of law as well as the development of a market economy. At the same time, the agency invests further in critical physical infrastructure, environmental protection, social development and the strengthening of civil society. Thus it aims at reinforcing the region's own reform processes by strengthening the 'state machinery' of central and local administration, the police, the judiciary, public finances and state utility providers. The areas that the EAR covers – Kosovo, Serbia and Montenegro and FYROM (Macedonia) – can also benefit from European Commission assistance not managed by the agency – which includes macro-financial, humanitarian, democratisation, customs and fiscal planning aid, support for higher education cooperation programmes, a Western Balkans' regional programme, and support for the European Union's contribution to the UN administration in Kosovo. Several EU member states also offer bilateral contributions to the region.

In 2005, the EU adopted a Civilian Capability Improvement Plan, which was followed by a Civilian Headline Goal 2008, to develop rapidly deployable civilian aid capabilities. Member states nominated 260 experts, of which the EU selected 100. Also EU police units were placed for rapid deployment. For military contributions to crisis management, the Headline Goal 2010 was set and possible contributions by member states were listed. A crucial weakness appeared to be strategic (large) airlift capacity. The EU continued to depend on other NATO members for such airlift capacity, especially the US.

7.3 FINANCING EU PEACEBUILDING ACTIVITIES

7.3.1 CFSP

The budget of the CFSP was still quite small, only € 62.6 million for the year 2005. This was considered inadequate for crisis management, which is a rapidly developing activity of the EU. Much larger in financial volume are the humanitarian assistance activities of the EU, and the sums managed by EU institutions for development, peacebuilding and human rights, as we will see below. In 2006, the total funds of the EU and its member states for development assistance amounted to € 58 billion, which forms well over half of the total Overseas Development Assistance from rich OECD countries, making the group of EU states the largest donor group in the world.

Georgia became independent from the USSR in 1991. Secessionist wars and severe economic crisis, as well as crime and corruption hampered statebuilding. The bloodless Rose Revolution of 2003 installed a new, reformist government, whose aspirations to join NATO and attempts at bringing breakaway territories back under Georgia's control led to poor relations with Russia. New elections in 2004 brought Saakashvilli to power with the National Movement party.

The secessionist regions Abkhazia and South Ossetia are ruled by unrecognized governments, supported by Russia. Russian-led peacekeeping operations continue in both regions. Georgia put forward a new peace initiative for the status of South Ossetia in 2005. Most of the troops have already been withdrawn by 2007, with the last remaining base in Batumi due to be evacuated in 2008.

The conflict in Abkhazia, strategically located on the Black Sea, began with social unrest and attempts by local authorities to separate from the Republic. It escalated into armed confrontations in 1992 when Georgia deployed 2,000 troops in Abkhazia. Fierce fighting resulted in some 200 dead, hundreds wounded and more than 20,000 Georgian refugees.

In the 13-month war between Georgian forces and separatist Abkhazians, Armenians and Russians, separatists were supported by North Caucasian and Cossack militants and Russian troops from Gudauta.

Russia and Georgia have agreed on 80 percent of their common border, leaving small, strategic segments and the maritime boundary unresolved; OSCE observers monitor volatile areas such as the Pankisi Gorge in the Akhmeti region and the Argun Gorge in Abkhazia. The UN Observer Mission in Georgia (UNIMOG) has maintained a peacekeeping force in Georgia since 1993. The boundary with Armenia remains undemarcated. Ethnic Armenians in the Javakheti region of Georgia seek autonomy from the Georgian government. Azerbaijan and Georgia continue to discuss their boundary.

Between 220,000-240,000 people are displaced from Abkhazia and South Ossetia (2006). A peacekeeping force of Russian troops is deployed in the Abkhazia region of Georgia with a UN military observer group (UNIMOG); a Russian peacekeeping battalion is deployed in South Ossetia.

The Georgian-Abkhaz peace process has remained stalled. UNOMIG continues daily

patrols, except in the upper Kodori Valley, where patrolling was suspended for security reasons. The local population in both sectors feels terrorised by armed groups. The Ceasefire Agreement of 1994 is repeatedly violated and restrictions on the freedom of movement of UNOMIG continue. Local law enforcement agencies are unable to curb serious crime.
There are acute food and medical needs of vulnerable segments of the population. Mine clearance and small-scale rehabilitation activities are hindered. There are serious human rights violations in Abkhazia and the Gali region.

7.3.2 ECHO

The European Community Humanitarian Aid Office (ECHO) – the European Commission's department for humanitarian aid – was established in 1992. In 1996 the office was given the mandate to provide emergency assistance and relief to the victims of natural disasters or armed conflict outside the European Union.[26] Seven objectives were defined:

(a) to save and preserve life during emergencies and their immediate aftermath and natural disasters that have entailed major loss of life, physical, psychological or social suffering or material damage;
(b) to provide the necessary assistance and relief to people affected by longer-lasting crises arising, in particular, from outbreaks of violence or wars, producing the same effects as described in (a), especially where their own governments prove unable to help, or where there is a vacuum of power;
(c) to help finance the transport of aid and efforts to ensure that it is accessible to those for whom it is intended, by all logistical means available, and by protecting humanitarian goods and personnel, but excluding operations with defence implications;
(d) to carry out short-term rehabilitation and reconstruction work, especially on infrastructure and equipment, in close association with local structures, with a view to facilitating the arrival of relief, preventing the impact of the crisis from worsening and starting to help those affected regain a minimum level of self-sufficiency, taking long-term development objectives into account where possible;
(e) to cope with the consequences of population movements (refugees, displaced people and returnees) caused by natural and man-made disasters and carry schemes to assist repatriation to the country of origin and resettlement there when the conditions laid down in current international agreement are in place;
(f) to ensure preparedness for risks of natural disasters or comparable exceptional circumstances and use a rapid early-warning and intervention system;
(g) to support civil operations to protect the victims of fighting or comparable emergencies.

ECHO has been financing emergency aid, food aid and aid to refugees and displaced persons amounting to more than € 500 million per year.[27] Aid has been provided in more than 85 countries through hundreds of partner organisations such as the Federation of Red Cross and Crescent Societies and the International Committee of the Red Cross (ICRC), the United Nations High Commissioner for Refugees (UNHCR) and the World Food Programme (WFP).

ECHO has two sources of funding: the general EC budget and the European Development Fund. These funds are also used to carry out studies for humanitarian operations, to monitor humanitarian projects, to provide training for humanitarian operations, to set up coordination, to provide technical assistance for humanitarian projects, to finance information campaigns and to fund mine-clearance operations.[28]

7.3.3 ERRM

The European Rapid Reaction Mechanism discussed above offers another financial source for peacebuilding activities. This mechanism was created in 2001 within the first pillar of the EU to allow the community to respond immediately to urgent situations.[29] The mechanism can be used when there is a threat to public order or public safety or in other circumstances that destabilise a country. It can provide financial aid in the short term – for no longer than six months – and it encompasses the activities that are not covered by ECHO. For instance, the ERRM was used to launch the EU contribution to the political, economic and social rebuilding of Afghanistan.

7.3.4 THE EUROPEAN INITIATIVE FOR DEMOCRACY AND HUMAN RIGHTS

The European Initiative for Democracy and Human Rights (EIDHR) encourages human rights and democracy in countries outside the European Union. This was prompted in 1994 by the European Parliament. A human rights and democracy committee started its work in July 1999. The committee assists the European Commission by advising on aid projects of at least € 1 million. Most of the aid is channelled through non-governmental organisations. About € 100 million is available per year for human rights, democratisation and conflict prevention support carried out with NGOs and other international organisations. Its support also includes international criminal tribunals and the International Criminal Court. EIDHR has also carried out training courses to create a pool of civilian experts in the rule of law and civilian administration and for deployment in crisis management missions. It has established a European network of professional training institutes and elaborated curricula for civilian crisis management courses, conflict prevention and peacebuilding. An evaluation of the training project showed no clear link to actual deployment in EU missions, however. The evaluation report recommended courses and seminars which are more tailored to specific missions.[30]

The European Union started sending observer missions to foreign elections in 1993 in Russia and in 1994 in South Africa. Since then, election assistance and observation have taken place in several other countries.

The EIDHR has four priorities for its financial aid: 1. democratisation, good governance and the rule of law; 2. abolition of the death penalty; 3. fighting torture and impunity, supporting international tribunals and criminal courts, and 4. fighting racism and discrimination against minorities and indigenous peoples. The funds of EIDHR for NGOs can be used without host government approval.

7.4 CONCLUSION

The EU is nowadays engaged in development assistance, improvement of civilian administration, and military peace operations in dozens of fragile, troubled states. The European Union and its members have, in comparison to other donors, a relatively large potential to encourage post-conflict peacebuilding, state building, democratisation, human rights and the rule of law. Almost all of the 27 member states are rule-of-law societies, even though the newest members still have an internal agenda of reform to carry out.

The EU is based on the common goal of the rule of law and full respect for human rights. The EU and its members are the largest source of international financial assistance to poor countries and represent 55 percent of the flow from rich OECD states to poor other states[31]. One-fifth of this 55 percent is managed by the European Commission, the other four-fifth through bilateral and other multilateral donor institutions. The resources of the EU for external assistance consist of joint assistance programmes (PHARE[32], TACIS[33], ALA[34], MEDA[35]), which amount to about € 5 billion per year. The European Development Fund spent an additional € 13.5 billion in the period 2000-2007 in African, Caribbean and Pacific countries. A small part of these assistance flows is available for the promotion of human rights, democracy and the rule of law.

In December 2006, the European Parliament approved a new budget law, enabling the European Development Cooperation Instrument DCI to commit almost € 12 billion between 2007 and 2013 for Asia, Latin America, the Middle East and South Africa. Another € 6 billion of this DCI budget is destined for additional thematic programs, cutting across countries, like health, education, gender equality, environment, food security and refugees. Other countries in Africa and the Caribbean and Pacific, which have a special relation with EU members, can receive commitments from the separate European Development Fund during 2008-2013 totalling € 22.7 billion.

Most of the EU assistance is for projects of recipient governments, and the larger part of this money is used for projects that aim to reduce poverty. Financial help for countries which are candidates for accession to the European Union gives relatively more attention for human rights and democracy questions than aid to other, third countries.

If the EU and its members would follow similar, coordinated policies, the EU could be the prime actor in rule-of-law support to troubled countries. This would even become much stronger if and when the EU members carry out their 2005 promise to devote 0.7 percent of their GNP to official development assistance. In 2006, only 4 out of 27 EU states were doing this. Those that lagged behind promised to increase aid to reach a level of 0.56 percent of GNP by 2010 and 0.7 percent by 2015. If this decision is implemented, it will increase resources for peacebuilding considerably.

The policy decisions and institutions created by the EU have prepared the EU in principle for an increase in rule-of-law support, which also enables the EU to shift more resources from economic aid to institution-building for the rule of law.

The attractiveness of membership of the EU to non-EU states gives the EU a special influence on applicant countries. To qualify for membership, applicants have to comply with the Copenhagen-criteria (in brief: democracy and human rights, stability, market economics, and good governance). The EU has large funds to help achieve these requirements. This offers the EU a strong influence in favour of democracy, rule of law, and human rights.

Strengthening border controls, police and other means to reduce trafficking of persons, drugs, weapons and illegal movement of money is a good example of assistance for the rule of law in other countries that directly serves also the national interests of the donors.

Support for the rule of law in weak states outside the EU offers the EU a possibility to advance its enlightened self-interest in the rule-of-law in neighbouring areas and carry out its vision and mission for European values as democracy and human rights. In doing so, it could give substance to its desire for a European identity, both distinct from and supportive of the foreign policies of other main democratic powers on the global scene.

There are, of course, also serious weaknesses of the EU, which limit the potential which was just outlined. First, the EU needs near-unanimity to take decisions on many subjects in the realm of external political affairs. EU members were deeply divided on the US-UK intervention in Iraq, which aimed at the removal of a dictatorship. The main difference was not on the values supporting this purpose, but on the basis which this intervention had in international law and the political prudence of this military action. The EU has shown greater coherence in other foreign policy goals, such as its European neighbourhood policy.

The requirement of near-unanimity continues to slow down possibilities to act swiftly. The draft constitution for the EU, rejected in referenda in France and the Netherlands, would have opened in due course some possibilities to further develop a European Common Foreign and Security Policy, which might lead to a stronger peacebuilding effort.

A crucial improvement of the role the EU can play has to await a new intergovernmental agreement which would improve the decision-making of the EU in external political affairs. An agreement to take foreign policy decisions by qualified majority voting seems unlikely in the foreseeable future, however. It might be possible to agree on a restricted form of qualified majority voting on foreign aid, in particular peacebuilding activities. Member states could determine the main goals and means for such assistance by consensus or near-unanimity (minus one or two members) and decide the implementation of that policy by qualified majority. The decision of the European Council of June 23, 2007 to negotiate a new treaty for the EU offers a new opportunity to strengthen the provisions for a peacebuilding role in the world which would measure up to the self-proclaimed vocation of the European Union in the 21st century as advocate of peaceful development.

In the absence of real improvements, a minimum of 8 members might use the option offered by the Treaty of Nice to enhance their cooperation in a particular field, under the conditions of this treaty, which exclude military action. Even as long as the possibilities for enhanced cooperation remain unutilised, the EU has many practical instruments and possibilities at its disposal to enlarge its peacebuilding role in support of the rule of law and human rights, as were shown in this chapter.

NOTES

1 Treaty of the European Union, Title V, Article 11.
2 Ibidem, Article 12.
3 Treaty of the European Union, Title V, Article 13.
4 Council Joint Action of 13 April 2000 (2000/298/CFSP).
5 Council Joint Action of 7 March 2005 (2005/190/CFSP).
6 Youri Devuyst, *De Nieuwe Europese Unie. Een Heldere Gids door de Europese Doolhof*: Brussels: Brussels University Press, 2004, p. 224.
7 Idem.
8 Common Strategy of the European Union of 4 June 1999 on Russia (1999/414/CFSP).
9 The First Pillar consists of the European Community for Coal and Steel, the European Community (before 1993 the European Economic Community), the European Community for Atomic Energy and the Economic and Monetary Union. In this pillar, decision-making on many issues is determined by weighted majority voting. Since 1999, also a part of the justice and internal affairs cooperation has been brought under the first pillar. The so-called Third Pillar regulates police and judicial cooperation among EU members.
10 Article 207.
11 Treaty of the European Union, Title V, Article J.4.
12 Amsterdam Treaty, 1997, Article 17.
13 West European Union Council of Ministers, Bonn, 19 June 1992, 'Petersberg Declaration', http://www.weu.int/documents/920619peten.pdf.
14 'Joint Declaration issued at the British-French Summit, Saint-Malo, France, 3-4 December 1998'.
15 'Helsinki Headline Goal', http://ue.eu.int/uedocs/cmsUpload/Helsinki%20Headline%20Goal.pdf. (consulted 12 March 2006).
16 Chris Lindborg, *The EU Rapid Reaction Force: Europe Takes on a New Security Challenge*, British American Security Information Council, Paper No. 37, 2001, http://www.basicint.org/pubs/Papers/BP37.htm (consulted 26 March 2006).
17 Idem.
18 Nice Treaty, 2001, Article 25.
19 *Presidency Report to the Göteborg European Council on European Security and Defence Policy*, 2001, p. 23-34, http://register.consilium.eu.int/pdf/en/01/st09/09526-r1en1.pdf.
20 Ibidem, p. 49.
21 Ibidem, p. 49-50.
22 Council Regulation (EC) of 5 December 2000 (No 2667/2000).
23 Council Regulation (EC) of 5 December 2000 (No 2666/2000).
24 Council Regulation (EC) of 10 December 2001 (No 2415/2001).
25 European Agency for Reconstruction, http://www.ear.eu.int/agency/agency.htm (consulted 3 April 2006).
26 Council Regulation (EC) of 20 June 1996 (No 1257/96).

27 ECHO, http://europa.eu.int/comm/echo/finances/budget_en.htm (consulted 3 April 2006). The total expenditure in 2005 ran up to € 654 million.

28 Council Regulation (EC) of 20 June 1996 (No 1257/96).

29 Council Regulation (EC) of 26 February 2001 (No 381/2001).

30 "Training on civilian aspects of crisis management", January 2006, Human European Consultancy in Utrecht. www.humanconsultancy.com.

31 www.europa.eu.int/comm/external_relations/gac/index.htm.

32 Assistance to EU candidate countries in Middle and Eastern Europe.

33 Assistance to countries of the Commonwealth of Independent States, many of which used to belong to the USSR.

34 Assistance to developing countries in Asia and Latin America.

35 MEDA is the assistance given to countries around the Mediterranean which participate in the Barcelona process.

Lebanon used to be a prosperous, multi-cultural state but was almost destroyed by foreign interventions and internecine wars. Its 4 million inhabitants are predominantly Arab with an Armenian minority. Nicknames for Beirut like 'Paris of the Middle East' and 'banking capital of the Arab world' signify the country's wealth during the twentieth century.

Lebanon gained independence in 1943. Its political system of confessional representation gave the Christian minority much influence. The Lebanese National Movement voiced Muslim leftist opposition. In 1975, sectarian civil war broke out. Palestinians assassinated two leading Maronites (Christians). Opposing sides formed militias. The Lebanese army could not contain inter-religious strife. On black Saturday, nearly 600 people were murdered, which led to all-out-fighting.

The war paused in 1976, after a Syrian dominated Arab Detention Force intervention, and Arab League mediation. The West was occupied by Christian militias, the East by Syrian troops and the South by Muslim militias receiving support from the Palestine Liberation Organization (PLO).

In 1977-1978 Palestinian attacks on Israel from Lebanese territory provoked retaliation. Israel occupied southern Lebanon. Israel violated the ceasefire in 1982 and invaded Lebanon after Palestinians had initiated a counterattack. Israel marched towards Beirut and forced the PLO's withdrawal causing many civilian casualties along the way. In the mid-eighties, two international interventions stabilized the country, but chaos returned after foreign troops left. Sectarian-strife re-emerged during the late eighties. Lebanon became a proxy battleground for other tensions in the Middle East.

The war ended in the early nineties when constitutional amendments created an equal distribution of parliamentary seats among Christians and Muslims. The majority of militias slowly disarmed. Hezbollah violently opposed Israeli occupation, which was lifted in 2000. In 2005 Hariri and other prominent Lebanese figures were assassinated. Mass protests led Syrian troops to retreat, known as the cedar revolution.

The 2006 July War between Hezbollah and Israel destroyed the largely rebuild economy, infrastructure and political stability. Both sides claimed success but lost considerably.
The UN decided to renew its peacekeeping mission UNIFIL and sent 13,000 UN soldiers from 30 countries who try to keep the peace in the south together with 15,000 Lebanese government troops.

Syrians, Palestinians, Israeli's, Iraqi's and Iranians used the Lebanese civil strife to carry on their own battles. The brief international interventions have not contributed much to solving the problems underlying the war. Lebanon would benefit more from a long-term international peace force that helps to build the rule of law and a political system of multi-party equilibrium. Interference of neighbouring states and regional extremist movements remains a constant threat.

8 CONCLUSIONS AND RECOMMENDATIONS

"Let there be a community of you who invite to what is good, advocate righteousness, and forbid evil. These are the winners."

Qur'an, Sura 3:104

What can be learned from the previous exploration of many attempts at peacebuilding and rule of law reform? How can policies be improved? There are neither sound-bite lessons nor quick fixes. We can only try to give an overview, based on our still incomplete reading of case studies (in 2005-7) and visits to a number of peacekeeping and peacebuilding operations (in the period 1984 – 2005). We refer to the limitations set out in chapter 1. Recent, very sobering experience in Iraq and Afghanistan could only be partially included. This exploration was written during the ongoing operations in those countries. These two unfolding, vexing cases and many current emergencies in Africa deserve further study. It seems possible, however, to give, on this incomplete basis, some suggestions for future improvement of peacebuilding operations.

8.1 GENERAL CONCLUSIONS

What can be observed in many peacebuilding programmes for helping countries establish rule of law after (civil) wars could be summarised as follows: the efforts are too little, too late, too short, too fragmented and too foreign. Yet peacebuilding projects are very necessary for humanitarian reasons (human security). They are extremely valuable investments in socio-economic progress.

1. The cost of a standard complete UN peacebuilding operation in a low-income country of 10 million inhabitants *with the consent of the parties* during 10 years is estimated at € 1.8 billion a year. The cost of a heavy complete peacebuilding operation *with military enforcement* in a similar country but a hostile environment is estimated at € 16 billion a year. We refer to section 6.8 for the sources, calculations and assumptions. If the world community undertook one heavy (green-helmet) and nine standard (UN blue-helmet) peacebuilding operations lasting on average 10 years in countries totalling 100 million people, the annual cost would amount to 3 percent of global military and development aid expenditures. Most of the states that enjoy peace themselves have a large financial and military capacity for peacebuilding in troubled states. At present, only 1.5 percent of active military troop strength in the world is used in all peace operations combined (even including the heavy US involvement in Iraq, which is not a UN peace operation.) These orders of magnitude show that UN peacebuilding operations need not be excessive in cost and may, on the contrary, be excellent investments in stability, rule of law, and human and economic progress.

2. The legitimacy under international law is an extremely important factor which strongly contributes to the chances of success. If there is no UN Security Council mandate, the acceptance the population and warring parties of the intervention by the international community may be low. Lack of cooperation and weak authority increase the duration, costs and casualties. International burden sharing among UN members and regional organisations is very uneven when legitimacy is disputed. This puts a heavy responsibility on the veto-holding Great Powers in the Security Council. They can make or break peace operations which many other nations would advocate, or would, on the contrary, deem ill-advised. We refer to the text-boxes on the responsibility to protect and criteria for military interventions.

3. It is important to avoid that UN peacekeepers, police and civilian personnel represent mostly the Western powers. Wide representative participation of personnel from various countries, cultures and religions is important to reflect the universalistic intent of peace operations. This puts a strong responsibility on non-Western nations with means to come forward and share burdens. The problem is not that OECD countries are doing too much, but that other countries are often doing too little. A particular scarcity is participation of Islamic countries in peace operations for the benefit of other Islamic countries in need. Reformist members of the Arab League and the Conference of Islamic States may want to play a much larger role in the near future.

4. From the previous observations follows that it would be ill-advised for NATO to aspire to the role of a global peacekeeping organisation. It is true that NATO is the largest and most capable military alliance in the world, which the UN Security Council can use to perform heavy peacekeeping operations for which it gives its mandate. The Security Council could consider making special combinations of NATO and non-Western states for complex peace missions outside the European area, for various reasons discussed above.

5. What is commonly underestimated in peace-operations is the need to rapidly impose basic public order and security after the end of combat. The population usually experiences a crime surge after cease-fire, while it yearns for personal security and emergency assistance. International organisations and foreign donors often leave a public security gap after a ceasefire is achieved and before peacekeeping and peacebuilding activities begin. This security gap coincides with the 'window of opportunity' to set the country on track towards new government and lasting reform. This window requires fast decisions and early action.

6. This means that an assessment of a country's needs has to be made well in advance, long before an intervention, and well before the end of combat operations between the warring parties. The warning signals are there of countries in trouble, of failing and collapsing states. Much of politics is unpredictable, but the indications in the international media and indices like the Failing States Index (Chapter 3) can help to avoid nasty surprises. Peacebuilding should start with a

thorough analysis of the history, politics, geography, culture, sociology and legal systems of the country. All countries and wars are different. Experience of previous peace operations gives guidance, but cannot offer solutions of the one-size-fits-all type. Before promises are made, a thorough feasibility study should answer the questions which limited goals should be set and what might be attained during a sustainable number of years (about 10) with reasonably available funds and personnel.

7. Peacebuilding needs to respond to the domestic demand of the local and national population groups for peace and justice. Domestic civil society must play a major role, and needs encouragement to develop and diversify. Donors should start by taking these domestic desires into account. They should impose neither the Westminster Model nor most other foreign inventions. If most of the population believes, for instance, in Islamic law, it is Islamic law that must provide the beginnings for domestic peacebuilding and legal reform, while those elements of Islamic or other law that are not in agreement with international human rights treaties, such as discrimination of women and harsh punishments, should be reformed step by step. Rapid imposition of very foreign laws and legal concepts is likely to fail after the donors leave. If the legal and justice sector is a heterogeneous mix of colonial heritage, local customary law, religious laws, communist laws and imported modern commercial law, the recipient government and political leaders must determine the desired nature of the future system. Foreign experts can analyse the options and give advice on their consequences, but generally cannot make the choices that national leaders have to make.

8. Too little international attention to the police and judicial sector is a common feature of development aid programmes since they started in the 1960s and '70s. After a war is ended, donors typically withdraw quickly from the security sector and focus instead on the economic development of the country. They tend to leave other areas of activity 'within the domestic jurisdiction' to the government of the country, thinking that the legal sector is very much the sovereign concern of the country, too political to meddle with, and not in their direct interest. This used to be an often repeated mistake, but since the middle of the '90s many assistance programs started to include reform of this sector. These efforts deserve to be stepped up.

9. Much of 'too late' is due to lengthy donor deliberations about new aid programmes. Donors need time to shift current activities that were not foreseen in their budgets, and valuable months can be lost after a cease-fire. Undefeated warlords and war profiteers continue to determine the scene for the new government and the police and judicial sector. Once international assistance arrives, many crucial positions are already taken. The old functionaries remain powerful. The formative phase or 'rebirth' of the country is going wrong. It is often impossible to correct afterwards the missed opportunities and mistakes made in the first three months after the new start. This means that 'first aid' policies should avoid determining the future reform track.

Democratic Republic Congo

The conflict in the DRC is one of the world's worst humanitarian crises since the late 1990s. Most armed clashes took place in the Eastern mineral-rich North- and South Kivu, Katanga and Ituri between militias from within and outside of Congo and the Congolese Army FARDC. The UN deployed a small peace-keeping mission since 2000 to reinforce state building and oversee the instalment of an elected government.

The conflicts have various economic, historical and cultural causes. The legacy of the Mobutu dictatorship with patronage networks caused an unequal distribution of income and access to land and resources along ethnic lines. Population movements from earlier conflicts in Uganda and the Rwandese genocide in 1994 intensified the pressure on the rich natural resources.

War broke out in 1998 when president Kabila moved to purge Rwandans from his government. Rwandan troops invaded backing Congolese Tutsi. Kabila called on Zimbabwe, Angola and Namibia for help. An estimated 4 million people died in the ensuing conflict between 1998 and 2004, mostly from war-related diseases and starvation. State parties, later joined by non-state actors, signed a ceasefire in Lusaka in July 1999, allowing the UN Security Council to send a peacekeeping mission (MONUC) in 2000. Violence continued, fuelled by Congo's mineral wealth. Peace negotiations continued throughout 2002 to get withdrawal of Rwandan and Ugandan troops in exchange for the demobilisation and disarmament of Rwandan Hutu rebels in DRC territory. By the end of 2002 Rwanda and Uganda claimed full withdrawal from the DRC, although proxies remained. In December 2002 all Congolese belligerents and political groups signed a peace deal which led to a transitional government. The son of Kabila became the first elected government in 40 years.

In the Eastern provinces, fighting continued over land and mineral wealth. Ethnic militias continued murderous raids on villages. The UN mission MONUC did not have the means and manpower to prevent all these attacks. This UN operation strongly combated criminal military gangs and spoilers of the peace and the election process with only a small UN force.

The country and its problems are too large, however, for a really effective peace- and state building operation which would have long-lasting results. The resources made available to the UN were too small. It is unclear how stable Congo will remain.

10. 'Too little, too late' also has another cause: it takes usually at least three months to free experts from current tasks to send them abroad on a peacebuilding mission. Experts from various countries need to learn to work together. Particularly in the area of police assistance, the language training and professional levels are often inadequate. Sometimes large numbers of 'experts' offered by some donor countries are hardly professional and should be refused for lack of basic abilities, but diplomatic considerations make rejection of incompetent personnel difficult. If international advisors establish little authority, they remain ineffective. A related problem is that many international functionaries who are accepted continue to follow national directives, rather than their international superiors, who derive their powers from the UN, EU, or other organizations.

11. In the first months after cease fire, all needs seem urgent and everything has to be done at once – which is simply not possible. Foreign aid is limited, promised experts are still to arrive, and the absorptive capacity of the indigenous administration and civil society organisations is still low. Keen sequencing of urgent actions is unavoidable. This sequence will differ from country to country. It may be useful, as a general guideline, to look at schedule 8.1

It goes without saying that optimal and feasible sequencing differs from case to case and depends heavily on the resources that are made available. The earlier certain subjects can be started, the better.

12. A frequent criticism of international aid is poor donor coordination. Peacebuilding requires a coherent approach, coordinated by an influential international organisation, or the largest, or most active member, of a group of like-minded states.
Donors want different things due to different interests, notably their national foreign policy goals, or the aid resources they happen to have available. They differ on the diagnosis of what the recipient needs. As international assistance is not just a humanitarian but also an economic activity, even the most idealistic organisations and people want to emphasise their identities, plant their flags and criticise others' short-sightedness and seeming self-interest. It is a Herculean task to combine all international donors, large and small, official and private, into one well-oiled machine. For example, in Bosnia after 1995, some 450 donor organisations were working next to each other. The EU and UN representatives had a hard time coordinating all this. Recipient governments are generally too weak and dependent to force donors to coherence. The few national unctionaries capable of organising productive donor visits and meetings may have a full-time job in receiving foreign delegations of ministers, experts, parliamentary committees and other dignitaries. It is the donors who should shoulder more responsibility for getting their act together, not the recipients.
External influence and assistance for improvement of the legal order in a country can only be strong if major external powers and international organisations act in unison.

Table 8.1 INDICATIVE TIME LINE OF OPTIMAL SEQUENCING

END OF COMBAT >>>	**STABILISATION >>>**	**REFORM >>>**
Negative peace >>>	*Secure public order >>>*	*Positive peace >>>*
PARTY NEGOTIATIONS		
MAIN POWER PRESSURE		
MEDIATION		
UN RESOLUTIONS AND MANDATE		
CEASEFIRE		
PEACE AGREEMENT		
PEACE IMPLEMENTATION FORCE		
CONSTABULARY FORCE		
EMERGENCY ASSISTANCE		
	INFRASTRUCTURE REPAIRS	
	DISARMAMENT, DEMOBILISATION, DEMINING, BASIC PUBLIC SERVICES	
	PUBLIC WORKS /EMPLOYMENT GENERATION	
	RESETTLEMENT OF IPD'S AND REFUGEES	
	ANTI-CORRUPTION PROGRAM	
	SECURITY SECTOR REFORM	
	POLICE REFORM	
	COURT REFORM	
		CONSTITUTIONAL REFORM
	TRANSITIONAL JUSTICE	
	RECONCILIATION MEASURES	
	WAR CRIMES TRIBUNALS	
		ECONOMIC REFORMS
		PRIVATE SECTOR
		ELECTORAL REFORM
		HUMAN RIGHTS REFORMS
		GENDER REFORMS
		BASIC HEALTH REFORMS
		EDUCATIONAL REFORMS
		OTHER REFORMS

13. If one or more major powers pursue very different purposes, like increasing the imports of oil, gas, precious metals or minerals from that country, and continue to support a 'cooperative' corrupt regime in the country concerned, the influence of others, who are acting in favour of the rule of law, will be severely undercut.

Increasing energy demand and competition among main importing states seriously undermines efforts to strengthen the rule of law and human rights in many weak or corrupt states, due to two mechanisms. First, large export revenues strengthen thedomestic regime and weaken reform-advocating donors which may also be dependent on these exports. Second, domestic advocates of reform are made powerless if a corrupt regime receives large revenues from foreign supporters. The quest for energy and other raw materials divides outside powers, by giving a premium to those who do not participate in an attempt to reform the regime. Coordination of the policies of major powers may become more difficult in the future vis-à-vis countries which possess large energy and metal resources. Coordination is the task of the UN Security Council, the G-8, and other multilateral forums. At the very least, NATO and EU members can avoid undercutting each other.

14. Coordination needs to be organised in concentric circles and should not exclude neighbouring states, even if they seem hostile to the peacebuilding operation. Brushing them aside as unwelcome guests and shunning them in international diplomacy, only makes things worse and pushes their actions into the dark. One could imagine four linked circles of coordination:

a. UN, host country government and main donors and international organisations;
b. all donor countries, large and small;
c. UN, NGOs and domestic civil society;
d. UN, organisations of the region and neighbouring states, including cultural and religious international organisations.

Of course, the composition, mix and interconnections have to be designed case by case.

15. Adding emergency and development projects to peacebuilding and rule-of-law support increases the participation and rewards for the population and local leaders and helps overcome past divisions. Examples are various basic needs projects (water, food, health care, shelter, education and employment). Rapid emergency aid may determine the chance of success of all following programs. A malnourished, desperate population, on the run because of counter-insurgency operations, may turn against international peacekeepers and foreign aid workers, to side with local insurgents.

16. Peacebuilding programmes need to be better evaluated during and after completion. Only a few donors have done so (notably Norway, Canada and the World Bank), and their experiences are varied. Our exploration of many different cases has led to the conclusion that similar mistakes are made over and over again.

17. Peacebuilding should be impartial in the sense that strict equality under the law is followed, but it should not be neutral by ignoring which groups and people continue to upset the peace and which are likely to strengthen it. Neutrality that turns a blind eye on warlords and hate mongers is likely to increase the risk of future violence by aiding unwittingly aggressor parties. All peacebuilding is intervention in the power relationships in a society full of violent tensions and conflicts.

Interior power players are jockeying for position and political, economic, military, tribal, ideological, religious and – foremost – personal gains. Foreign diplomats, politicians, donors and international organisations which negotiate and assist national and local leaders change the domestic power configuration, as they strengthen some and weaken others. This may be well-intended, but can be poorly informed, and can run counter to the feelings and convictions of many local and national groups. It is often difficult to assess how representative those leaders are who claim to represent 'their' parts of 'the population'. Financial and military aid strengthens some leaders and weakens others, who do not push themselves into the picture and are left out. Those leaders who see the aid dollars streaming, are inclined to please foreign donors with promises of peacebuilding behaviour and the rule of law, human rights and democracy. But will they keep those promises once the foreign donors leave? Even impartial international assistance for electoral democracy is not a neutral intervention. It strengthens some and weakens others. Are the candidates for elections really the most democratic and representative, and the most peaceful? Or do they use international support to usurp their offices soon after electoral legitimisation? This has happened too often to ignore. Foreign donors have to face and answer these difficult questions before they act.

18. The strong urge to intervene to counter human rights violations in failing states or oppressive governments is generally a response to indignation of media and public opinion. But is the urge to intervene militarily always guided by a thorough analysis of short and long term effects on the population at risk? Under the pressure of international publicity, there is sometimes a risk of political and diplomatic posturing. This can lead to half-hearted or ill-designed interventions. Moreover, good intentions can lead to bad results. Damage that may be done to another state or society may not be immediately discernable, and can manifest itself late, when opportunities for more prudent non-military action may have passed. The need to reflect on unintended consequences before intervening shows how important it is to make in time a *social and anthropological impact study*, next to the usual military assessment of intervention options.

19. Peacebuilding takes at least ten years, as a rule of thumb, if not two or three decades to achieve lasting results. Donors should realise this before they start. Projects that are prematurely aborted by donor fatigue and a short media attention span may in the end do more harm than good. Donors respond to needs as they are featured in the media, and the media soon turns to other, newsworthy crises. Policy makers in many Western countries prefer 'quick fixes'. There is often little understanding for the historical roots of the problems to be solved. Most donor governments and electorates do not like long-term commitments, so results have to be measurable in the short run. Funds are limited and there are, indeed, so many other needs elsewhere. Donors are sometimes content with the appearance of results and less worried about sustainability. Most diplomats and foreign experts serve only a few years in the recipient country.

The responsibility to protect

In recent years the debate about military intervention for humanitarian purposes has intensified. There are many examples of in-action (e.g. Rwanda), late action (e.g. Cambodia) or wrong and weak action (e.g. Bosnia 1993-5 and Darfur). Traditional views of state sovereignty conflict with modern views of the responsibility of states. The International Commission on Intervention and State Sovereignty (ICISS) was established to provide guidelines. It recommends 'The Responsibility to Protect' (2001). The international community embraced this principle at the UN World Summit 2005.

(1) Basic Principles

A. State sovereignty implies responsibility, and the primary responsibility for the protection of its people lies with the state itself.

B. Where a population is suffering serious harm, as a result of internal war, insurgency, repression or state failure, and the state in question is unwilling or unable to halt or avert it, the principle of non-intervention yields to the international responsibility to protect.

(2) Foundations

The foundations of the responsibility to protect, as a guiding principle for the international community of states, lie in:

A. obligations inherent in the concept of sovereignty;

B. the responsibility of the Security Council, under Article 24 of the UN Charter, for the maintenance of international peace and security;

C. specific legal obligations under human rights and human protection declarations, covenants and treaties, international humanitarian law and national law;

D. the developing practice of states, regional organizations and the Security Council itself.

(3) Elements

The responsibility to protect embraces three specific responsibilities:

A. **The responsibility to prevent:** to address both the root causes and direct causes of internal conflict and other man-made crises putting populations at risk.

B. **The responsibility to react:** to respond to situations of compelling human need with appropriate measures, which may include coercive measures like sanctions and international prosecution, and in extreme cases military intervention.

C. **The responsibility to rebuild:** to provide, particularly after a military intervention, full assistance with recovery, reconstruction and reconciliation, addressing the causes of the harm the intervention was designed to halt or avert.

(4) Priorities

A. Prevention is the single most important dimension of the responsibility to protect: prevention options should always be exhausted before intervention is contemplated, and more commitment and resources must be devoted to it.

B. The exercise of the responsibility to both prevent and react should always involve less intrusive and coercive measures being considered before more coercive and intrusive ones are applied.[1]

Programmes may fall to pieces after a few years. Excuses are easy to find: the recipient country does not have the proper culture, its people lack training, or corruption destroyed 'the good work we started'. Moreover, donors get worn out after a few years.

20. Improving the police and judicial sector should start with a profound analysis of the weakest spots in the system. Haphazard assistance to weak services may actually worsen the situation. If the police system is strengthened by international assistance, but the judiciary and the prisons remain as bad as they used to be, a well-intentioned programme to improve police capacity can actually strengthen the means of suppression.

21. Private military and security firms have become frequent and important participants in many operations. Their work, responsibility and liability need to be regulated in comprehensive contracts. Their tasks should be restricted as soon as possible to training and advising domestic security services. Private security services often serve for long periods of time to bolster indigenous police and detention capacity. The legal liability and who is responsible for their use of arms should always be clearly regulated in contracts.

22. Various weapons, particularly small arms, have to be collected and their possession restricted to reduce the risk that group violence erupts again. Buy-back programmes and exchange for much-desired goods (building materials, petrol, etc.) are required. This needs to be supported by a new international treaty limiting the sale and transportation of small and light weapons to others than legitimate authorities. We refer to the text box on the scourge of small arms.

23. A particularly difficult task of peacebuilding is re-socialising child soldiers. In Africa, there are armies of very young children, made orphans by war or kidnapped from their communities, who have not had normal upbringings, but are brainwashed by beliefs that turned them into 'warrior machines'. How to re-educate them, how to give them a normal sense of conscience and a feeling for values that are essential for constructive civilian life, is a daunting therapeutic task of social psychology. In the present brief study, the experience gained with this task was not evaluated. It is an extremely important question for peacebuilding in sub-Saharan Africa.

24. In or near many war zones, large numbers of refugees and displaced persons flock or are driven together, often for many years. They are 'warehoused' in camps or enclaves, which often turn into overcrowded, makeshift slum cities with very high levels of crime. Millions of people live there in limbo. The host country's resources and refugee aid organisations are usually not able to guarantee safety and minimal rule of law. These camps are recruiting grounds for political extremism and violent crime. Criminals hide among the refugees and often go unpunished. Some receive asylum in other countries and hide their

war records. The often near-explosive situation in these camps makes peace negotiations and peacebuilding very difficult. Refugee camps can spread civil war or 'state failure' to neighbouring states. New solutions should be found to resettle inhabitants of permanent refugee camps in more promising conditions elsewhere.

25. Peacebuilding is not just removing the causes of a distinct, incidental civil war or imposing peace and rule of law from the outside. Peacebuilding is encouraging the growth of domestic institutions, laws and attitudes needed for non-violent settlement of all kinds of conflicts. Conflicts will continue to arise. It is this institution-building, and the training of people to train others for the next generation, which enables peacebuilding to reach its objective: the rule of law in a state of peace, in both senses of the word 'state'.

8.2 RECOMMENDATIONS

The exploration in the previous chapters of main questions that arise in peacebuilding operations in countries that have suffered war, civil war, contemporary armed conflict and other forms of massive political violence, leads to some general recommendations for donor institutions (governments, international organisations and NGOs, where applicable).

8.2.1 STRENGTHEN INTERNATIONAL ORGANIZATIONS FOR PEACEBUILDING

1. It is of great importance that the new Peacebuilding Commission of the UN, a large new advisory body, focuses its work in smaller subcommittees of leading donors to coordinate the often fragmented contributions of various institutions, and that the European Union and its members provide leadership in this global institution by acting with one voice.

2. The European Union and its members form the *largest* source of funds for peacebuilding and rule-of-law support. To become also the most *effective* actor, the EU needs to improve the speed and consistency of its decision-making and the efficiency of its operations. The unanimity rule slows down and weakens the potential beneficial influence of the EU. With 27 and soon even more members, it is necessary to move from unanimity to consensus (near-unanimity) and gradually to qualified majority. This requires an improvement of the Nice-treaty. Such changes may become possible in the near future on the basis of the agreement of June 23, 2007 on an improved treaty. Even before such new legal possibilities are approved for the entire EU, the provisions of the Nice-treaty for enhanced cooperation of at least 8 members might be used for the purposes of post-conflict peacebuilding.
All EU-members may come to realise that they can be the strongest actor in the field of peacebuilding in the world once they overcome their fragmented decision-making. Such a role for the EU would also improve its influence in global international organizations that are important to the rule of law. A united EU

Darfur (Sudan)

One of the worst humanitarian crises of the early 21st century is in Darfur, a large western region of Sudan. Its 6 million inhabitants are mainly dependent on subsistence agriculture. Historical tensions between African farmer tribes and Arab nomads about scarce water and land frequently led to conflicts. Desertification and periods of droughts reinforced this in recent years. Lake Chad to the east is shrinking.

In February 2003, two rebel groups, the Justice and Equality Movement (JEM) and the Sudan Liberation Army (SLA), attacked government installations. These groups accused the Sudanese government of political and economic marginalization of Darfur. The government had most of its own troops located in the south and encouraged Arab militias, Janjaweed, to fight opponents in Darfur. These militias launched a campaign that also targeted countless civilians. This devastating civil war between rebel groups and a coalition of government troops and Janjaweed militias has caused at least 200,000 deaths and more than 2 million refugees. A UN commission of inquiry found evidence that severe crimes against humanity were committed, including systematic killings of civilians, sexual violence, forced displacements, torture, and enforced disappearances. Human Rights Watch and Amnesty International confirm this. Some countries, including the US, called the situation in Darfur genocide. The conflict is also threatening the stability of eastern Chad.

The international community reacted slowly and failed to stop this crisis. The Security Council has been very slow to authorize a UN peacekeeping force. The peace negotiations that would end the war between the North and the South were almost finished and the international community feared that an intervention in Darfur would disrupt this peace process. China has large oil interests at stake in Sudan. China and Russia supply the government with weapons. These countries also adhere to the non-intervention principle. The US is already heavily engaged in Iraq. The controversial war in Iraq has increased reluctance towards military interventions in general.

International jurists and human rights organizations argued that the international community must act upon its recently accepted principle of 'the Responsibility to Protect' which states that "where a population is suffering serious harm (...) and the state in question is unwilling or unable to halt or avert it, the principle of non-intervention yields to the international responsibility to protect". However, it seems that stopping the humanitarian crisis in Darfur is not in the direct interest of members of the Security Council.

Although the Security Council did not yet send a UN peacekeeping mission, it did establish an arms embargo and referred the situation in Darfur to the International Criminal Court. It has also authorized an African Union peacekeeping mission (AMIS) to monitor the ceasefire of N'Djamena (2004). This mission largely failed because of a lack of resources and a weak mandate. Insufficient troop levels, training, equipment, and logistics make it almost impossible for AMIS to respond to attacks. AU capacities in command, planning, and information management should be strengthened.

After a new peace agreement in 2006, a combined UN and AU peacekeeping force is being prepared, but this will not be operational before 2008. Jan Pronk, the UN Special Representative and head of UNMIS, was expelled by the government of Sudan at the end of 2006. Questions remain about the willingness of the government of Sudan to really stop the slaughter and hunger. Khartoum has hindered and delayed a UN peacekeeping force, and has not implemented the peace agreement (including the disbanding of the Janjaweed militias).

could be the prime mover in most international financial organisations which have become active in peacebuilding programmes and rule-of-law support.

3. The mandate of a peacebuilding operation should be determined by the UN Security Council separately from the prior military peace operation. Disagreement on the latter may hinder fair and broad burden sharing in the post-conflict phase. Civilian peacebuilding should generally be able to count on much wider support than the military peace operation.[2]

4. International and national donors would do well to set up peacebuilding funds within their own budgets to jump-start activities when needed and encourage rapid cooperation of emergency aid, peacekeeping activities and development cooperation. The EU's financial instruments are relatively large, but decision-making is fragmented. Some bilateral donors like the UK and the Netherlands have set up peacebuilding funds in which development aid and peacekeeping expenses are joined. Their experience is encouraging. The slow and incidental manner in which many donor countries and institutions finance peace operations

from regular budgets results in long delays at crucial times, causing lost windows of opportunity after a cease-fire.

5. The UN Stand-By Agreement System for military peacekeeping units earmarked by member states for UN duty needs to be further enlarged with many more police units, civilian administrators, health workers and technical engineering experts, as well as prosecutors, judges, trainers of legal personnel and other experts who are often in short supply and can only be freed for international service after several months. Police, legal and judicial reform assistance is, of course, not simply an activity which can be added on the back of a military peacekeeping operation. It requires professional expertise and management of individual experts' work to achieve best results. Such personnel need to be prepared and trained for international operations well in advance. It is necessary to have three systems of rapidly deployable police officers who can monitor, advise and train local police forces. These should be available at the national, the regional and the global level.

6. The military and police forces play the crucial role in the early stages of peacebuilding and rule-of-law reform, as they have to provide the country with the security so necessary for the return to normalcy. The military role should decrease as soon as possible, and the police and civilian role grow as quickly as feasible. What is needed is a doctrine for post conflict security reconstruction involving main donors and international agencies engaged in peacebuilding operations.[3] This doctrine needs to be agreed upon by military and civilian agencies. Without active support of Justice, Interior and Police ministries, it cannot work effectively.

This doctrine will have to be based on experience in various international settings, and apply the lessons learned from many failures. A general doctrine needs to be translated to specific situations with the aid of country specialists, especially knowledgeable nationals of the country concerned. Such doctrine needs to comprise both the immediate task of providing basic public security and order, as well as the more time-consuming task of police and justice sector reform. It would be useful to develop this as a mixed civilian-military doctrine for stabilisation operations which sets out what to do after violent military operations are concluded and before the time that peacekeeping forces can be withdrawn. This stabilisation doctrine aims at filling the void between war and peace, between chaos and order, between the rule of violence and the rule of law.

7. Prior to any peace operation, a social-anthropological analysis is needed for the country in trouble, in order to make a civilian impact study and to formulate a plan to help establish personal security for the population. This approach helps to balance the current over-emphasis on military operations planning.

8. It is recommended that the UN, the EU and individual donors set up pools of police and justice sector experts who are prepared for rapid international duty. This can be done by pre-arranging selection and training for possible missions

and making 'headquarter formations' beforehand, much like the SHIRBRIG formula, which was designed for military peacekeeping.[4]

9. Consideration should be given to establishing a global rule-of-law support fund, attached to influential international donor organisations like the EU or the World Bank, to coordinate and finance legal reform programmes in peacebuilding operations.

10. A major question in peacebuilding programmes is: who takes the lead and who will be boss or 'coordinator'? Generally, a representative of the UN Secretary General should perform this task. It can be delegated or mandated to a special envoy of another major international organisation, such as the World Bank, the EU, UNDP or, in the peacekeeping phase, to NATO. Donors should meet immediately after a cease-fire to establish donor coordination and divide responsibilities in the aid structure. This aid coordination meeting also requires agreement on division of tasks and specialties, i.e. which donors will do what: security sector reform, police reform, justice sector reform, assistance to transitional justice, restoring infrastructure, etc. Donors' comparative advantages and interests have to be taken into account from the outset. In the beginning, due to international media attention, many donors will be inclined to do a little bit of everything. This adds to the confusion and also explains, in part, the short duration of many aid programmes.

11. It is recommended that donors conclude agreements with recipient governments (or, where no government is available, with the interim administration) on long-term (ten-year) plans of what is to be achieved, who will help with what, and which donors will take over certain assistance tasks after a number of years. Pre-arranged rotation of tasks among donors for the medium and longer term helps to share burdens, avoid donor fatigue and finish the long-term tasks.

12. Neighbouring states and potential spoilers of the peace should be invited to the peacebuilding program from the start by forming a consultative group. This improves communication and can reduce temptations to disturb peacebuilding by clandestine operations to exploit a chaotic situation. Shunning neighbouring states has short-term isolation effects, but will later on undermine the peace process once the foreign donors leave and the usual geopolitical influences of the neighbours re-assert themselves. Lasting peacebuilding should aim for equilibrium of political forces both inside and around the war-ravaged country. The purpose of patient, transparent consultation is to show that nations' enlightened self-interests are served by construction and stability rather than renewed war.

13. The UN might prepare a standard mandate for interim administration in countries without the beginning of an effective government. This mandate can be adapted to specific circumstances as the need arises. Such interim administration need not be implemented in all cases by the UN itself. It can also be delegated by the UN to regional organisations or coalitions on the basis of a UN mandate. These groups of states should, however, report regularly to the Security Council.

14. Expertise centres for constitutional reform should be set up by a number of international organisations able to borrow advisors at short notice from different academic and governmental institutions to assist the negotiators in their efforts[5]. A related recommendation is to formulate, in the framework of the UN, the standards for a constitution of a pluralistic state guaranteeing basic human rights, available for adaptation to national circumstances.

15. If all OECD countries would implement the internationally agreed goal for aid of 0.7 percent of GNP, the volume of available aid would more than double. An additional $120 billion would become available every year. In fact, the development assistance level could become even higher, if many non-OECD countries (formerly developing countries which have become middle income countries), which have similar aid capabilities once they reach a per capita annual income of, say, € 5000, would also pitch in. There is no good reason to apply the UN donor target of 0.7 percent of national income (GNP) only to so-called Western industrialised countries. Middle income and energy exporting countries with high revenue relative to their population have aid capabilities that are proportional to their wealth.

16. More non-Western countries could be encouraged to participate in peacebuilding. They have large human and often financial resources. Also reformist Arab and Islamic states can contribute more military, police, legal and administrative experts to suitable peace operations, particularly in Islamic countries. This would broaden the expertise, widen the political support in the UN, and reduce a Western bias in such operations. Engaging more non-Western states will take time, but also save time in the end, when peace operations turn out to be more broadly based and less vulnerable to criticism against 'neo-colonial or human rights imperialism'.

17. The means for peace operations could be greatly increased if the reorganisation of armed forces that started after of the Cold War, and is not yet completed in many countries, were sped up to expand the expeditionary capacity for peacekeeping and peacebuilding. This applies not only to OECD-type countries, but also to developing countries with professional armed forces that are trained to abide by the rule of law, like India. Japan is a highly developed large country which can contribute significant means. The considerable resources of other Asian countries like China can also be engaged constructively.

18. As 'good government' is required to create respect for and enforcement of the most essential human rights pertaining to human security, which is the ultimate purpose of peacebuilding, an international manual with standards of good governance could help civil servants, media commentators, educators, field workers and others to improve conditions in various countries. Such a manual would ideally be adopted by UN organisations. Several elements are already available or can be derived from international treaties on human rights, the convention against corruption, and many other treaties and codes of conduct. Adminis-

Principles for military intervention

The report 'The Responsibility to Protect' formulates the following guidelines for intervention:

(1) The just cause threshold

Military intervention for human protection purposes is an exceptional and extraordinary measure. To be warranted, there must be serious and irreparable harm occurring to human beings, or imminently likely to occur, of the following kind:

A. **large scale loss of life,** actual or apprehended, with genocidal intent or not, which is the product either of deliberate state action, or state neglect or inability to act, or a failed state situation; or
B. **large scale 'ethnic cleansing'**, actual or apprehended, whether carried out by killing, forced expulsion, acts of terror or rape.

(2) The precautionary principles

A. **Right intention:** The primary purpose of the intervention, whatever other motives intervening states may have, must be to halt or avert human suffering. Right intention is better assured with multilateral operations, clearly supported by regional opinion and the victims concerned.
B. **Last resort:** Military intervention can only be justified when every non-military option for the prevention or peaceful resolution of the crisis has been explored, with reasonable grounds for believing lesser measures would not have succeeded.
C. **Proportional means:** The scale, duration and intensity of the planned military intervention should be the minimum necessary to secure the defined objective.
D. **Reasonable prospects:** There must be a reasonable chance of success in halting or averting the suffering which has justified the intervention, with the consequences of action not likely to be worse than the consequences of inaction.

(3) Right authority

A. There is no better or more appropriate body than the United Nations Security Council to authorize military intervention for human protection purposes. The task is not to find alternatives to the Security Council as a source of authority, but to make the Security Council work better than it has.
B. Security Council authorization should in all cases be sought prior to any military intervention action being carried out. Those calling for an intervention should formally request such authorization, or have the Council raise the matter on its own initiative, or have the Secretary-General raise it under Article 99 of the UN Charter.
C. The Security Council should deal promptly with any request for authority to intervene where there are allegations of large scale loss of human life or ethnic cleansing. It should in this context seek adequate verification of facts or conditions on the ground that might support a military intervention.
D. The Permanent Five members of the Security Council should agree not to apply their veto power, in matters where their vital state interests are not involved, to obstruct the passage of resolutions authorizing military intervention for human protection purposes for which there is otherwise majority support.

E. If the Security Council rejects a proposal or fails to deal with it in a reasonable time, alternative options are:
   I. consideration of the matter by the General Assembly in Emergency Special Session under the 'Uniting for Peace' procedure; and
   II. action within area of jurisdiction by regional or sub-regional organizations under Chapter VIII of the Charter, subject to their seeking subsequent authorization from the Security Council.

F. The Security Council should take into account in all its deliberations that, if it fails to discharge its responsibility to protect in conscience-shocking situations crying out for action, concerned states may not rule out other means to meet the gravity and urgency of that situation – and that the stature and credibility of the United Nations may suffer thereby.

(4) Operational principles

A. Clear objectives; clear and unambiguous mandate at all times; and resources to match.

B. Common military approach among involved partners; unity of command; clear and unequivocal communications and chain of command.

C. Acceptance of limitations, incrementalism and gradualism in the application of force, the objective being protection of a population, not defeat of a state.

D. Rules of engagement which fit the operational concept 'are precise', reflect the principle of proportionality, and involve total adherence to international humanitarian law.

E. Acceptance that force protection cannot become the principal objective.

F. Maximum possible coordination with humanitarian organizations.

Source: The Responsibility to Protect: Report of the International Commission on Intervention and State Sovereignty. Ottawa: International Development Research Centre for ICISS, 2001

trative law in several OECD countries also contains the rules which could become applicable gradually at the national and international level in less-organised societies. Academic institutions can help design such a UN Convention on Good Governance. Ideally, good governance should be codified in a single internationally accepted set of norms, if possible in treaty form, by the United Nations.[6]

8.2.2 DEVELOP COMPARATIVE ADVANTAGES OF DONOR COUNTRIES

The 'international community' consists of changing groups of active, like-minded countries and international organisations. It is useful, particularly for medium and smaller powers, to concentrate on special contributions for which that country has a particular reason and competence. Their expertise and funds can be contributed to the total of other countries' contributions. Not every donor state should try to cover the whole spectrum, as this is not an efficient use of scarce resources.

1. A country the size of the Netherlands cannot be prominently active in all fields of international assistance. Concentration on rule-of-law assistance in peace-building operations can be further developed into a specialty and a comparative

advantage. This can be financed with relatively small shifts in the ODA budget, partially at the cost of some lower-priority economic assistance to developing countries. The constitutional task of the Netherlands' government is to strengthen the international legal order. But in countries of chaos, where a national legal order does not function, the international legal order cannot function either. It follows that helping to build or improve the legal order in other countries is central to fulfilling the wider constitutional task of strengthening international law. The Netherlands enjoys a reputation of having a modern legal order. The presence of the International Court of Justice, the International Criminal Tribunal for the former Yugoslavia, the International Criminal Court and other international and national legal institutions, lends the country a comparative advantage. The Hague takes pride in the name 'legal capital' of the world (a phrase coined by UN Secretary-General Boutros Ghali). There are many renowned training and research institutes for international legal activities that can contribute to this comparative advantage.

2. The task of post-conflict peacebuilding is almost unlimited in geographical and functional terms. It is, therefore, necessary to concentrate on presently accepted tasks, to bring them to a reasonably successful conclusion. For the future, it is necessary to clearly prioritise among possible tasks, according to national, EU, NATO and UN interests. Chapter 6 discussed criteria for allocation. Among the many deserving cases, it is important to bring peacebuilding programmes in the Balkans to a good conclusion. This task was started by the EU in 1991 and is still to be completed. In the meantime, many additional, urgent tasks have been taken on, particularly in Afghanistan and Africa. It is important to bring as many as possible to acceptable conclusions or find other donors willing to take over the Dutch contributions after a number of years (rotation of responsibilities among donors) before heavy other tasks are added to the agenda.

3. Peacebuilding deserves to be the focus of development aid. Socio-economic progress which reduces poverty is not possible during (civil) war. A reorientation of development cooperation, to helping to build institutions for stable states, the rule of law and peaceful conflict settlement is advisable.
Funds for peacebuilding assistance can be found through re-allocation of present budget items and through an increase of 'Other Official Flows' (in addition to concessional Official Development Assistance). Other Official Flows ('non-ODA') was set as a proportion of Gross National Product (0.3 percent) in 1995, but this benchmark was left behind in 1999, resulting in a gradual relative decline. It is recommended to again set such a benchmark, to facilitate active participation by the Ministries of Justice, the Interior, and Education in joint policies for promotion of the rule of law in peacebuilding programmes.

4. If the foregoing is correct, it follows that in the broad field of peacebuilding, the Netherlands can best focus on support for rule of law institutions, especially police and the judiciary. The comparative advantage of the Netherlands and The Hague lies in the rule of law. To further develop this comparative advantage, it is

recommended to establish a Hague Centre for Peacebuilding, which can start as a coalition of already existing elements.

5. In most peacekeeping missions and the following peacebuilding operations, the lack of professional police with international peacekeeping experience is an important obstacle. It is recommended to increase the size and training of the Netherlands' Marechaussee (constabulary forces) for international missions, relative to other expeditionary forces.

6. It is recommended that the example of the joint policy paper of 2005 on 'Peace Building after a Conflict' of the Ministries of Foreign Affairs (Development Cooperation) and Defence be followed by a joint policy paper with the Ministries of Justice, Interior, and Education, Culture and Science. The purpose would be to define an active role of the Justice Department in international legal reform and training assistance, for the Interior Department in police monitoring, advice and training, and for the Education Department in further developing academic institutions in the Netherlands with an up-to-date analytical and training capacity for international reform of the legal sector, notably Islamic law.

8.3 SOME SUGGESTIONS FOR FURTHER STUDY

The previous pages touched upon many questions that need further contemplation and require more policy research than was possible during this explorative study. Institutions for policy analysis and advice may want to consider adding one or more of these subjects to their agenda. These suggestions are listed in order of urgency and importance. The reasoning leading to these recommendations is based on chapters 3 to 7. Subjects for further study are in particular:

1. The size, policies and training of a European Union rapid deployment facility for police assistance to countries emerging from violent conflict, or in danger of falling into anarchy. The EU has made such a decision, but its implementation needs further consideration.

2. Widening the possibilities for UNHCR to maintain basic rule of law in large refugee camps with local and internationally recruited police capacity, temporary courts and detention facilities.

3. An UN-led international police facility for peacekeeping and peacebuilding operations, similar to suggestion 1 and also available for carrying out suggestion 2.

4. A study of the possibilities for forming an international coalition of governmental and NGO bodies (a global policy action network) which aim to encourage legal reform and its many related subjects, such as transitional justice. The need for peacebuilding and rule-of-law assistance is growing, but the activities of the main donors (official and private) are still very fragmented.

A Small Arms Treaty?

About 500,000 people are killed each year by small arms and light weapons. It is urgent to curb their spread. About 300,000 p.a. die because of political violence and 200,000 by non-political criminal violence and accidents. Women suffer disproportionately from firearms violence. Small arms make so many casualties each year that they should be viewed as weapons of mass destruction in slow motion. Their effects are, up to now, no less serious than nuclear, biological and chemical weapons.

Each year, more than 8 million small and light weapons are produced. The majority ends up in the hands of civilians. Each year an average of 22 billion dollars is spent on weapons by countries in Africa, Asia, the Middle East and Latin America. These amounts could help achieve the Millennium Development Goals of the United Nations, such as primary education for all children and the eradication of child and maternal mortality and HIV/AIDS. The top five exporters of weapons in the world are all members of the UN Security Council: Russia, the US, France, the UK and China.

Thousands of people suffer from the effects of unregulated global arms trade. Many people are killed or suffer because they are injured, raped or forced to flee their homes. The Control Arms campaign calls for an international, legally-binding Arms Trade Treaty to ease the suffering caused byirre-sponsible weapons transfers. Since its start in October 2003, 'Control Arms' has gathered the support of over one million people worldwide. In December 2006, 153 governments voted at the UN to start work on developing an international Arms Trade Treaty.

The treaty would establish common international standards for the import, export and transfer of all conventional arms. This would make a major contribution to the attainment of humanitarian, human rights and development objectives worldwide. The Economic Community of West African States (ECOWAS) and the Council of the European Union (EU) expressed support for stringent regulation of the global arms trade. The UN often declares separate arms embargoes to curb violence in crisis regions. But arms embargoes are systematically violated without punishment. During the last ten years none of the 13 UN arms embargoes managed to stop the flow of weapons to countries or armed groups subject to these embargoes. UN reports show that individuals and companies operating in at least 30 countries across the world were involved in embargo busting.

Only a few of the arms embargo breakers have been successfully prosecuted. The authority of the UN is greatly undermined by persistent violations. The Security Council should improve the design of arms embargoes based on a common set of criteria for arms transfers that would be consistent with international law. The UN Sanctions Committees, the UN Secretariat and UN investigative teams require better support to improve verification, especially from Member States close to the embargoed entity, UN peace-keeping missions operating in the vicinity, and other intergovernmental organisations.

International treaties are needed to outlaw step-by-step various categories, and limit possession and trade at least to legitimate authorities (police and armed forces) rather than persons and private non-state parties.

Sources: www.controlarms.org, www.paxchristi.nl, www.oxfam.org

This could be undertaken as a national study, focussed on possibilities and capabilities in and of the Netherlands, or could be done jointly with like-minded countries in the EU. One could also conceive of a joint study with one or more similar institutions outside the EU, especially with think tanks from developing countries. Such a multilateral report would lessen the often-heard criticism by non-western observers that Western proposals do not take 'non-Western values' and interpretations of the rule of law into account. The possibilities of reform of Islamic law have been highlighted in the report by the Netherlands Scientific Council for Government Policy.[7] It might be considered to carry out suggestion 4 with one or more policy research institutes in reformist Islamic countries.

5. A different object in need of further study is the idea of an Organisation of Democratic States. There are already some good, small initiatives, but also a number of half-hearted, weak or failing initiatives in this direction. Deserving special study are: how existing institutions like the International Institute for Democracy and Electoral Reform could be strengthened, how the activities of the Council of Europe could be widened to non-European democracies, or whether the US-sponsored idea of a Concert or Community of Democracies should be given priority.
   The main functions of such an 'ODS' might be:
   a. to advise other states on how to introduce and develop democracy, and how to anchor it in rule-of-law systems;
   b. to act as a caucus of democracies of all continents within the UN system, encouraging joint action and democratisation of other states as well;
   c. to help bridge some of the gaps among the US, various European states, and a number of important non-western democracies, e.g. India.

The mere existence of an ODS would encourage democracy, as many semi-democratic states would like to be admitted and recognised as fully democratic. This is somewhat comparable to the strong reformist effect the EU has on countries that are in its waiting room for membership. An important subject to ponder about is what criteria should be applied for the minimum requirement of membership. Also, what should be done if a member slides back into authoritarianism or political violence: assist the member to improve, freeze membership if the government refuses to cooperate, or start procedures to terminate membership? Clear criteria for membership may encourage, by themselves, some further democratisation, as most governments want to avoid loss of international prestige.

8.4 IN CONCLUSION

Are the words of John Rawls, the main philosopher on the nature of justice, quoted at the outset of this book, really wise counsel? Should it be the long-term goal of relatively well-ordered societies to bring burdened societies, like outlaw states, into the 'Society of well-ordered Peoples'? We leave the question of what is 'well-ordered' aside and refer to chapters 3, 4 and 5 for some observations on legal order and human rights.

The present exploration dealt with only a part of Rawls' observation, i.e. helping those societies that are torn apart by massive political violence to rebuild themselves into more peaceful states. The previous chapters suggest that it is in the interest of 'well-ordered societies' to reduce the frequency of (civil) wars in others, and assist them in peacebuilding and development of the rule of law. But it also became clear that the possibilities of bringing lasting fundamental improvements to foreign cultures and political systems are limited. Risks of failure are considerable. A rational allocation is necessary of increased resources, to well-chosen countries, after a thorough assessment of the likely effects of foreign assistance to the people in trouble. We hope the foregoing analysis may help to limit mistakes and improve results.

NOTES

1 *The Responsibility to Protect: Report of the International Commission on Intervention and State Sovereignty*. Ottawa: International Development Research Centre, 2001.

2 Advisory Council on International Questions, *Failing States*, The Hague, 2004.

3 Rand 2005, p. xviii and 226-228.

4 SHIRBRIG is the Stand-by High Readiness Brigade, a group of a dozen countries that have earmarked military units for rapid deployment in UN peacekeeping operations under pre-arranged multinational headquarters. The units have trained together. SHIRBRIGs responsibilities are in principle limited to actions under Chapter 6 of the Charter and the member states reserve the right to refuse participation in specific actions.

5 Like the Venice Commission of the Council of Europe.

6 See Hirsch Ballin, WRR report 58, pp. 232-4.

7 WRR, *Dynamism in Islamic Activism. Reference Points for Democratization and Human Rights*. Amsterdam University Press, 2006.

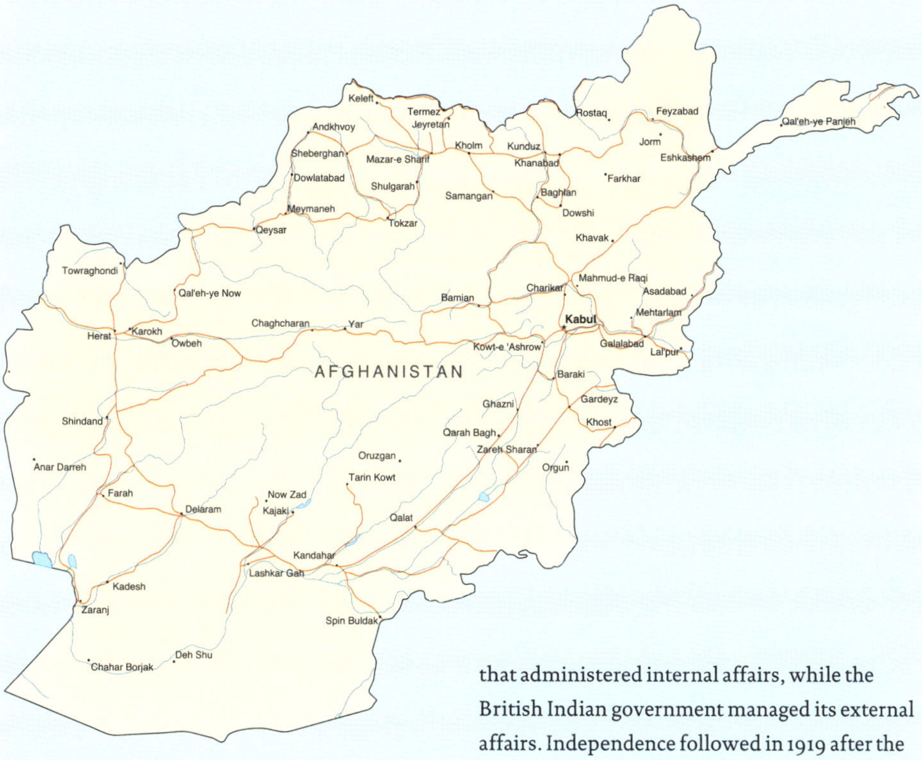

Afghanistan is a war torn, landlocked, Islamic country. The population is a mixture of 42 percent Pashtun, 27 percent Tajik, 9 percent Hazara, 9 percent Uzbek, 4 percent Aimak, 3 percent Turkmen, 2 percent Baloch, and 4 percent of other origins. The country counts approximately 26 million Sunni Muslims, 6 million Shi'a Muslims and 32,000 citizens of other or no religious affiliation (figures are changing due to refugees).

Its strategic position in Eurasia and Southern Asia caused a history of war, invasion and occupation. Current borders originate from the late nineteenth century when the United Kingdom tried to occupy Afghanistan from 1878 to 1919. The British created Afghanistan as a buffer zone between British India and Czarist Russia. The so-called Durand Line divided the Pashtun tribal area between Afghanistan and the later Pakistan. British support enabled Amir Abdur Rahmad Khan to establish a central Afghan government that administered internal affairs, while the British Indian government managed its external affairs. Independence followed in 1919 after the Third Anglo-Afghan War.

During subsequent years warlords fought to gain power. A period of stability commenced when Pashtun King Zair Shah gained power in 1933 after his father was assassinated. Support of the Pashtun tribes to the south and the elite of Kabul enabled him to adopt a new constitution in 1964. Religious militants opposed his policies and modernizing reforms that were discriminatory to non-Pashtuns.

In 1964, Afghanistan voted against Pakistan's UN membership because Pashtuns in the border region had not been given the opportunity to vote on independence. Strong ethnic links with Afghan Pashtun caused Pakistani fears for a breakup of the North of Pakistan along ethnic lines. King Zair Shahs policies and other Afghan leaders encouraged Pashtun revolts.

Zair Shah's policies undercut much of the country's economy and infrastructure. Daoud Khan seized power in 1973, creating the Afghan Republic whilst making himself president. Daoud was assassinated by the communist People's Democratic Party of Afghanistan in 1978. Afghanistan then became a Cold War zone of confrontation between communism and western influence. Whilst the US supported the anti-government *Mujahedin* forces, the Soviet Union (SU) closed a Treaty of Friendship, Cooperation and Good Neighborliness with Afghanistan. The Treaty provided the SU an excuse for the 1979 invasion, when 100,000 Soviet troops backed by another 100,000 Afghans overthrew the Daoud Khan government in the Great Saur Revolution.

Communist rule lasted until 1989 when mass casualties led to the Sovjet Union's departure. During the occupation, the West had supported and armed the opposition against communist occupation. Pakistan played a key role by distributing funds and weapons among mostly Islamic Pashtun warlords.

Six years of battles among Afghan warlords followed, destroying many lives. On the one hand, the Taleban, by origin an Islamic student movement, struggled to gain power, supported by Pakistan. The opposition to the Taleban was incidentally supported by the United States. The Taleban seized Kabul in 1996 and imposed a strict interpretation of Islamic Law. By 2000, the Taleban controlled nearly 95 percent of Afghanistan. The Taleban leadership allowed anti-American terrorist training camps to arise. On the 11th of September 2001, the Al-Qaeda organization led by Osama bin Laden destroyed the Twin Towers in New York, causing about 3500 dead. The US identified Afghanistan as the hide out of Bin Laden's terrorist organization. When Taleban refused to extradite Al Qaeda, the US invaded Afghanistan with Operation Enduring Freedom.

The US contacted reformist Afghan leaders to encourage establishment of democracy. Hamid Karzai became Interim President, which was confirmed by the 2002 *Loya Jirga* (a formal meeting of elders in which most ethnic groups are represented). In 2003, the constitutional *Loya Jirga* drafted a new constitution which was ratified in 2004. Karzai won the presidential elections that year and in 2005 democratic parliamentary elections followed.

Afghanistan is currently struggling to establish a functioning state with the support of a NATO led, UN-mandated ISAF mission. State building is frustrated, among others, by Taleban fighters, influx from Northern Pakistan of Pashtun Islamic fundamentalist resistance, local leaders, anti-western feelings, arms traders, terrorists from other countries, abundant poppy cultivation and opium trade, presence of landmines, a poor infrastructure, and a very weak economic position.

Afghanistan's ethnic diversity makes it highly sensitive to foreign interference. Pakistan supported the US intervention, but did not stop the Taleban's resurrection from the North-West Frontier Province, which enabled the increase of insurgent attacks in 2006-2007. Militants have also entered from other countries.

LIST OF COUNTRY ILLUSTRATIONS

LIST OF TABLES

LIST OF TEXT BOXES

MAPS

ACKNOWLEDGEMENTS

I am especially grateful for the encouragement by Dr. Herman Tjeenk Willink, vice-president of the Council of State of The Netherlands, Dr. Ernst Hirsch Ballin, former chairman of the Department of Administrative Law of this Council, and Dr. Wim van de Donk, chairman of the Scientific Council for Government Policy WRR. Students who assisted with research are Wouter van Cleef, Christel Koop, Saskia Rademaker, Jan-Willem Oosterbroek, Petra Vergeer, Veerle van Doeveren and Reinout Pieneman. The maps in country boxes are from Map Resources (www.mapresources.com). Permission to print the Failed States Map (pp. 38-39) was granted by Foreign Policy and The Fund for Peace. Permission to print the Global Peace Map was given by visionofhumanity.com. Several persons helped to prepare the typescript: Marjolein Hanssen, Dinet Jurrien, Yvonne de Graaf and Melanie van Soolingen. Dr. Nathalie Wlodarczyk (London School of Economics and Political Science) improved parts of the editing and commented on the draft. Mirjan van Leijenhorst and Kinnema van Eik assisted with the completion. Comments on various draft chapters were received from members and staff of the WRR, as well as Dr. Peter Baehr (Professor Emeritus of International Relations and Human Rights), Dr. Pieter van Dijk (Council of State), John Heck (PUA), Dr. Richard Lauwaars (Council of State), Kees Kouwenaar (Center for International Legal Cooperation), Christa Meindersma LL.M (Hague Center for Strategic Studies), Gerrit Jan van Oven LL.M, Dr. Richard Soudriette (Director of IFES), Paul van Tongeren (European Centre for Conflict Prevention), Dr. Alex Voorhoeve (Dept. of Philosophy, London School of Economics and Political Science), and Daniel Voorhoeve (Ministry of Foreign Affairs, The Hague). Conversations with many people active in peacebuilding helped to develop this analysis. I am very grateful for their insights. Any short-comings in this text are my responsibility. Suggestions for improvement are very welcome at j.voorhoeve@raadvanstate.nl.

ABOUT THE AUTHOR

The author (1945) is professor of International Organizations at Leiden University and International Security at the Netherlands' Defence Academy. He is member of the Netherlands' Council of State since 1999. He chairs Oxfam-Novib and the World Population Foundation and is a member of the Trilateral Commission. Previously, Joris Voorhoeve served in the Policy Planning Division of the World Bank, as a member and floor leader of the Dutch Parliament, director of The Netherlands' Institute for International Relations Clingendael, and minister of Defence. Previous books are *Peace, Profits and Principles: A Study of Dutch Foreign Policy* (The Hague, Martinus Nijhoff, 1979) and *Labiele Vrede* (Unstable Peace), (Amsterdam, Balans, 1995) and various reports and articles on foreign affairs, development cooperation, disaster assistance and international conflicts.

FURTHER READING
limited to works in English

General (Works marked * contain case studies)
Andy Knight, W. and T. Keating (eds) (2004) *Building Sustainable Peace*, Alberta: University of Alberta Press.*
Brinkerhoff, D.W. (2005) 'Rebuilding Governance in Failed States and Post-Conflict Societies: Core Concepts and Cross-cutting Themes' in: *Public Administration and Development* 25: 3-14.
Carothers, T., et al. (2006) *Promoting the Rule of Law Abroad: In Search of Knowledge*, Washington DC: Carnegie Endowment for International Peace.
Chesterman, S., Ignatieff, M. and R. Thakur (eds) (2005) *Making States Work: State Failure and the Crisis of Governance*, Tokyo: UNU Press.*
Crocker, C.A., Hampson, F.O. and P. Aall (eds.) (1996) *Managing Global Chaos: Sources of and Responses to International Conflict*, Washington DC: United States Institute of Peace Press.*
Fearon, J.D. and D. Laitin (2004) 'Neotrusteeship and the Problem of Weak States', *International Security* 28, 4.
Fukuyama, F. (2004) *State-building: Governance and World Order in the 21st Century*, Ithaca: Cornell University Press.
Holm, T.T. and E.B. Eide (eds) (2000), *Peace building and Police Reform*, London: Frank Cass.*
International Commission on Intervention and State Sovereignty (2001), *The Responsibility to Protect*, Ottawa: International Development Research Centre.
Junne, G. and W. Verkoren (eds) (2005) *Post-conflict Development*, Boulder: Lynne Rienner.*
Milliken, J. (ed.) (2003): *State Failure, Collapse and Reconstruction*, Oxford: Blackwell (Development and Change book series) originally published in *Development and Change* 33, 5.*
Netherlands Min. of Foreign Affairs (2004) *Handbook Good Government*, The Hague.
Rand Corporation (2005) *The UN's Role in Nation Building, From Congo to Iraq*. Santa Monica.
Rand Corporation (2007) *The Beginners Guide to Nation Building*, Santa Monica.
Reychler, L. and T. Paffenholz (eds) (2001) *Peace building: A Field Guide*, Boulder: Lynne Rienner.*
Tongeren, P van, et al (2005) *People Building Peace II*, Boulder: Lynne Rienner.
United Nations General Assembly Resolution (2005) *2005 World Summit Outcome*, UN document A/60/L.1.
Zartman, I.W. (ed.) (1995) *Collapsed States: The disintegration and restoration of legitimate authority*, Boulder: Lynne Rienner.*

Security Sector Reform
Ball, N. (2005) 'Strengthening Democratic Governance of the Security Sector in Conflict-affected Countries' in: *Public Admin. and Development* 25: 25-38.
Ball, N., Bouta, T. and L. van de Goor (2003) *Enhancing Democratic Governance of the*

Security Sector: An Institutional Assessment Framework, The Hague: Clingendael Institute.

Schnabel, A. and H.G. Ehrhart (eds) *Security Sector Reform and Post-Conflict Peace building*, Tokyo: UNU Press.*

United Nations (2000) *Disarmament, Demobilization and Reintegration of Ex-Combatants in a Peacekeeping Environment: Principles and Guidelines*, New York: Department of Peacekeeping Operations.

Legal reform

Call, C.T. (ed.) (2007) *Constructing Justice and Security after War*, Washington DC: US Institute of Peace.

Center for International Legal Cooperation (2003), *Law and Development*, conference proceedings of 16 December 2003, The Hague.

Luz, M.A. (1998) *Peace building and Legal Reform: Priorities and Directions*, Canadian Department of Foreign Affairs and International Aid.

Samuels, K. (2006). *Rule of Law Reform in Post-Conflict Countries*, Conflict Prevention & Reconstruction, Paper 37, The World Bank.

Skaar, E., et al (2004) *Aid to Judicial Reform*, Michelsen Institute, Bergen (Norway).

Democracy and elections

Carothers, T. (1999) *Aiding Democracy Abroad: The Learning Curve*, Washington DC: Carnegie Endowment for International Peace.

Diamond, L. and M. Plattner (2006) *Electoral Systems and Democracy*, Baltimore: Johns Hopkins University Press.

Halperin M., Siegle, J. and M. Weinstein (2004) *The Democracy Advantage: How Democracies Promote Prosperity and Peace*, Washington DC: Routledge Press.

IDEA (2005) *Electoral System Design: The New International IDEA Handbook*, Stockholm: International IDEA.

IDEA (2006) *Democracy, Conflict and Human Security: Pursuing Peace in the 21st Century*, Stockholm, Sweden.

McMahon, E. and s. Baker (2006) *Piecing a Democratic Quilt: Regional Organizations and Universal Norms*, Bloomfield, Connecticut: Kumarian Press.

Soudriette, R., and A. Ellis (2006) 'Electoral Systems Today: A Global Snapshot', *Journal of Democracy 17*, 2: 78-88, Washington DC.

Humanitarian Relief

Anderson, M.B., (1999) *Do No Harm: How Aid Can Support Peace-or War*, Boulder, London, United Kingdom: Lynne Rienner Publishers Inc.

Do No Harm Project (2004) *The Do No Harm Handbook (Framework for Analysing the Impact of Assistance on Conflict)*, Cambridge, USA: Collaborative for Development Action Inc. and CDA Collaborative Learning projects.

Goodhand, J. and B. Klem with Fonseka, D., Keethaponcalan, S.I. and S. Sardesai (2005) *Aid, Conflict, And Peacebuilding in Sri Lanka 2000-2005*, For the governments of the Netherlands, Sweden, and the United Kingdom, in collaboration with the Asia Foundation and the World Bank, Sri Lanka: www.asiafoundation.org.

Hess, G. and M. Pfeiffer (2007) *Comparative analysis of WHO 'Health as a Bridge for Peace' case studies*, World Health Organization, http://www.who.int/hac/techguidance/hbp/comparative_analysis/en/index.html.

High-Level Forum on the Health MDGs (2005) *Health Service Delivery in Post-Conflict States*, Paris, 14-15 November 2005, http://www.hlfhealthmdgs.org/Documents/HealthServiceDelivery.pdf.

Inter-Agency Standing Committee Task Force on HIV/AIDS in Emergency Settings (2003) *Guidelines for HIV/AIDS in emergency settings*, UNFPA, http://www.unfpa.org/upload/lib_pub_file/249_filename_guidelines-hiv-emer.pdf.

MacQueen, G. and J. Santa-Barbara (2000) 'Conflict and health: Peace building through health initiatives', *BMJ* 321: 293-296, http://www.bmj.com/cgi/content/full/321/7256/293.

Medecins Sans Frontieres (1997) *Refugee Health: An approach to emergency situations*, London: Macmillan Education Ltd.

Rushton, S (2005) 'Health and Peacebuilding: Resuscitating the Failed State in Sierra Leone', *International Relations* 19, 4: 441-456, SAGE publications. On line available at: http://ire.sagepub.com/cgi/content/abstract/19/4/441.

Shuey, D.A., Qosaj, F.A., Schouten, E.J. and A.B. Zwi (2003) 'Planning for health sector reform in post-conflict situations: Kosovo 1999-2000', *Health Policy* 63, 3: 299-310, Elsevier Science.

Silove, D., Ekblad, S. and R. Mollica (2000) 'The rights of the severely mentally ill in post-conflict societies', *The Lancet* 335, 9214: 1548-1549, Science Direct.

Sondorp, E., Kaiser, T. & A. Zwi (2001) 'Editorial: beyond emergency care: challenges to health planning in complex emergencies', *Tropical Medicine and International Health* 6, 12: 965-970, Blackwell Science.

The Sphere Project (2004) *Humanitarian Charter and Minimum Standards in Disaster Response*, http://www.sphereproject.org/.

United Nations Office for the Coordination of Humanitarian Affairs, *Coordination of Humanitarian Response*, http://ochaonline3.un.org/Coordination/tabid/1085/Default.aspx.

United Nations *Security Council resolution 1308 on the responsibility of the Security Council in the maintenance of international peace and security: HIV/AIDS and international peacekeeping operations,* http://daccessdds.un.org/doc/UNDOC/GEN/N00/536/02/PDF/N0053602.pdf?OpenElement.

University of New South Wales Health and Conflict Project and the School of Public Health and Community Medicine (2004) *Background paper I: Health and Peace-building: Securing the Future*, The University of New South Wales, Sydney, Australia. See also: http://healthandconflict.sphcm.med.unsw.edu.au.

University of New South Wales School of Public Health and Community Medicine (2003) *Health and Peace-building Filter- Case Study Paper*, The University of New South Wales, Sydney, Australia.

Vass, A. (2001) 'Peace through health; This new movement needs evidence, not just ideology, *BMJ* 323: 1020. Available online: http://www.bmj.com/cgi/content/full/323/7320/1020?ck=nck.

Waters, H., Garrett, B. and G. Burnham (2007) *Rehabilitating Health Systems in Post-Conflict Situations- Research Paper No. 2007/06*, UNU-WIDER, http://www.

wider.unu.edu/publications/rps/rps2007/rp2007-06.pdf.
World Health Organization (2003) 'Health Systems: principled integrated care' chapter 7 in *The World Health Report 2003 – Shaping the Future*, http://www.who.int/whr/2003/en/.
World Health Organization, Dept. Emergency and Humanitarian Action (2001) *Health as a Potential Contribution to Peace; 'Realities from the field: what has WHO learned in the 1990s' – Working Material*, http://www.who.int/hac/techguidance/hbp/en/health-poster.pdf.
Zwi, A.B and N.J. Grove (2006) 'Challenges to Human Security: Reflections on Health, Fragile States and Peacebuilding', in Mellbourn, A. (ed.) *Health and Conflict Prevention* 119-139, Gidlunds, Sweden: Anna Lindh Programme on Conflict Prevention.

Gender and Women Issues

IRIN: Office for the Coordination of Humanitarian Affairs Integrated Regional Information Networks (2007) *The Shame of War: Sexual Violence Against Women and Girls in Conflict*, A United Nations OCHA/IRIN publication, http://www.irinnews.org/pdf/sow/IRIN-TheShameofWar-fullreport-Mar07.pdf.
OECD (2003) *GE: United Nations Inter-agency Network on Women and Gender Equality and the OECD-DAC Network on Gender Equality*, OECD, Paris 10-11 July 2003, United Nations, http://www.un.org/womenwatch/ianwge/taskforces/communique03.htm.
Office of the Special Adviser on Gender Issues and Advancement of Women, IANWGE (2003) *Communiqué: Gender and post-conflict reconstruction: lessons learned from Afghanistan, Joint workshop of IANW*.
OXFAM, *OXFAM International Strategic Plan 2007-2012: Demanding Justice*, http://www.oxfam.org/en/files/oi_strategic_plan_2007.pdf.
OXFAM, *What We Do – Gender; Introduction*, http://www.oxfam.org.uk/what_we_do/issues/gender/introduction.htm.
Porter, F. and C. Sweetman (eds.) (2005) *Mainstreaming Gender in Development: A Critical Review*, OXFAM Publishing, http://publications.oxfam.org.uk/oxfam/display.asp?isbn=0855985518
UNECE, United Nations Economic Commission for Europe, *Gender Issues: Policy areas 'Crime & Violence – Trafficking in humans'*, http://www.unece.org/stats/gender/genpols/keyinds/crime/traffic.htm.
UNFPA: United Nations Population Fund (2006) *Sexual Violence Against Women and Girls in War and Its Aftermath: Realities, Responses, and Required Resources; A Briefing paper Prepared for Symposium on Sexual Violence in Conflict and Beyond, 21-23 June 2006*, Brussels (Belgium): Ward, J. and M. Marsh, http://www.peacewomen.org/resources/Human_Rights/PDF_files/SGBV inWar.pdf.
UNIFEM (2004) *Getting it Right, Doing it Right: Gender and Disarmament, Demobilization and Reintegration*, http://www.womenwarpeace.org/issues/ddr/gettingitright.pdf.
UNIFEM (2005) *Securing the Peace: Guiding the International Community towards Women's Effective Participation throughout Peace Processes*, http://www.unifem. org/attachments/products/Securing_the_Peace.pdf.

UNIFEM (2005) *UNIFEM at a Glance: Achieving Gender Equality in Democratic Governance*, http://www.unifem.org/attachments/stories/AAG_Governance-PeaceSecurity.pdf.

UNIFEM (2007) *News release: UNIFEM Launches Community-Based Programme to Support Women in Peacebuilding and Prevention of Sexual Violence*, http://www.unifem.org/news_events/story_detail.php?StoryID=574.

UNIFEM (2007) *Women, Peace & Security: CEDAW and Security Council Resolution 1325: A Quick Guide*, http://www.womenwarpeace.org/UNIFEM_CEDAW_and_1325.pdf.

UNIFEM: United Nations Development Fund For Women (2006) *Gender and Conflict Analysis: UNIFEM policy briefing paper,* http://www.womenwarpeace.org/UNIFEM_Conflict_Prevention.pdf.

Some case studies

Afghanistan

Donini, A., Niland, N. and K. Wermester (eds) (2004) *Nation-building Unravelled?: Aid, Peace and Justice in Afghanistan*, Bloomfield: Kumarian.

Normand, R. (2002) *Human Rights and Reconstruction in Afghanistan*, Brooklyn, NY: Center for Economic and Social Rights, http://www.reliefweb.int/library/documents/2002/cesr-afg-31may.pdf.

Sedra, M. (2002) *Challenging the Warlord Culture: Security Sector Reform in Post-Taliban Afghanistan*, Bonn, Germany: Bonn International Center for Conversion.

Bosnia and Herzegovina

International Crisis Group (1999) *Rule of Law in Public Administration: Confusion and Discrimination in a Post-Communist Bureaucracy.*

International Crisis Group (2002) *Policing The Police In Bosnia: A Further Reform Agenda.*

International Crisis Group (2005) *Bosnia's Stalled Police Reform: No Progress, No EU.*

Burundi

Ferguson, C. and J. Isima (2003) *DDR Framework: Burundi*, Shrivenham: GFN-SSR. Available online: http://www.gfn-ssr.org/edocs/gfn005_isima_ferguson_ddr_burundi_2003.pdf.

International Crisis Group (2004) *End of the Transition in Burundi: The Home Stretch.*

Haiti

Harvard Law Student Advocates for Human Rights and Centro de Justiça Global (2005) *Keeping the Peace in Haiti?* Available online: http://www.reliefweb.int/library/documents/2005/harvard-haiti-mar05.pdf.

International Crisis Group (2005) *Spoiling Security in Haiti.*

Kumar, C. (1998) *Building Peace in Haiti*, Boulder: Lynne Riener.

Stromsen, J.M. and J. Tricellito (2003) *Building the Haitian National Police: A Retrospective and Prospective View*. Available online: http://www.trinitydc.edu/academics/ depts/Interdisc/International/PDF%20files/HNP.final.pdf.

Iraq

Day, G. and C. Freeman (2003) 'Policekeeping is the key: Rebuilding the internal security architecture of postwar Iraq', in: *International Affairs* 79: 299-313.

International Crisis Group (2003) *Iraq: Building a New Security Structure.*

Phillips, D.L. (2005) *Losing Iraq: Inside the Postwar Reconstruction Fiasco*, Boulder, CO: Westview Press.

United States Institute of Peace (2003), *Establishing the Rule of Law in Iraq*, available on http://www.usip.org/pubs/specialreports/sr104.html.

Rwanda

Alusala, N. (2005) *Disarmament and reconciliation Rwanda 's concerns*, available on http://www.iss.co.za/pubs/papers/108/Paper108.htm.

International Crisis Group (1999) *Five Years After the Genocide in Rwanda: Justice in Question.*

Kimonyo, J.P., Twagiramungu, N. and C. Kayumba (2004) *Supporting the Post-Genocide Transition in Rwanda: The Role of the International Community*, The Hague: Clingendael Institute.

SOME RELEVANT WEBSITES

African Union
Asia Foundation
Canadian International Development Agency
Carnegie Endowment for Peace
CIA
Clingendael, Netherlands Institute of International Relations
Department for International Development
Electoral Institute of Southern Africa
European Union
European Parliament Democracy Caucus
European Commission
European Foundation for Democracy through Partnership
European Network of Political Foundations
European Peace Building Liaison Office
Ford Foundation
Friedrich Ebert Foundation
Friedrich Naumann Stiftung
IDEA
Institute for Democracy in South Africa (IDASA)
InterAmerican Development Bank (IDB)
International Republican Institute
Konrad Adenauer Foundation
League of Arab States
National Democratic Institute
NATO
Netherlands Institute for Multiparty Democracy (NIMD)
Netherlands Development Organisation (SNV)
Netherlands Ministry of Defence
Netherlands Ministry of Foreign Affairs
OECD
Organisation of American States (OAS)
Organisation of the Conference of Islamic States
Organisation for Security and Cooperation in Europe, Office for Democratic Institutions and Human Rights
Southern Africa Development Community
United Nations (UN)
UN Democracy Fund
UNDP
UNIFEM
USAID
US Department of State
World Bank